Reducing Poverty and Investing in People

DIRECTIONS IN DEVELOPMENT
Human Development

Reducing Poverty and Investing in People

The New Role of Safety Nets in Africa

Victoria Monchuk

THE WORLD BANK
Washington, D.C.

Contents

Boxes

Figures

Map

Tables

Preface

Over the past two decades, Africa's strong economic growth has paved the way for poverty reduction. Nevertheless, high poverty levels persist, especially in rural areas, and the gap between income groups in terms of human capital and access to basic services is growing. In addition to chronic poverty, there is widespread vulnerability as environmental, economic, and other shocks frequently affect many households.

Safety nets are an important tool in a country's development strategy because they can increase the momentum toward sustainable poverty reduction. By providing regular and reliable support to poor households and helping the poor to invest in productive and capital-forming activities, targeted interventions such as safety nets can help to reduce the high levels of persistent poverty and reverse the trend of increasing inequality across Africa. Safety nets can also provide additional support in times of crisis to those who have temporarily fallen into poverty and assist them with boosting their resilience so they are not forced to deplete their assets during times of hardship.

During 2009–13, the World Bank's Africa Region, together with country governments, undertook social safety net assessments in a number of countries in Sub-Saharan Africa. So far, assessments have been completed for 22 countries (Benin, Botswana, Burkina Faso, Cameroon, Ethiopia, Ghana, Kenya, Lesotho, Liberia, Madagascar, Malawi, Mali, Mauritania, Mauritius, Mozambique, Niger, Rwanda, Sierra Leone, Swaziland, Tanzania, Togo, and Zambia). These assessments analyze the status of safety nets in Africa and their strengths and weaknesses. They also identify areas for improvement with the aim of helping governments and donors to strengthen African safety net systems to protect and promote poor and vulnerable people. This review synthesizes the findings of these 22 assessments and other recent studies of safety net programs in Africa in a regional review.

Until recently, safety nets were implemented only on an ad hoc basis in Africa. However, the safety net assessments find that in the wake of the global economic and food and fuel price crises, policy makers in Africa are increasingly viewing safety nets as core instruments for reducing poverty and managing risk. Hence, social safety nets are on the rise in Africa and are beginning to evolve from fragmented stand-alone programs into integrated safety net systems. Social protection programming has started to change from largely emergency food aid programs to one-off safety net interventions and, in some countries, becoming regular and predictable safety nets consisting of targeted cash transfers and cash-for-work programs. Some countries, such as Ghana, Kenya, Mozambique, Rwanda, and Tanzania, are now beginning to consolidate their programs into a national safety net system. Many countries are also making progress toward articulating national social protection strategies to serve as the basis for implementing effective safety net systems. In addition, impact evaluations of safety net programs in Africa are increasingly being undertaken. These impact evaluations, as well as recent research into the productive aspects of cash transfer programs, have yielded encouraging evidence that safety nets are effective in reducing poverty and vulnerability in Africa.

The timely analysis of the state of safety nets in each country provides a solid, reliable foundation for evidence-based policy dialogue and programming. As a result of these assessments and of the growing body of evidence showing that safety nets reduce poverty and contribute to inclusive growth, decision makers in Africa are now putting safety nets high on their development agendas.

Acknowledgments

This review is a product of the World Bank's Africa Region Social Protection Unit. Victoria Monchuk was the task leader and is the principal author. Monchuk is an economist whose fields of interest include social protection, labor, and children and youth. Her current work at the World Bank includes supporting governments in West and Central Africa in building safety net systems. She has also carried out evaluations of cash transfer, public works, and skills development programs. She previously worked in the Fiscal Affairs Department at the International Monetary Fund, where she did analytical work on public expenditure efficiency of health and education spending. Her research has focused on the impact of child labor on school achievement in Latin America.

The review benefited from significant inputs from Sarah Coll-Black, Siddharth Sharma, and Frieda Vandeninden. Fiona Mackintosh edited the document, and Ana Lukau provided editorial support. The review was conducted under the overall direction of Deon Filmer, Stefano Paternostro, Manuel Salazar, and Lynne Sherburne-Benz.

This review is heavily based on 22 country-level safety net and social protection assessments undertaken by the World Bank from 2009 to 2013. These assessments analyzed the status, as well as the strengths and weaknesses, of safety nets in Africa. They also identified areas for improvement with the aim of helping governments and donors strengthen African safety net systems to protect and promote poor and vulnerable people. These assessments were prepared together with the respective country governments, and some of the assessments are published as joint World Bank and government products. Several of the assessments benefited from support from the United Kingdom's Department for International Development and the Rapid Social Response Program. The Rapid Social Response Program is the result of a concerted effort by several donors (Australia, Norway, the Russian Federation, and the United Kingdom) that seek to help developing countries implement efficient social protection systems to better protect poor and vulnerable people against serious shocks, such as food, energy, and financial crises.

Several World Bank staff members in the Africa Region Social Protection Unit were involved in preparing the country-level assessments, including Philippe Auffret, Anush Bezhanyan, Emily Weedon Chapman, Sarah Coll-Black, Carlo del Ninno, Randa El-Rashidi, Qaiser Khan, Alex Kamurase, Ida Manjolo,

Emma Mistiaen, Nina Rosas Raffo, Setareh Razmara, Manuel Salazar, Cornelia Tesliuc, Fanta Touré, John van Dyck, and Will Wiseman. In addition, a large number of international and local consultants prepared the data and drafted the reports. Patrick Premand also provided input, especially related to impact evaluation and the research agenda.

Andrew Dabalen, Margaret Grosh, and Ruslan Yemtsov provided external peer-review comments on the document. Social Protection colleagues also provided helpful guidance and comments to the review, including Harold Alderman, Anush Bezhanyan, Carlo del Ninno, Marito Garcia, Camilla Holmemo, Alex Kamurase, Phillippe G. Leite, Cem Mete, Emma Mistiaen, Setareh Razmara, Dena Ringold, Cornelia Tesliuc, Andrea Vermehren, and Will Wiseman.

Abbreviations

AIDS	acquired immunodeficiency syndrome
CCT	conditional cash transfer
CSG	child support grant
CT-OVC	Cash Transfer for Orphans and Vulnerable Children (Kenya)
DRMFSS	Disaster Risk Management and Food Security Sector (Ethiopia)
EDPRS	Economic Development and Poverty Reduction Strategy (Rwanda)
FARG	Fond d'Assistance aux Rescapées du Génocide, or Assistance Fund for Genocide Survivors (Rwanda)
FISP	Farmer Input Support Program (Zambia)
GDP	gross domestic product
HIV	human immunodeficiency virus
HSNP	Hunger Safety Net Programme (Kenya)
ICT	information and communication technology
LEAP	Livelihood Empowerment against Poverty (Ghana)
LIC	low-income country
M&E	monitoring and evaluation
MASAF	Malawi Social Action Fund
MIC	middle-income country
MIS	management information system
MOARD	Ministry of Agriculture and Rural Development (Ethiopia)
NGO	nongovernmental organization
NHIS	National Health Insurance Scheme (Ghana)
NISSA	National Information System for Social Assistance (Lesotho)
NSNP	National Safety Net Program (Kenya)
NSPS	National Social Protection Strategy (Rwanda and Kenya)
OAP	Old-Age Pension (Lesotho)
OPSF	Oil Price Stabilization Fund (the Philippines)
OVC	orphans and vulnerable children
PAD-Y	Projet d'Assainissement de Yaoundé, or Yaoundé Sanitation Project (Cameroon)

PASD	Programa Apoio Social Directo, or Direct Social Assistance Program (Mozambique)
PEJHIMO	Programme d'Emploi des Jeunes par l'Approche Haute Intensité de Main d'Œuvre, or Employment Program for Youth by High Labor Force Intensity (Mali)
PMT	proxy means testing
PRSP	Poverty Reduction Strategy Paper
PSA	Programa Subsidio de Alimentos, or Food Subsidy Program (Mozambique)
PSNP	Productive Safety Net Program (Ethiopia and Tanzania)
PUSH	Peri-Urban Community Self-Help (program) (Zambia)
SALOHI	Strengthening and Accessing Livelihood Opportunities for Household Impact (Madagascar)
SAVS	Stock Alimentaire Villageois de Sécurité, or village cereal banks (Mauritania)
SPLASH	Sustainable Program for Livelihoods and Solutions for Hunger (Zambia)
SSN	social safety net
STEPS	Sustainability through Economic Strengthening, Prevention, and Support (Zambia)
TASAF	Tanzania Social Action Fund
VUP	Vision 2020 Umurenge Program (Rwanda)
WFP	World Food Programme
YES	Youth Employment Skills (project) (Liberia)

Executive Summary

Over the past two decades, Africa's strong economic growth has paved the way for poverty reduction. Between 1995 and 2008, the percentage of the African population living in poverty fell from 58 percent to 48 percent (World Bank 2011). Nevertheless, high poverty levels persist, especially in rural areas, and the gap between income groups in terms of human capital and access to basic services is growing. In addition to *chronic poverty*—a situation where households are not able to improve their living standard and move out of poverty over time—vulnerability is high because environmental, economic, individual, and governance shocks frequently affect many households.

In the effort to increase the momentum in the progress toward sustainable poverty reduction, safety nets are an important tool in any country's development strategy. The high levels of persistent poverty and the increasing inequality suggest that in speeding up poverty reduction, targeted interventions such as safety nets, which provide regular and reliable support to poor households and help the poor invest in productive and capital-forming activities, may be important (see box ES.1). Safety nets can also provide additional support in times of crisis to those who are temporarily thrown into poverty and can help them develop strategies to build their resilience and thus avoid drawing down on their assets during times of hardship. Hence, safety nets will be essential to achieve the new World Bank goals.[1]

Until the recent urgency to strengthen safety nets for the poorest in the face of the global crisis and repeated droughts, social protection has been implemented only on an ad hoc basis in Africa. Over the past few years, in the wake of the global economic and food and fuel price crises, a number of countries have started to coordinate their separate safety net programs into a national system. There is also momentum throughout the region to rationalize public spending to provide more adequate and targeted support to the poorest. This effort responds to the growing body of evidence indicating that safety nets reduce chronic poverty and vulnerability and promote inclusive growth. Impact evaluations of safety net programs in Africa show that safety nets help households meet their basic consumption needs, protect their assets, and enable them to invest in human

Box ES.1 Definition of Terms

Safety nets refer to noncontributory transfer programs targeted in some way to the poor or vulnerable (Grosh *et al*. 2008). Safety nets aim to increase households' consumption—either directly or through substitution effects—of basic commodities and essential services. Safety nets are targeted to the poor and vulnerable—that is, individuals living in poverty and unable to meet their own basic needs or in danger of falling into poverty, because of either an external shock or socioeconomic circumstances, such as age, illness, or disability. *Safety nets* form a subset of broader social protection programs along with social insurance and social legislation. Hence, social protection includes both contributory and noncontributory programs, whereas safety nets are noncontributory.

capital. Moreover, recent research on the productive aspects of cash transfer programs in Africa suggests that these programs may have the potential to boost well-being in the future through productive investments (see box ES.2).

Objectives and Methods

This review assesses the current status of safety nets in Africa. The World Bank Africa Social Protection Strategy for 2012–22 highlights the need for a strong evidence base to inform the design and implementation of social protection programs in Africa (World Bank 2012). This review aims to contribute to that goal. It reviews and analyzes the objectives, features, systems, performance, and financing of safety nets in 22 countries in Sub-Saharan Africa (see map ES.1).[2] Through this analysis, it identifies areas for improvement to guide governments and donors in strengthening African safety net systems and helping them protect and promote poor and vulnerable people. The audience for this review is country governments that want to compare their countries' systems with those in other African countries, World Bank staff members, and personnel of other donor organizations that support safety net programs in Africa. The main data sources used are the 22 country-level safety net and social protection assessments undertaken by the World Bank between 2009 and 2013 as well as other relevant reviews of specific safety net program types (cash transfers, public works, and school feeding programs) in Africa.

In synthesizing this material, the review first summarizes the poverty and vulnerability profiles in the 22 countries. Second, it lays out the most common types of programs that exist in the region and the systems and institutional contexts in which they operate, such as the role of safety nets in the poverty reduction agenda, the existence of social protection strategic frameworks, and the extent to which the programs within a given country are coordinated. Third, it discusses the most common performance criteria used to assess safety nets. These criteria include the targeting effectiveness, coverage, generosity (benefit level), flexibility, and effects of social safety nets. Finally, the review discusses the cost

Box ES.2 The Productivity of Cash Transfers in Africa

Most safety net programs focus on reducing current levels of poverty. However, they may also have the potential to increase productivity and reduce poverty in the long term. Public works are considered productive even in the short term because, besides transferring income to disadvantaged households, they help create small community investments. Cash transfer programs (often conditional) can help poor families invest in the human capital of their children, for example, through more regular school attendance. However, some groups of the very poor and destitute may not be able to participate productively in society and may use income support to purchase food and other necessities (the protective role of safety nets). Improving consumption could be considered productive in itself; for instance, better nutritional intake helps children develop and improve their future prospects. Old-age assistance to grandparents in Kenya and South Africa has been shown to support the schooling of their grandchildren.

Helping households become more productive is an increasingly important aspect of safety nets in Africa. This potential remains to be fully exploited, but some findings from impact evaluations and other research in a number of African countries show promising results. Initial findings of this work (further detailed in chapter 4 in box 4.5) show that even a small amount of regular income support—even without any conditions—can help households diversify livelihoods and increase their consumption of "goods" (such as investment in assets, human capital, and small enterprise development) and move away from "bads," or negative coping strategies (such as reducing exploitive or risky employment and asset sales in times of distress). As such, safety nets can allow households to invest in higher-productivity, higher-return activities. Also, cash transfers were shown to boost the local economy through multiplier effects because beneficiaries spend transfers in the local market.

and financing sources of African safety net programs as well as their political, institutional, and financial sustainability.

The review attempts to compare and explain why various countries in the region approach safety nets differently and why they have different programs and objectives. The aim is to enable those lessons to be extrapolated to other countries. Moreover, the review provides insights on what drives safety net developments in different contexts and why establishing safety nets in Africa remains challenging. Throughout the analysis, the review identifies specific aspects of safety net systems that are in need of improvement. In parallel, it highlights examples from countries that have developed plans to make their safety nets more effective.

Importantly, however, safety nets are changing rapidly in a number of the countries reviewed, often in response to the findings of these assessments. Many of the safety net assessments were carried out with the explicit aim of informing governments' safety net–related policies and programs. In many cases, the analysis and resulting recommendations have led governments to reform existing programs or to launch new safety net instruments that provide more predictable support to poor and vulnerable households (for example, in Cameroon). In addition, advances in information and communication technology are quickly

Map ES.1 The 22 Countries Covered in This Review

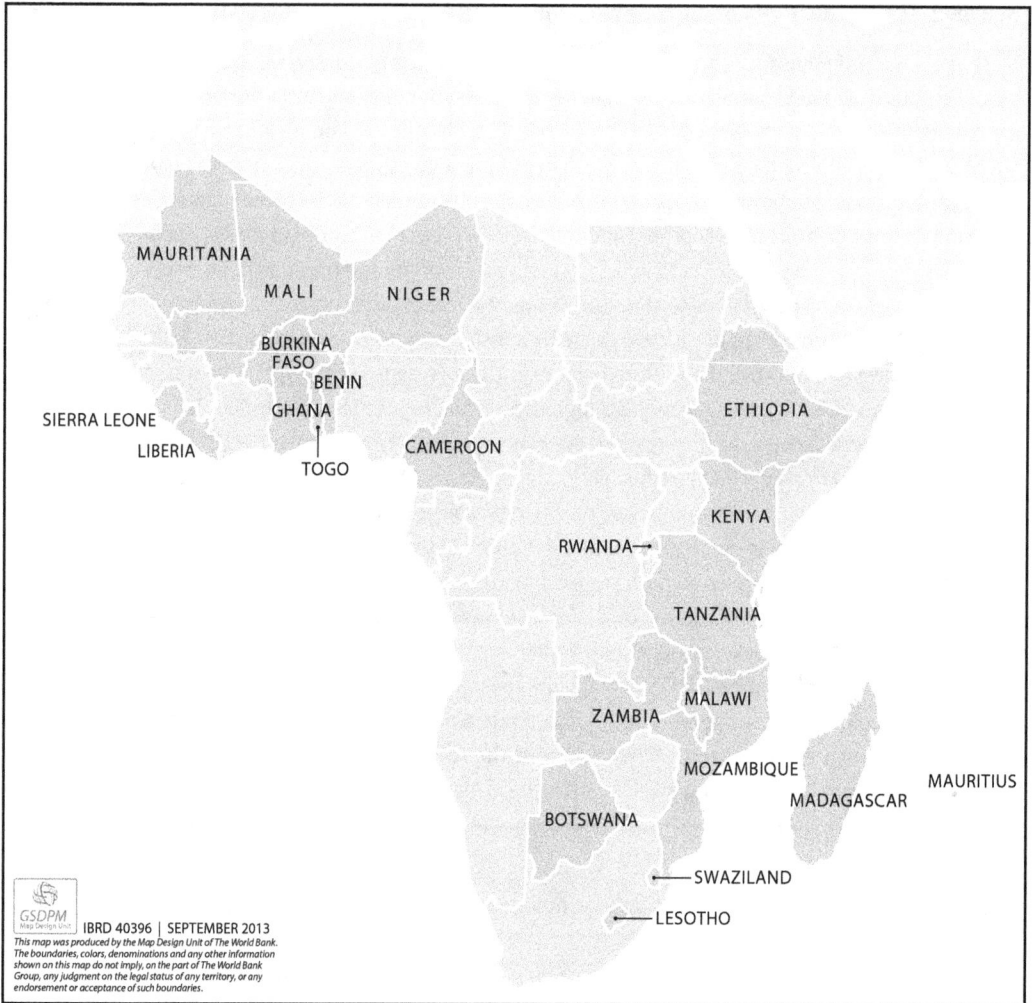

GSDPM
Map Design Unit
IBRD 40396 | SEPTEMBER 2013
This map was produced by the Map Design Unit of The World Bank.
The boundaries, colors, denominations and any other information
shown on this map do not imply, on the part of The World Bank
Group, any judgment on the legal status of any territory, or any
endorsement or acceptance of such boundaries.

creating opportunities for African countries to adopt international best practices with regard to the use of management information systems, single beneficiary registries, and payment systems, among others. Throughout the book, these cases are highlighted.

Conclusions Based on the Experience in the 22 Countries

Safety nets are needed in Africa both to support the poor and to help them weather shocks. Africa has a long tradition of family and community-based safety nets. As countries prosper, inequalities rise and social structures may erode as a result of economic and social change. In most African countries, government-led social safety nets are a relatively new phenomenon, but governments have become aware of the need to provide safety nets for the poor and vulnerable to help them cope with crises and to rise out of extreme poverty over time. However, given the vast extent of poverty and vulnerability in Africa, safety nets cannot reach all of the poor. They need to focus on the extremely poor and on specific vulnerable groups for maximum effect and affordability—not only helping protect them but also providing a ladder out of poverty in the longer term.

Safety nets have evolved differently across Africa in response to the specific political economy and sociocultural background in each country. Hence, the policy frameworks, approaches, and institutional arrangements that govern safety net systems are not homogeneous across the continent. For instance, middle-income countries (MICs) in southern Africa have strong government-led systems based on horizontal equity, whereas in fragile states and low-income countries (LICs), such as those in West Africa, the social protection agenda tends to be more donor influenced. Any measures to strengthen safety nets need to be designed in ways that take into account these context-specific factors.

Despite this heterogeneity across the continent, safety nets are taking hold as core poverty reduction instruments in Africa. More and more African countries are preparing social protection strategies to serve as the foundation on which to build effective and efficient safety net systems. Safety nets are also being placed higher on government agendas. The review shows that about three-fourths of the countries studied include safety nets as a component of their overall poverty reduction strategy and over half have prepared or are preparing a social protection strategy. Experience from some African countries, such as Rwanda, shows that clear action plans with careful costing and implementation plans are crucial for putting strategies into operation.

Although safety nets in Africa generally lack strong institutional homes and coordinating bodies, examples of robust implementation arrangements exist. Responsibility for government safety net programs is generally spread over a number of different ministries, such as the ministries of social affairs, women and family, and employment, as well as other cross-sectoral ministries that often lack significant political decision-making power within the government. The Ethiopia Productive Safety Net Program (PSNP) is, however, an example of how countries could create effective implementation arrangements that span multiple ministries. Meanwhile, fragmented donor support often leaves LICs with a host of small and isolated programs that lack coordination or a political champion. For instance, both Liberia and Madagascar have more than five different public works programs, each operated by different donor organizations and government agencies.

The results of this review show that few African countries have well-planned safety net systems that are capable of taking a strategic approach to reducing poverty and vulnerability. Instead, a multitude of interventions exist that are fragmented, typically donor driven, and together do not effectively target the poor. In LICs, for example, in West Africa, safety nets are focused on emergency relief and food-related issues. Few provide continuous support to the large number of chronically poor, although such programs are more common in MICs (such as in Botswana, South Africa, and Swaziland) because of the prevalence of social assistance and social pension programs in those countries. Looking across countries, we find that the most common kinds of programs are school feeding programs, public works programs, in-kind emergency and nonemergency programs, categorical transfer programs, and general subsidies. National poverty-targeted cash transfer programs are not common, although some of the significant number of small programs are currently being expanded. For example, Rwanda is expanding the coverage of the Vision 2020 Umurenge Program, and in Kenya, the government is bringing five cash transfer programs into the National Safety Net Program.

Lacking long-term, development-oriented safety nets, many LICs and fragile states still react to crises and disasters by providing emergency relief. These shock-response mechanisms tend to be weak, inflexible, and unpredictable. Moreover, very little information is available about the effectiveness of food distribution and emergency relief programs that are common in West Africa (for example, in Benin, Burkina Faso, Cameroon, Mali, and Mauritania). Countries are increasingly looking to the positive experience of the risk-financing component of Ethiopia's PSNP.

More monitoring data on safety net programs in Africa would help assess their effectiveness. In general, little is known about the effectiveness of safety net programs in Africa, and lack of basic program information systems and data is a crucial weakness. Many countries do not have accurate administrative data on the number of beneficiaries reached and benefit levels provided by each of the programs. Programs that distribute food, for instance, in response to emergencies, particularly lack data.

Coverage of the poor and vulnerable by existing safety net programs is low, although growing in some countries. Taken together, each country's safety net programs cover only a very small share of the total number of poor and vulnerable people. For example, in Benin, the net coverage rate of all safety net programs is estimated to be only about 5–6 percent of the poor. In Kenya, estimates show that cash transfers reached about 9 percent of the poor population in 2010, but the government is planning to expand coverage so that by 2018, 17 percent of the poor will be reached. The exception is universal social pension programs common in southern Africa, which cover a large share of the elderly population. However, the coverage of poverty-targeted programs in many MICs is still limited. To achieve their goals at a reasonable cost, safety nets need to be well targeted, cover the identified groups, provide adequate benefits, and be flexible enough to adjust to changing needs and to respond to the types of shocks that are now being faced by many countries.

Targeted programs are still not widely available in Africa. Poverty-targeted programs are rare and mainly practiced in small and new pilot initiatives, with only 20 percent of the programs reviewed using some form of means testing (based on actual consumption income) or proxy means testing to target the poor.

Evidence shows that, in some cases, community-based targeting can identify the poorest households for safety net support. A key question is how well African safety nets are able to identify and reach the poor and vulnerable, especially those in extreme poverty and vulnerability, given data and capacity constraints. Improving the extent to which safety nets can reach the poor also depends on political viability.

With better analysis of safety nets, in part from safety net assessments, several countries are on a path toward developing more effective safety net systems. Our review suggests that 36 percent of the countries analyzed are building a system whereas half still need to make more progress. A number of countries are actively increasing the effectiveness and the scale of their existing programs, including some that are relatively well targeted (such as the programs run by the Tanzania Social Action Fund, Ghana's Livelihood Empowerment against Poverty program, and Kenya's Cash Transfer for Orphans and Vulnerable Children program). In a handful of countries, such as Rwanda and Tanzania, sustainable and more institutionalized programs are starting to appear, backed by influential ministries such as the ministries of finance, economy, and planning. Also, more countries are moving toward building safety net systems and programs that are predictable and are flexible enough to respond to crises (for example, Cameroon, the Republic of Congo, Guinea, Mali, Mozambique, Niger, and Senegal). Ethiopia's PSNP has long been a pioneer in this respect.

Well-targeted safety nets are affordable in Africa, especially if inefficient universal and categorical spending can be reduced and redirected to the extremely poor and to specific vulnerable groups and if fragmented programs can be harmonized.

- In LICs, because poverty is high and government income low, attracting donor funds to support the safety net agenda will continue to be vital in both the short run and the longer run. With the exception of universal programs such as old-age benefits and general subsidies, donors finance a large share of safety nets in Africa—for example, over 80 percent of safety net spending in Burkina Faso, Liberia, Mali, and Sierra Leone.
- In MICs, however, current public budgets are sufficient to provide adequate support to the poorest. For instance, in Cameroon, estimates indicate that it would cost only 0.5 percent of gross domestic product to provide an adequate safety net to half the chronic poor.
- General subsidies are costly mechanisms for redistributing income and often do not benefit the poor, as is true, for example, of the fuel subsidies in Cameroon, Mauritania, and Sierra Leone and the Farmer Input Support Program in Zambia. Reducing poorly targeted programs and subsidies can make fiscal space for more effective and better-targeted safety nets. Likewise, well-performing safety nets providing support to the most vulnerable groups can be important mitigating mechanisms to facilitate reform of expensive general subsidies.

- Growing natural resource discoveries across Africa (see World Bank 2013) are likely to provide additional fiscal space for safety nets.

Moving Forward to Strengthen Safety Nets in Africa

Data collection and the monitoring systems that support safety net programs need to be improved systematically across Africa. Basic and core data on the number and type of beneficiaries reached and information about program outcomes and impact are imperative to improve the design and coordination of programs, to keep decision makers informed, and to attract financial resources and donor support. The impact of safety nets on poverty and welfare indicators, where known, has generally been positive but mixed. More and more impact evaluations are being undertaken, thereby contributing to a growing body of evidence on safety net programs in Africa. Although in the past most impact evaluations have been for small donor pilots for research purposes, such as Malawi's Zomba cash transfer program or Mali's Bourse maman, larger programs, such as those in Ethiopia, Kenya, and Tanzania, are now benefiting from impact evaluations.

Harmonizing and coordinating safety net programs into a coherent system should be a priority. Within a given country, a small number of coordinated and well-functioning programs can effectively and feasibly meet the needs of the poorest, as happens in Rwanda. Also, African governments, with the support of international donors, should continue to prepare social protection strategies that link, consolidate, and harmonize programs and put the strategies into operation.

Safety nets should be built on the basis of strong operational tools to ensure effective program implementation and monitoring and establishment of institutional and coordinating bodies in charge of organization and planning. Basic operational tools, such as beneficiary registries, targeting methods, payment systems, and monitoring and evaluation systems, provide a platform that enables programs to deliver support effectively to targeted groups. More work is needed to understand how existing food-based programs and their infrastructure should play a part in new and improved safety net systems in Africa.

These systems need to be built during stable times so that they are ready and can respond quickly to crisis. Establishing such systems takes time. Most countries in Africa (including Benin, Cameroon, Mauritania, and Sierra Leone) did not have safety nets capable of effectively responding to the recent global crises but had to resort to inefficient and expensive universal handouts.

More accurate targeting of African safety net programs is likely to involve a combination of targeting methods that together can distinguish the appropriate households and individuals. Which targeting approach is chosen will depend on the program's objective and the institutional capacity of the implementing agencies, and the approach will have to be customized to the particular poverty profile and political economy of the country in question. Household-level income and consumption data are often not precise enough to be reliable as the sole basis for identifying those most in need. Assessing the targeting accuracy of programs is important, irrespective of which targeting method is used.

Programs that are well targeted and are serving the poor effectively should be scaled up, whereas ineffective programs should be gradually phased out. As mentioned previously, because of Africa's widespread poverty and vulnerability, safety nets cannot reach all the poor but need to focus on the poorest and most vulnerable to ensure maximum influence and affordability. The allocation of safety net spending on scattered emergency programs shows that, typically, neither donors nor governments have focused on safety nets for addressing long-term chronic poverty. This situation is now starting to change. Ethiopia, Kenya, Mozambique, Rwanda, and Tanzania are moving to harmonize programs for enhanced efficiency and coverage.

The role of safety nets in the context of subsidy reform and use of mineral resource proceeds should be further explored with the unique political economy of each country in mind. In moving forward with efforts in Africa to rationalize public spending for better reaching the poorest, safety nets are an important mitigating aspect that countries may want to have in place. Careful political economy considerations are important when balancing tightly targeted programs with other investments that can benefit a wider set of people and contribute to improved social outcomes. As more and more African countries are benefiting from newfound mineral resource wealth,[3] getting the balance right between effectively targeting those funds to the poorest through safety nets or other investments in social services and building both a fiscally and politically sustainable social protection system will be especially important.

Implementing the Vision: What Can Other Countries Learn?

Countries need to pursue the reform agenda most suitable to their context. One size does not fit all. The path of safety net development and reform should be based on careful analysis of each country's specific needs and challenges. The 22 safety net assessments provide thoughtful country-specific recommendations for doing so. However, using the country typology chosen for this review (see table 1.1 in chapter 1), we can make some general recommendations. These recommendations are intended to serve as guidance for other African countries on how to develop their safety net systems and to learn from the experience in the 22 countries.

The following recommendations apply to countries that are classified in the typology used in this review as "early stage or no plans." Such countries have no solid plans for a national safety net system or no adequate programs in place.[4] They mainly consist of LICs and fragile states but also include some MICs whose main form of income redistribution is through general subsidies.

- *Develop and put into operation a safety net strategy.* This strategy should assign clear institutional responsibilities for safety net programs and policies, with specific roles and responsibilities for involved ministries and agencies. The strategy should be used as the basis for building strong financial and political support for the safety net agenda. It should also be embedded in the country's broader poverty reduction agenda.

- *Build key organizational tools on which safety net programs should be based.* These tools include basic targeting mechanisms, a registry, a payment system, and a strong monitoring system. They can channel transfers from various programs to the targeted poor and vulnerable groups that enhance efficiency accountability and transparency. Multiple programs should migrate toward using a single registry, a common payment system, and a coordinated monitoring and evaluation system, even though the programs may support different groups of people.

- *Coordinate scattered donor support.* Safety net development in this group of countries will continue to depend on donor support, at least in the medium term. With the long-term view of moving toward a coordinated system of safety nets, these countries must begin harmonizing the funding given and approaches taken by donors, guided by the government's safety net strategy and the establishment of underlying systems. In postconflict countries, establishing government systems to track and monitor existing donor programs can offer a practical foundation for government interventions and can build country ownership in low-capacity and fragile contexts.

- *Develop a few key safety net programs that are based on a careful analysis of the country's needs.* This small number of key safety net interventions should (a) provide regular support to people in chronic and extreme poverty and (b) be able to expand and contract to provide assistance to poor and vulnerable households in the case of emergencies or seasonal fluctuations in income and consumption. Which programs are chosen and how they are implemented should be based on the country's poverty profile, the experience of pilot programs, and feasibility studies. Particular efforts should be made to develop robust targeting methods for these programs so that, when the programs are considered functioning well and when the political economy and fiscal resources allow, they can be scaled up to become efficient national programs. However, this expansion does not necessarily have to take place right away. Other existing smaller programs should be strengthened, especially to gather basic monitoring data to inform decisions about their future.

- *Other context-specific recommendations.* Countries with generous general subsidies and with emergency aid programs should consider reallocating some of those funds to more targeted interventions. Moreover, because human development outcomes tend to be poor in this group of countries, policy makers should seek to establish synergies between safety nets and health, education, and nutrition interventions.

The following recommendations apply to countries that are classified as "emerging" because their safety net systems are in the process of being developed.[5] They consist mainly of LICs but also include some MICs.

- *Continue to reform existing categorical, universal, and ad hoc food emergency programs to make them more effective and efficient tools for reducing poverty.* Improving poverty targeting is especially important. For instance, social pension programs could be more cost-effective if they were targeted only to elderly people and people with disabilities who are also poor, and grants for orphans and vulnerable children as well as other children should target only those in poor and vulnerable families. Efforts to reallocate universal subsidies and expensive ad hoc emergency programs toward better-targeted and development-oriented safety net support should continue.

- *Continue scaling up a few key, relatively well-targeted programs.* Experience from the 22 countries shows that a small number of complementary and well-coordinated programs is often sufficient for meeting the needs of the poor. Which programs are selected will vary by country, but they should provide regular support to chronically poor families or individuals and be flexible enough to scale up and down to provide shorter-term or repeated support to poor and vulnerable groups in response to shocks. As these programs are being scaled up, they should be continuously assessed to ensure that vulnerable groups are being adequately supported. It may also be appropriate to supplement these core programs with smaller complementary programs and services that focus on helping beneficiaries engage in productive and promotive activities, such as investing in the health and education of children.

- *Continue harmonizing and consolidating fragmented safety net programs.* Even if countries have prepared safety net or social protection strategies, they also need to prepare well-costed action plans. While the core programs are being implemented, these countries should continue to harmonize and consolidate the objectives and operational tools of their various programs. Unique beneficiary registration systems should be explored to reduce duplication and overlap. The capacity to develop robust information systems, monitoring and evaluation systems, and payment systems will need to be strengthened or built.

- *Coordinate donor funding and technical assistance into one collective financing envelope or "basket."* As occurred in Ethiopia, such coordination can minimize duplication and maximize effectiveness as a first step toward the government taking over financing of the safety net system in the medium to long term. To build sustainability, countries must secure a medium-term funding envelope from domestic sources. Donor support and technical assistance are likely to remain important in the short and medium run to strengthen systems and scale up programs.

The following recommendations apply to countries that are classified as "established" and that already have a national safety net and social protection system in place.[6] They consist mainly of MICs.

- *Strengthen the existing safety net and social protection system to ensure that it is reaching the extremely poor.* Even when countries have well-established programs, large overlaps in programs often occur along with significant inclusion errors, and some gaps can remain, with some members of the poorest and most excluded groups not receiving sufficient support. Within the existing budget, it is entirely possible to refine the targeting mechanisms used by universal and categorical programs to provide adequate support to the poorest families and individuals within these groups.

- *Continue harmonizing and consolidating fragmented safety net programs.* As in countries with emerging systems, more effort is needed even in this group of countries to integrate the individual programs into one national system. This effort may require policy makers to reduce the number of existing programs by assessing their individual targeting effectiveness and impact compared with other interventions within the safety net system.

- *Continue strengthening the effectiveness of targeting, unique registry systems, payment systems, monitoring and evaluation systems, and grievance systems.* This task includes incorporating information technology for better management, accountability, and governance of programs and linking program eligibility and registries to national identification databases.

An Agenda for Learning

Strong monitoring and information systems are necessary elements of the safety net learning agenda, but they will need to be complemented by analysis based on nationally representative surveys and rigorous impact evaluations. Although this basic information is critical and generated only through program monitoring systems, it is only a part of the necessary information and will have to be complemented by other types of data and analysis, such as (a) data collection and analysis through representative household surveys of how safety net benefits reach households and (b) impact evaluations and testing of various delivery mechanisms and program features for closing knowledge gaps and providing more information of what works for safety nets in Africa. Potential areas for future evaluation and research in Africa, some already ongoing, include the productive aspect of safety nets, the relative effectiveness of conditional and unconditional cash transfers, and synergies between climate change and social protection.

The World Bank is contributing to this learning agenda by promoting and facilitating knowledge generation and sharing. The Bank is helping generate new knowledge through new analytical work. Currently, more than 20 World Bank–supported impact evaluations are ongoing in the social protection sector in

Africa, and several more are in the planning stages. Moving beyond the 22 safety net assessments included in this review, future country-level assessments should cover the broader social protection sector, including contributory social insurance and labor market programs. Many opportunities for South-South learning exist within and beyond the continent. The World Bank is already actively supporting this kind of exchange of knowledge through the annual South-South Learning Forum on social protection and by supporting initiatives such as the recent Communities of Practice on cash transfers among researchers and implementers and bilateral study tours and visits. Nineteen countries regularly meet in the Community of Practice for cash transfer programs in Africa, and another nine countries will soon join.

Notes

1. During the spring meetings in April 2013, the Development Committee endorsed the World Bank Group's new goals of reducing the number of people living on less than US$1.25 per day of purchasing power parity to 3 percent by 2030 and boosting shared prosperity by focusing on the bottom 40 percent of the population.

2. The countries are Benin, Botswana, Burkina Faso, Cameroon, Ethiopia, Ghana, Kenya, Lesotho, Liberia, Madagascar, Malawi, Mali, Mauritania, Mauritius, Mozambique, Niger, Rwanda, Sierra Leone, Swaziland, Tanzania, Togo, and Zambia. See box 1.4 in chapter 1.

3. It is estimated that over the next 10 years, about 30 countries in Sub-Saharan Africa will be dependent on mineral resources (over 20 percent of exports), not counting oil and gas exports (World Bank 2013).

4. Among the 22 countries, this group includes Benin, Burkina Faso, Cameroon, Liberia, Madagascar, Malawi, Mauritania, Sierra Leone, Togo, and Zambia, although countries can change groups over time.

5. Among the 22 countries, this group includes Ethiopia, Ghana, Kenya, Lesotho, Mali, Mozambique, Niger, Rwanda, Swaziland, and Tanzania, although countries can change groups over time.

6. Among the 22 countries, this group includes Botswana and Mauritius, although countries can change groups over time.

References

Grosh, Margaret, Carlo del Ninno, Emil Tesliuc, and Azedine Ouerghi. 2008. *For Protection and Promotion: The Design and Implementation of Effective Safety Nets.* Washington, DC: World Bank.

World Bank. 2011. *Africa's Future and the World Bank's Support to It: Africa Regional Strategy.* Washington, DC: World Bank.

———. 2012. *Managing Risk, Promoting Growth: Developing Systems for Social Protection in Africa—The World Bank's Africa Social Protection Strategy, 2012–2022.* Washington, DC: World Bank.

———. 2013. "Securing the Transformational Potential in Africa's Mineral Resources." PowerPoint presentation, World Bank, Washington, DC.

CHAPTER 1

The Changing Landscape: An Introduction

The Rise of Safety Nets in Africa

Given its recent strong economic growth, Africa has the momentum to sustainably reduce poverty levels. Since the 1990s, growth has been rapid in most African countries. As a consequence, the percentage of the African population living in poverty fell from 58 percent to 48 percent between 1995 and 2008 (World Bank 2011a).[1] African countries also made significant progress in improving social indicators during that period. However, chronic poverty remains high despite this strong growth, and most African countries can still be characterized as having low incomes. Low-productivity employment and subsistence farming dominate economic activity. Over one-quarter of the region's population lives in countries that are fragile or conflict affected, and despite recent expansions in the availability of infrastructure and services, a significant portion of the population still lacks access to basic services.

Recent gains in poverty reduction remain fragile because of the increasing volatility and risk. Negative shocks arising from the global economic slowdown and climate change could undermine the recent progress in poverty reduction. The vast majority of Africans make their living from the land, which means that they are particularly vulnerable to climate shocks and natural disasters. During the 2008–10 global economic crisis, a 50 percent increase in food prices resulted in an increase in poverty rates in West and Central Africa of 2.5–4.4 percentage points (World Bank 2011a). More recently, in July 2012, the World Bank's Food Price Index reached its all-time peak, 1 percent higher than the previous peak in February 2011. The high prices threaten the well-being of millions of people, especially in many African countries. Frequent natural disasters such as droughts and floods also increase the risks faced by the poor.

These findings point to the fact that economic growth may not be enough to substantially reduce extreme poverty in Africa. As prosperity increases, societies often become more unequal, and social structures may erode as a result of shocks and economic and social developments. This phenomenon is occurring in Africa today. In Tanzania, for example, the poorest 10 percent of the population has not benefited from recent economic growth. The northern savannah area of Ghana has been left behind in the growth process, with the share of the poor living in the rural savannah increasing from 32.6 percent in 1991/92 to 49.3 percent in 2005/06.

Evidence from a number of countries shows that safety net support can reduce poverty and inequality. Studies have found, for example, that Bolsa Família, the largest conditional cash transfer program in the world, was responsible for one-fifth of Brazil's remarkable reduction in inequality, while having no negative impact on economic growth. The old-age pensions in South Africa have reduced the poverty gap ratio between the richest and poorest citizens by 13 percent. At the same time, the country's comprehensive system of cash transfers has doubled the share of national income that the poorest 20 percent of the population receives. In Africa, it is increasingly clear that safety net support is needed as a complement to economic growth to enable the poorest households to meet their immediate needs and to strengthen their ability to rise out of poverty.[2] In this review, the term *safety nets* refers to noncontributory transfer programs targeted in some way to the poor or vulnerable (Grosh *et al.* 2008; see box 1.1).

However, until the recent urgency to protect the poor and vulnerable affected by the global economic crisis and the food and fuel price crises, safety nets in Africa have largely been implemented on an ad hoc basis. Africa has a long history of informal, traditional safety nets that are family and community based. Recent analysis has shown that these informal support networks are increasingly inadequate for the challenges that the region faces (World Bank 2012a). Social assistance ministries tend to be weak, and spending on targeted safety net programs is much lower than is needed given the extent of poverty. As a result, the effectiveness of Africa's safety net systems and their ability to

---

Box 1.1 The Definition of Social Safety Nets

In this review, the term *safety nets* refers to noncontributory transfer programs targeted in some way to the poor or vulnerable (Grosh *et al.* 2008), whereas *social protection* refers to both contributory and noncontributory programs. The definition is further discussed in appendix A, which specifies the types of safety nets that are included in this review.

Safety nets aim to increase the consumption of basic commodities and essential services, either directly or through substitution effects. Safety nets are targeted to the poor and vulnerable—in other words, individuals who are living in poverty and are unable to meet their own basic needs or who are in danger of falling into poverty because of either an external shock or socioeconomic circumstances such as age, illness, or disability. *Safety nets* are a subset of broader social protection policies and programs along with social insurance and social legislation such as labor laws and safety standards that set minimum civic standards to safeguard the interests of individuals.

Source: Grosh *et al.* 2008.

respond to crises vary by country. As in other regions of the world, middle-income countries in Africa (such as Botswana, Mauritius, and South Africa) have well-developed safety nets. In contrast, most low-income countries and fragile states have had only small, fragmented programs that have tended to be donor driven, although this situation is changing quickly as countries increasingly invest in programs that have demonstrated results and as they adopt international best practices.[3]

African governments now have a growing interest in developing safety nets. Although the concept is still relatively new in Africa, formal safety nets, especially cash transfers, are emerging as governments are increasingly recognizing that food aid has not been effective and that informal safety nets have weakened as a result of migration, urbanization, the spread of HIV/AIDS, and the recent global crisis.[4] At the same time, a number of safety net programs in Africa are demonstrating a range of positive results, including improved consumption, investments in productive assets, and poverty reduction.[5] Since 2009 (and even earlier in some countries such as Ethiopia), safety net programming has increasingly been changing from emergency food aid and one-off safety net interventions mainly focused on food insecurity to regular and predictable safety nets such as targeted cash transfers and cash-for-work programs.

Several countries are now seeking to turn individual programs into national safety net systems. The World Bank's Africa Social Protection Strategy (2012–22) aims to support countries as they reform their safety net programs into more effective systems (World Bank 2012b). Ghana, Kenya, Mozambique, Rwanda, and Tanzania, among other countries, are seeking to move in this direction. Box 1.2 describes how Kenya is moving from fragmented programs to a safety net system. Even conflict-affected states such as Liberia have programs that target ex-combatants, youths, and the chronically poor and are now looking at developing broader national social protection strategies. Indeed, the 2011 *World Development Report* (World Bank 2011c) identified safety nets as an effective means of delivering early, tangible results, which are required to restore confidence in postconflict states.

The Need for Safety Nets in Africa

The most important rationale for safety nets in Africa is the large share of people who are vulnerable, poor, and food insecure.[6] Strong economic growth has not translated into lower poverty for most Africans, and the gap between the extremely poor and the rising middle class is widening in many countries. In addition, growing social, environmental, and economic fragility on the continent makes it increasingly important for governments to maintain social peace and economic equilibrium. To sustain the great increases in growth that have been achieved in many African countries, governments are eager to ensure that no one is left behind. Given the vast extent of poverty in Africa, safety nets cannot reach all of the poor with the limited resources that are available. Such programs must therefore focus on reaching the extremely poor and the most vulnerable.

Box 1.2 The World Bank's Africa Social Protection Strategy: Moving toward Systems in Kenya

The World Bank's Africa Social Protection Strategy (2012–22) aims to support countries moving from fragmented approaches to social protection to more harmonized systems that ensure more effective coordination across programs. Although the approach varies across countries, the strategy suggests that efforts usually focus on three areas: building basic management and administrative systems; integrating, harmonizing, or coordinating programs; and ensuring policy coherence and a long-term vision.

Kenya provides an excellent example of how to put this strategy into operation. In the area of building basic management and administrative systems, the National Safety Net Program (NSNP), which the World Bank is supporting through Program-for-Results financing, will extend good practices developed by two pilot programs to the NSNP and strengthen targeting, payments, and complaint and grievance systems. Support to the integration, harmonization, and coordination of programs will be achieved by developing a strategy to consolidate the four programs currently managed by the Ministry of Gender, Children, and Social Development; the adoption of a common monitoring and evaluation framework; and the establishment of a single registry. Notably, the broader policy context for social protection in Kenya envisions this shift from programs to systems for both social assistance and social protection more broadly. With regard to building a social protection system more generally, beyond the NSNP, the government is considering how to extend the single registry to all poverty-targeted programs and how to create links between the NSNP and the National Health Insurance Fund and youth employment schemes.

In many areas, the NSNP is replicating international good practice with regard to the delivery of safety net support. The single registry, which is a new concept in Africa, builds particularly on Brazil's experience with such a registry. The delivery of payments electronically to bank accounts using biometric smart cards points to how innovations in information and communication technology can be harnessed to improve the security and reach of safety nets to hard-to-reach populations. Finally, the NSNP provides a clear demonstration of how African countries can move beyond the current fragmentation of safety nets, with many small donor-financed programs providing limited, time-bound coverage, to a government-managed system.

Source: World Bank 2012b.

Weak risk management and historical social exclusion further justify the need for safety nets in Africa. Repeated shocks, such as rising food prices, droughts, and floods, also increase the risks faced by the poor. Nevertheless, formal risk management mechanisms such as credit markets are generally not accessible to the poorest, and informal systems may not adequately protect against systemic (communitywide) risk (see chapter 2). Hence, even a temporary loss of income because of a shock can lead vulnerable households to fall into poverty, depleting their productive assets further without strategies to build up their resilience and avoid drawing down on assets. Box 1.3 summarizes the economic theory behind safety nets with examples from developing countries around the world.

Box 1.3 The Economic Theory: When Markets Fail to Support Investments in the Poor

A market failure opens up the possibility of more efficient investments in the poor in many situations. Under certain types of credit market imperfection and if economies of scale exist, the poor may be unable to take advantage of profitable opportunities because they do not have access to the required scale. Thus, they may be trapped in a low-productivity sector in the economy, even as more productive opportunities go unexploited, because they are unable to commit to repayment in credit markets. Investments in the poor may raise their ability to take advantage of more profitable investments, thereby reducing both inequality and inefficiency.

This possibility was first modeled by Loury (1981), who introduced credit constraints into a model of intergenerational mobility. Galor and Zeira (1993) further noted the link between aggregate efficiency and reduced inequality under nonconvex production sets. Banerjee and Newman (1993) exploited long-term implications of the same types of basic mechanisms by noting the effect of initial levels of inequality on patterns of occupational choice and subsequent inequality trajectories. All these papers demonstrate the theoretical plausibility that some redistribution may increase efficiency.

Empirical examples of aggregate underinvestment arising from the inability of the poor to access credit and insurance markets on equal terms now abound. In one striking case from Africa, Goldstein and Udry (1999) document the failure of many farmers to switch from a low-return maize and cassava intercrop to a more profitable pineapple culture in southern Ghana. Despite the expected return of 1,200 percent, only 190 of 1,070 plots in the study sample made the switch. When farmers were asked why, the model answer was, "I don't have the money." In Sri Lanka, de Mel, McKenzie, and Woodruff (2008) used a randomized experimental design to estimate the return on capital for microenterprises that generally are thought to be credit constrained. They found average monthly real rates of return of 5.7 percent—much higher than the market interest rate. The existence of investment projects (in preexisting firms) that are profitable at the prevailing market rate but that do not take place (before the intervention) is prima facie evidence that the credit market is imperfect.

Until the underlying causes of failures in the credit and insurance markets can be corrected, this kind of evidence suggests that targeted cash transfers can be useful not only in reducing inequality and current poverty, but also in reducing inefficiencies in the economywide allocation of resources.

Sources: Fiszbein and Schady 2009; box 2.1.

Safety nets promote resilience, equity, and opportunity among poor and vulnerable people in Africa. The literature describes social safety nets as having two mandates: (a) protection to support households that are coping with chronic poverty or the effects of shocks, and (b) promotion to help households rise out of poverty by enabling them to make investments that will increase their human and physical capital (see, for example, Fiszbein and Schady 2009; Grosh *et al.*

2008; World Bank 2012b). Moreover, the World Bank's Africa Social Protection Strategy describes how social protection reduces poverty and contributes to sustainable, inclusive growth through three functions: resilience, equity, and opportunity (World Bank 2012b). These multiple functions are reflected in the multiple objectives of safety net programs in Africa. Many safety net programs aim to protect immediate consumption and to guarantee individuals and households a minimum level of well-being while helping reduce the socioeconomic harm that results from acute inequality, as well as promote productivity in a more permanent way. Yet safety nets have many other complementary objectives, such as (a) helping the poor cope with shocks and manage risk; (b) allowing them to invest in their own human capital and break the cycle of intergenerational poverty; (c) providing them with support during agricultural slack seasons so they do not have to resort to selling assets that are needed for longer-term growth; (d) allowing the poor to build up some capital, thereby enabling them to diversify their income-generating activities; and (e) injecting funds directly into the local economy, thus creating multiplier effects in poor areas. These objectives and the effectiveness of programs to achieve them are explored in later chapters of this book.

Safety net programs will be essential for achieving the World Bank Group's new goals to end extreme poverty. During the spring meetings in April 2013, the Development Committee endorsed the World Bank Group's new goals of reducing the number of people living on less than US$1.25 per day (purchasing power parity) to 3 percent by 2030 and boosting shared prosperity by focusing on the bottom 40 percent of the population. Given the increase in mineral resource discoveries in many African countries (see World Bank 2013), reaching these objectives through transfer programs such as safety nets is becoming increasingly feasible financially.

The World Bank's Africa Social Protection Strategy explains that the question is no longer whether low-income African countries can afford to provide safety nets but rather whether they can afford not to do so (World Bank 2012b). In addition to the fact that safety nets can contribute to reducing poverty and promoting inclusive growth, the costs of not protecting poor households from the negative effects of shocks and chronic poverty are high and last far into the future, disproportionately affecting children. Safety nets can be affordable in Africa by making social protection spending more efficient and by relying on the support of international donors in the short to medium term (World Bank 2012b).

Objectives, Methodology, and Typology

This review assesses the status of safety nets in Africa, considers their strengths and weaknesses, and identifies areas for improvement to guide governments and donors in their efforts to strengthen African safety net systems to better protect and promote poor and vulnerable people. The review summarizes and cross-analyzes the safety net experiences in 22 Sub-Saharan African countries.[7] The main data (qualitative and quantitative) presented in this book are drawn from

22 individual country safety net and social protection assessments unless otherwise indicated. (For a list of the 22 countries, see box 1.4.) Trends and contrasts are discussed, and specific country experiences are used for illustration. The review also draws on analyses that have been done of specific cash transfer programs (Garcia and Moore 2012), public works programs (McCord and Slater 2009; Milazzo and del Ninno 2012), and school feeding programs (Bundy *et al.* 2009) in Africa. The landscape is quickly changing, however, and a number of countries are making big strides toward more effective safety nets.

Box 1.4 Country Safety Net Reports Used in This Review

1. **Benin:** World Bank. 2011. "Les Filets Sociaux au Benin: Outils de Réduction de la Pauvreté—Rapport de Synthèse." World Bank, Washington, DC.
2. **Botswana:** World Bank. 2011. "Botswana: Challenges to the Safety Net—Preparing for the Next Crisis." World Bank, Washington, DC.
3. **Burkina Faso:** World Bank. 2011. "Burkina Faso: Social Safety Nets." Washington, DC: World Bank.
4. **Cameroon:** World Bank. 2012. "Cameroun: Filets Sociaux." World Bank, Washington, DC.
5. **Ethiopia:** PSNP (Productive Safety Net Program). 2010. "Designing and Implementing a Rural Safety Net in a Low-Income Setting: Lessons Learned from Ethiopia's Productive Safety Net Program 2005–2009." Addis Ababa: Government of Ethiopia.
6. **Ghana:** World Bank. 2011. "Republic of Ghana: Improving the Targeting of Social Programs." Washington, DC: World Bank.
7. **Kenya:** Ministry of State for Planning, National Development, and Vision 2030. 2012. "Kenya Social Protection Sector Review." Nairobi: Republic of Kenya.
8. **Lesotho:** World Bank. 2012. "Lesotho: A Safety Net to End Extreme Poverty." Washington, DC: World Bank.
9. **Liberia:** World Bank. 2012. "A Diagnostic of Social Protection in Liberia." Washington, DC: World Bank.
10. **Madagascar:** World Bank. 2012. "Madagascar: Three Years into the Crisis—An Assessment of Vulnerability and Social Policies and Prospects for the Future." Main report, vol. 1. Washington, DC: World Bank.
11. **Malawi:** World Bank. 2011. "Review of Targeting Tools Employed by Existing Social Support Programs in Malawi: Final Report." World Bank, Washington, DC.
12. **Mali:** World Bank. 2011. "Mali: Social Safety Nets." Washington, DC: World Bank.
13. **Mauritania:** World Bank. 2013. "Islamic Republic of Mauritania: Summary Analysis of Safety Net Programs and Costs." World Bank, Washington, DC.
14. **Mauritius:** World Bank. 2010. "Mauritius: Social Protection Review and Strategy—Final Report." World Bank, Washington, DC.
15. **Mozambique:** World Bank. 2011. "Mozambique: Social Protection Assessment—Review of Social Assistance Programs and Social Protection Expenditures." Washington, DC: World Bank.

box continues next page

Box 1.4 Country Safety Net Reports Used in This Review *(continued)*

16. **Niger:** World Bank. 2009. "Niger: Food Security and Safety Nets." Washington, DC: World Bank.
17. **Rwanda:** World Bank. 2012. "Rwanda Social Safety Net Assessment: Draft Report." World Bank, Washington, DC.
18. **Sierra Leone:** World Bank. 2012. "Sierra Leone: Social Protection Assessment." World Bank, Washington, DC.
19. **Swaziland:** World Bank. 2012. "Swaziland: Public Transfers and the Social Safety Net." World Bank, Washington, DC.
20. **Tanzania:** World Bank. 2011. "Tanzania: Poverty, Growth, and Public Transfers—Options for a National Productive Safety Net Program." Washington, DC: World Bank.
21. **Togo:** World Bank. 2011. "Les Filets Sociaux au Togo: Rapport de Synthèse." World Bank, Washington, DC.
22. **Zambia:** World Bank. 2012. "Zambia: Using Productive Transfers to Accelerate Poverty Reduction." World Bank, Washington, DC.

To compare safety net systems between country groups, one may find it useful to categorize different country contexts into a typology. The countries can be categorized by their enabling (exogenous) environment, including their income level, their socioeconomic context, their colonial heritage, and any governance factors that may affect their approach to safety nets. The typology can also be based on the status of the existing safety net system in the country (endogenous), including its capacity to protect the poor, its readiness to respond to crises, and the extent to which the safety net programs are coordinated and organized into an overall system. The different typologies are discussed in detail in appendix B.

In this review, we use a method that uses a combination of the exogenous and endogenous typologies for grouping countries. This method combines a proxy for the enabling environment in which safety nets operate (income level)[8] and a judgment about the status of the existing safety net systems based on the classification done by the World Bank's Africa Region. The country group typology is presented in table 1.1. This typology is used throughout the analysis to illustrate some important underlying differences between the safety net systems of the different groups of countries and to explain why some countries have been more able to establish effective and efficient safety net systems than others. The typology is used to compare safety net objectives, policies, programs, and measures of effectiveness across the region, and these lessons can be extrapolated to other countries not covered in this review.

In many countries, safety nets have continued to evolve since these assessments were carried out. The 22 safety net assessments and the analysis in this review present a detailed picture of the state of safety nets among a large number of African countries. Importantly, in many countries, the analysis presented in the safety net assessments catalyzed a response from government, the World Bank, and development partners to reform the existing safety nets into more productive and predictable support to poor and vulnerable populations. For example,

Table 1.1 Country Typology Used in This Review

Level	Low-income countries	Lower- and upper-middle-income countries
Level 1: "Established"—national safety net system in place	None	Botswana, Mauritius
Level 2: "Emerging"—safety net system development in progress	Ethiopia, Kenya, Mali, Mozambique, Niger, Rwanda, Tanzania	Ghana, Lesotho, Swaziland
Levels 3 and 4: "Early stage or no plans"—no solid plans for a national safety net system or no adequate programs in place	Benin, Burkina Faso, Liberia, Madagascar, Malawi, Mauritania, Sierra Leone, Togo	Cameroon, Zambia

Sources: World Bank 2011b; World Bank World Development Indicators database.
Note: Compared to the original model used by the Bank's Africa Region, the number of levels is reduced to three: "Established" = level 1, "Emerging" = level 2, and "Early stage or no plans" = levels 3 and 4.

in Cameroon, the government is now preparing a cash transfer and a public works program and is putting in place operational building blocks for an integrated overall safety net system as recommended by the assessment. As a result, the information presented here does not always reflect the current status of safety nets among African countries. Where appropriate, the review refers to the evolution in safety nets that has occurred since these assessments were carried out.

Following this introductory chapter, which lays out the definitions, context, and rationale for social safety nets in Africa, chapter 2 discusses the poverty and vulnerability profile of the 22 countries. Chapter 3 reviews the existing safety net policies and programs in the 22 countries, including their institutional and implementation arrangements. Chapter 4 analyzes the performance of the programs, including their targeting effectiveness, generosity, coverage, monitoring and evaluation systems, and crisis preparedness, while chapter 5 summarizes the cost and financing aspects of safety net programs in Africa as well as important political economy considerations. Finally, chapter 6 provides recommendations for strengthening safety nets in Africa and lays out a forward-looking agenda.

Notes

1. Calculations are based on PovcalNet, April 2012. Poverty is defined at US$1.25 per day. See the PovcalNet poverty analysis tool at http://iresearch.worldbank.org /PovcalNet/.

2. There is robust and growing evidence indicating how safety nets reduce poverty and enable poor households to participate in the growth process. This evidence is explored in chapter 4.

3. A notable example is the Productive Safety Net Program in Ethiopia, which was designed to be a reliable safety net for chronically poor households that would cost one-third the amount spent on Ethiopia's previous ad hoc responses to drought. It was scaled up in 2008 to provide additional transfers to existing beneficiaries who were negatively affected by the global crisis and local drought and again in response to severe droughts in 2009 and to the Horn of Africa crisis in 2011.

4. In 2006, the African Union summit called on all African governments to develop national social protection frameworks, which started an effort by several African

countries to systematically develop targeted and effective safety nets (Garcia and Moore 2012; World Bank 2012b).

5. This evidence is discussed in chapter 4.

6. The World Bank's Africa Social Protection Strategy (2012–22) discusses the need for and the rise of safety nets in Africa in more detail (World Bank 2012b).

7. Between 2009 and 2013, the World Bank's Africa Region undertook country-level social safety net assessments in 22 countries. In 2014, a couple more country assessments will be completed and may be added to later versions of this book to make it as representative as possible of safety net systems in the Africa Region as a whole. Note that the review does not include countries in North Africa (such as Algeria, the Arab Republic of Egypt, Djibouti, Morocco, and Tunisia). It also does not include the large Sub-Saharan countries of South Africa and Nigeria, because they do not have safety net assessments.

8. Using income level as a proxy for level of development is consistent with how the World Bank's Africa Social Protection Strategy (2012–22) categorizes country systems in lower- and middle-income countries (World Bank 2012b).

References

Banerjee, Abhijit V., and Andrew F. Newman. 1993. "Occupational Choice and the Process of Development." *Journal of Political Economy* 101 (2): 274–98.

Bundy, Donald, Carmen Burbano, Margaret Grosh, Aulo Gelli, Matthew Jukes, and Lesley Drake. 2009. *Rethinking School Feeding: Social Safety Nets, Child Development, and the Education Sector*. Washington, DC: World Bank.

de Mel, Suresh, David McKenzie, and Christopher Woodruff. 2008. "Returns to Capital in Microenterprises: Evidence from a Field Experiment." *Quarterly Journal of Economics* 123 (4): 1329–72.

Fiszbein, Ariel, and Norbert Schady. 2009. *Conditional Cash Transfers: Reducing Present and Future Poverty*. Washington, DC: World Bank.

Galor, Oded, and Joseph Zeira. 1993. "Income Distribution and Macroeconomics." *Review of Economic Studies* 60 (1): 35–52.

Garcia, Marito, and Charity M. T. Moore. 2012. *The Cash Dividend: The Rise of Cash Transfer Programs in Sub-Saharan Africa*. Washington, DC: World Bank.

Goldstein, Markus, and Christopher Udry. 1999. "Agricultural Innovation and Resource Management in Ghana." Yale University, New Haven, CT.

Grosh, Margaret, Carlo del Ninno, Emil Tesliuc, and Azedine Ouerghi. 2008. *For Protection and Promotion: The Design and Implementation of Effective Safety Nets*. Washington, DC: World Bank.

Loury, Glenn C. 1981. "Intergenerational Transfers and the Distribution of Earnings." *Econometrica* 49 (4): 843–67.

McCord, Anna, and Rachel Slater. 2009. *Overview of Public Works Programmes in Sub-Saharan Africa*. London: Overseas Development Institute.

Milazzo, Annamaria, and Carlo del Ninno. 2012. *The Role of Public Works Programs in Sub-Saharan Africa*. Washington, DC: World Bank.

World Bank. 2011a. *Africa's Future and the World Bank's Support to It: Africa Regional Strategy*. Washington, DC: World Bank.

———. 2011b. "Safety Nets in Africa." Brief to Robert Zoellick, Annex 1, World Bank, Washington, DC.

———. 2011c. *World Development Report 2011: Conflict, Security, and Development.* Washington, DC: World Bank.

———. 2012a. "Informal Safety Nets: A Literature Review of the Evidence in Africa." World Bank, Washington, DC.

———. 2012b. *Managing Risk, Promoting Growth: Developing Systems for Social Protection in Africa—The World Bank's Africa Social Protection Strategy, 2012–2022.* Washington, DC: World Bank.

———. 2013. "Securing the Transformational Potential in Africa's Mineral Resources." PowerPoint presentation, World Bank, Washington, DC.

CHAPTER 2

Poverty and Risk

The role played by safety nets in any country depends on several factors, including the government's vision of social policy, the social contract between the state and its citizens, and fiscal space in the budget. Nevertheless, the main rationale for safety nets in Africa is the existence of high levels of vulnerability, chronic poverty, and food insecurity. The profile of a country's poverty and vulnerability as well as the level and distribution of its economic growth are key determinants of what type of safety net system may be appropriate. In Africa, the strong economic growth of recent decades has not reduced poverty levels for the masses, and the gap between the extremely poor and the rising middle class is growing in many countries. Moreover, the increasing frequency and severity of shocks repeatedly undermine the sustainability of any reductions in poverty. This chapter reviews the incidence of poverty and vulnerability of African countries in an effort to determine how safety nets could reduce chronic poverty and poverty caused by shocks and help poor households invest in their livelihoods and their children's development over the long term.

The chapter's main findings indicate that despite economic growth, high poverty levels persist in Africa, which makes safety nets vital for supporting those who are not benefiting from economic growth. Given the vast extent of poverty and vulnerability in Africa, safety nets cannot reach all of the poor but need to focus on the extremely poor and on specific vulnerable groups for maximum impact and affordability. A careful analysis of the poverty profile of each specific country is needed to design safety nets that are appropriate for its circumstances.

Growth and Poverty Incidence

Despite the recent global crisis, economic growth has been strong and stable across the African region in the past decade, averaging around 5.0 percent per year (figure 2.1).[1] Soaring prices for oil, minerals, and other export commodities have helped increase gross domestic product (GDP) since 2000. In addition, improved macroeconomic management and market-oriented policies have

Figure 2.1 Average Annual GDP Growth Rate, 2000–10

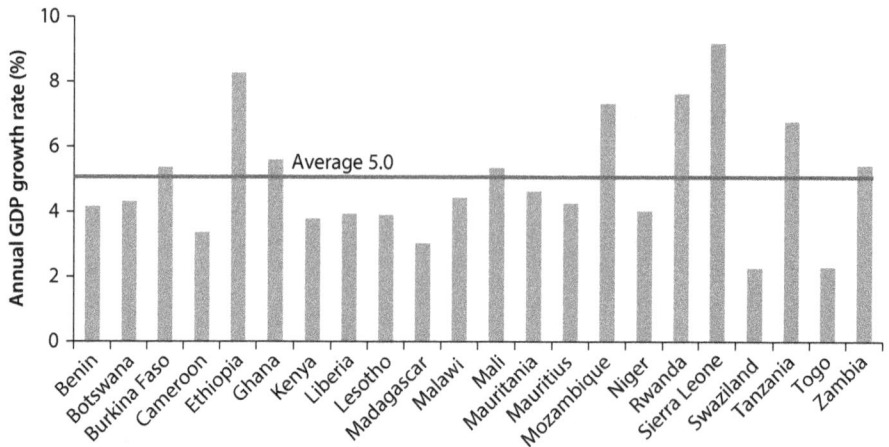

Source: World Bank's World Development Indicators database.

spurred domestic markets, including the wholesale and retail, transportation, telecommunications, and manufacturing sectors. Finally, increased peace and stability have helped countries prosper.

Although some African countries, such as Botswana, Ethiopia, and Rwanda, have enjoyed an unparalleled reduction in poverty rates over the decade, in many African countries poverty rates remain stubbornly high and poverty reduction is slow (figures 2.2 and 2.3).[2] Between 2003 and 2009, the poverty headcount in Burkina Faso declined only slightly from 51.0 percent to 46.7 percent. In Tanzania, poverty hovered at 34–35 percent both in 2000 and 2007 (see box 2.1 for an analysis of growth and poverty in Tanzania). In Mozambique, poverty rates increased from 54.0 percent in 2003 to 54.7 percent in 2008. Hence, despite economic growth, not all Africans are receiving their share of the pie, and inequality is on the rise. In Kenya, for instance, large differences exist among income groups in terms of access to basic services and human capital outcomes. Mortality rates for infants and children younger than 5 years of age among those in the poorest two deciles are 50 percent higher than rates for those in the richest two deciles. In Lesotho, rapid economic expansion that has resulted in relatively high levels of GDP has not significantly reduced poverty because a large part of the labor force is still stuck in the stagnant agricultural sector. One consequence of this sluggish response to growth in Lesotho has been extreme income inequality (a Gini coefficient of 0.53), more typical of that found in Latin America and South Africa than in other countries in Sub-Saharan Africa. Similarly, in Zambia, where the Gini coefficient is about 0.52, the poorest 20 percent of the population receives less than 1 percent of total monthly household income. This high inequality means that safety net programs that invest in the poor can play a significant role in reducing poverty.

Figure 2.2 Poverty Headcount, Latest Year Available

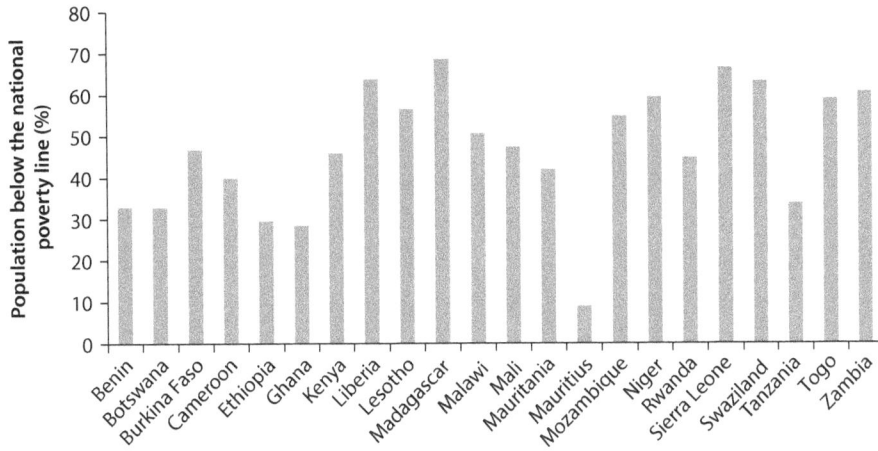

Source: World Bank's Africa Region poverty database, March 2013.
Note: The figure uses the national poverty line defined for each country (PovcalNet data in purchasing power parity presented in appendix C).

Figure 2.3 Poverty Headcount, Early and Late 2000s

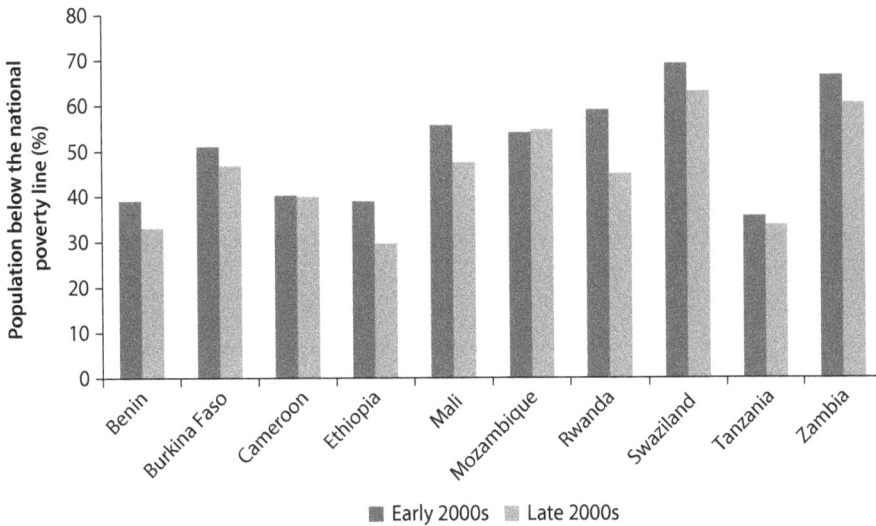

Source: World Bank's Africa Region poverty database, March 2013.

Box 2.1 Growth and Poverty Reduction in Tanzania

Although some debate exists about the data, researchers nonetheless widely agree that the impact of growth on poverty in Tanzania has not been as great as it might have been. What is interesting from a safety net point of view is the distributional impact of growth and the extent to which it reaches (or fails to reach) the poorest. Figure B2.1.1 shows the growth incidence

box continues next page

Box 2.1 Growth and Poverty Reduction in Tanzania *(continued)*

Figure B2.1.1 Growth Incidence, Tanzania Mainland, 2001–07

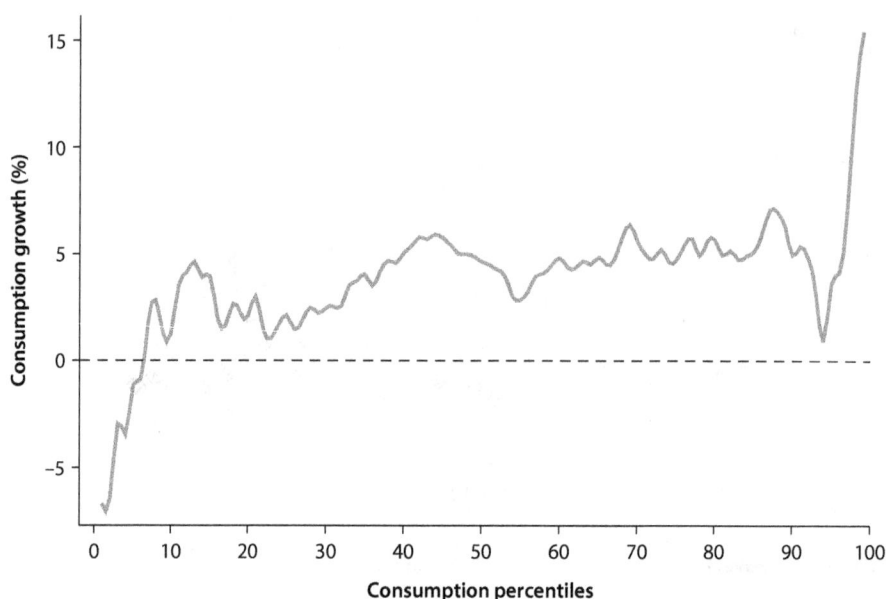

curve, which illustrates the impact of economic growth on consumption by income group. The curve is relatively flat, suggesting that all income groups benefited equally from growth, with the notable exception of the poorest 10 percent, who became worse off, and the richest 10 percent, whose consumption grew relatively fast. This finding is significant for safety net strategy because it suggests—at least according to the data for 2001–07—that the very poorest are those who are not benefiting from growth and who are most likely to be in need of sustained transfers.

Source: World Bank 2011.

Large variations occur in poverty incidence between countries, and rural areas have much higher poverty rates than urban areas. In many countries, poverty is highly concentrated in some geographic areas, usually rural areas (figure 2.4). In West African countries such as Ghana and Togo, the northern Sahel regions are much more poverty stricken than the coastal areas. In Kenya, poverty incidence is the highest in the Coast and North Eastern provinces. In Mozambique, it is highest in the northern provinces. In Mali, the northern Timbuktu region has the highest nonmonetary poverty rate[3] (over 92 percent). However, in some countries, such as Liberia and Sierra Leone, even urban poverty is above 45 percent. Only in Mauritius, the richest country in the group of countries considered in this review, is urban poverty higher than rural poverty, because the most vulnerable groups tend to be urban slum dwellers.

Figure 2.4 Urban and Rural Poverty Headcount, Latest Year Available

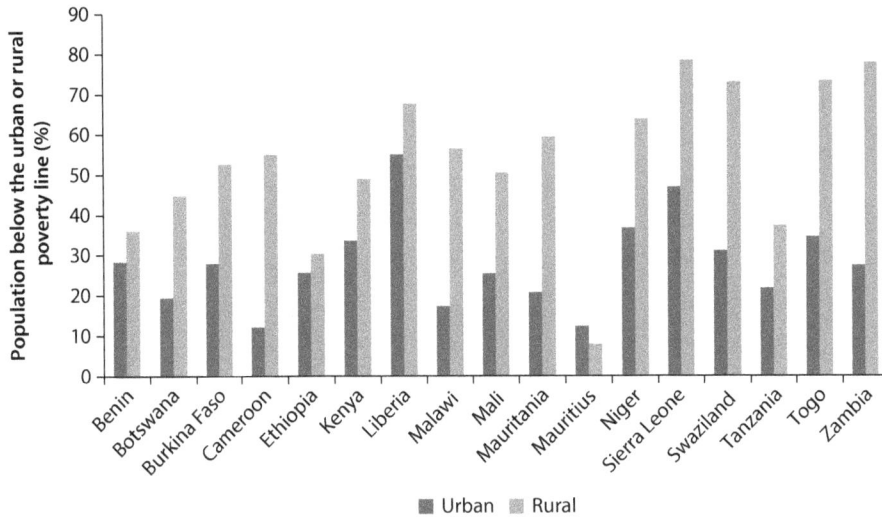

Source: World Bank's Africa Region poverty database, March 2013.

Figure 2.5 Urban Poverty Headcount, Early and Late 2000s

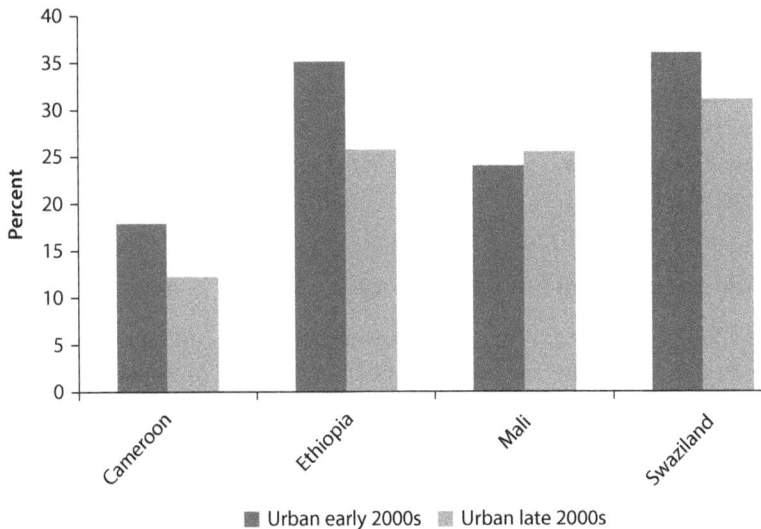

Source: World Bank's Africa Region poverty database, March 2013, selected countries.
Note: Among these countries, the largest decline, of 9.4%, occurred in Ethiopia from early 2000s to late 2000s.

Changes in poverty incidence within countries vary and are often driven by shifting standards of living and migration between urban and rural areas. In Cameroon, Ethiopia, and Swaziland, urban poverty dropped significantly during the past decade, whereas rural poverty remained high and even increased in Cameroon (figures 2.5 and 2.6). In Mali, the opposite happened: urban poverty has remained constant, and rural poverty has been reduced by nearly

Figure 2.6 Rural Poverty Headcount, Early and Late 2000s

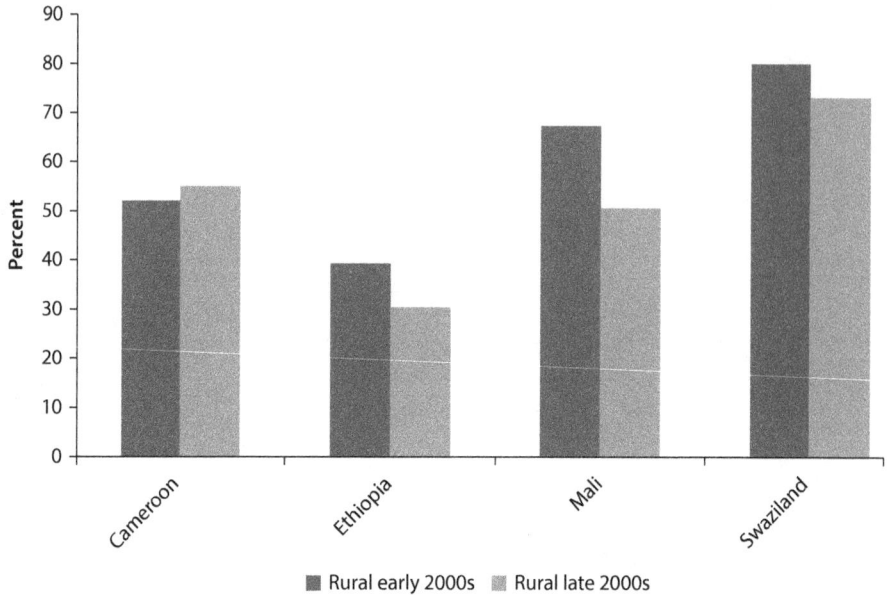

Source: World Bank's Africa Region poverty database, March 2013, selected countries.

17 percentage points but remains at a very high level. In Botswana and Kenya, although poverty incidence is on average higher in rural areas than in urban areas, residents of informal settlements in big towns such as Gaborone and Nairobi have been found to experience higher levels of deprivation, sometimes far more than in rural areas.

Vulnerability and Food Insecurity

In addition to being in persistent poverty, the poor and near poor are highly vulnerable because the vast majority of them depend on subsistence agriculture. In rain-fed subsistence economies, the consumption of the poor varies by the time of year, depending on the abundance of food and of paid agricultural work. The poor are usually the most vulnerable group in any society because they do not have enough assets or savings to respond to adverse shocks; therefore, they remain poor and may become even poorer. In addition, the near poor (those living close to the poverty line) may risk falling below the poverty line.

An important consideration when planning safety net interventions is whether people are chronically poor or whether they are moving in and out of poverty—in other words, whether the same households need continuous, comprehensive support or different households need help at different points in time. In some countries, such as Mozambique, Swaziland, and Zambia, income distribution across those in the bottom three to four deciles is relatively flat, with few household variables that explain the depth of poverty. For instance, in Mozambique, a large share of the population is near the poverty line. Although 54 percent of Mozambicans fall below the national poverty line, more than 60 percent are below the poverty line plus 10 percent, and two-thirds are below the poverty line plus 25 percent. In Cameroon, 26 percent are considered to be chronically poor, and another 9.9 percent are considered to be in transitory poverty. Transitory poverty is more pronounced in urban than in rural areas. In Madagascar, transient poverty is higher in urban areas (23 percent) than in rural areas (15 percent), whereas chronic poverty is very widespread in rural areas (78 percent) and much lower (19 percent) in urban centers. In Tanzania, about equal shares of the population fell into or rose out of poverty in a 5- to 10-year period. According to panel data, just over one-half of the poor remained in poverty over a 5-year period, while about 46 percent rose out of poverty and about one-third of families who were not poor in the first round of the panel survey had fallen into poverty five years later.

The most common shocks affecting poor and vulnerable people in the countries analyzed are environmental shocks (such as droughts, floods, and infestations) and individual shocks (such as the illness or death of a family member). Fluctuations in food prices, most significantly during the 2007–08 food price crisis, have also affected the poor and near poor in many African countries, because those groups spend a large share of their budget on food items. In Ethiopia, many households find it extremely difficult to accumulate the cash savings, livestock, or food stores that are sufficient to weather the bad seasons. In times of drought, agricultural production declines by 25 percent on average, and cereal yields can go down by as much as 75 percent at local levels. Livestock losses as high as 70 percent have also been recorded using case study data. Repeated droughts have caused high rates of malnutrition as households seek to survive in the short term by decreasing their consumption to protect assets (PSNP 2010). In Togo, as a result of devastating rains in 2006 and the rise in food and fuel prices in 2007, more than 13 percent of all households in the northern Savane region fell into severe food insecurity and over half of all households (300,000 people) were at risk of losing their livelihoods in the Savane, Kara, and Plateaux regions. To cope with shocks and crisis, households in most countries often resort to reducing their food intake (by eating a lower quantity or quality of food or by reallocating consumption within the household); to selling assets such as livestock, landholdings, or equipment; or to taking their children out of school and putting them to work. At times of crisis, households can sometimes draw on support from informal safety nets to some extent. Macroeconomic and governance shocks can also negatively affect household welfare in some countries. For example, Lesotho's economy depends heavily on revenues from the Southern African Customs Union, which are volatile and have recently declined sharply because of the global economic downturn. Also, the recurrence of internal governance crises is a major risk faced by the Malagasy population.

The risks faced by the poor vary depending on macroeconomic and sociocultural factors and are different in urban and rural areas. In countries with poorly diversified resource bases (such as Burkina Faso, Mali, Mauritania, and Niger), the poor are also particularly dependent on regional stability for imports and for a favorable export climate and favorable terms of trade. Moreover, fragile states, including Liberia and Sierra Leone, contain large numbers of displaced people, refugees, orphans, former combatants, and others suffering from war-related traumas. Vulnerability also varies within countries. People living in rural areas tend to be more susceptible to environmental risk because of their heavy reliance on agriculture for their livelihoods and on infrastructure to access markets. Meanwhile, in urban areas, economic and labor market fluctuations affect wage-workers, cash-crop farmers, and traders. Social risks such as forced marriages, early childbearing, and genital mutilation affect women in particular.[4] In southern Africa, where the HIV/AIDS epidemic is the most severe, many families are in a vulnerable position because of the deaths of so many working-age adults and the proliferation of orphans.

Food insecurity is highly correlated with poverty, especially in rural areas, and it affects both chronic and seasonal poverty. In Niger, more than half of the population consumes less than the minimum caloric intake,[5] and in Liberia, 41 percent of the population is classified as being food insecure (figure 2.7). In other countries, national food insecurity may be lower than average, but rural and arid areas are badly affected. Several different types of food insecurity were noted in those social safety net assessments that analyzed food security issues. In most countries, some groups of the population suffer from chronic food insecurity because of constant monetary poverty and the inability to buy enough food to meet their daily caloric needs. But food insecurity often manifests itself seasonally; groups of people are repeatedly food insecure during the agricultural lean seasons every year or when droughts and floods occur and recur, as in the Sahel. Temporary food insecurity is common in rural and remote areas during the agricultural lean season. Changes in international food prices also affect

Figure 2.7 Percentage of the Population Living in Food Insecurity, Latest Year Available

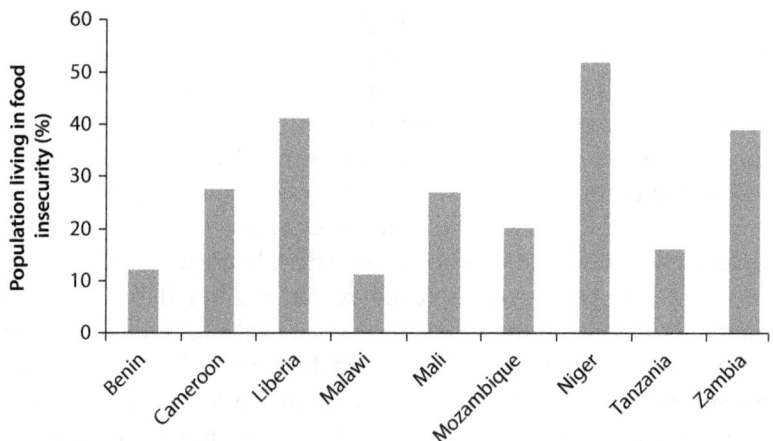

Sources: Secondary data; country safety net assessments.
Note: Data are based on the various definitions of food insecurity used in each country report.

Figure 2.8 Malnutrition Prevalence in Children under Five Years of Age, Latest Year Available

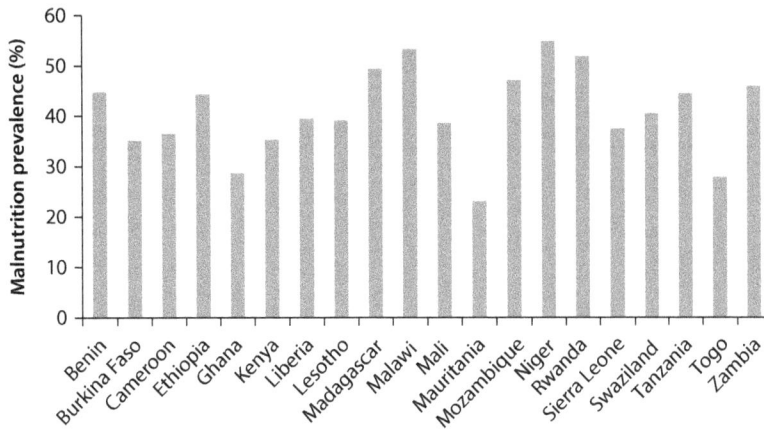

Source: World Bank's World Development Indicators database.
Note: *Prevalence of child malnutrition* is the percentage of children under age five whose height for age
(stunting) is more than two standard deviations below the median for the international reference population
of the same age.

the availability of food staples such as cereals, which constitute the bulk of the
diet of the poor. Even in agricultural areas where most people are farmers, many
also buy part of their food intake.

Shocks such as a reduction in income and a lack of access to food have long-
term consequences for household welfare. Although any shock experienced by
poor and vulnerable people, such as a loss of income or acute hunger, can imme-
diately have a negative impact on welfare, temporary shocks also cause people to
be more vulnerable to future shocks if they must deplete their assets to survive
the temporary shock. Reducing the nutritional intake of young children—even if
only temporarily—can lead to stunting and wasting. For instance, in Benin,
Ethiopia, Madagascar, Malawi, Mozambique, Niger, Rwanda, Tanzania, and
Zambia, malnutrition rates among children under five years of age are very high
(figure 2.8). In the long run, these consequences, in addition to disinvestments in
schooling and productive assets, can seriously affect future poverty and welfare
outcomes.

Determinants of Poverty and Vulnerability

Some clear trends emerged in terms of what determines household poverty and
vulnerability. As noted earlier, rural households are more prone to poverty
because they generally have less access to social and economic services and tend
to engage more heavily in agricultural activities than do urban households
(table 2.1). At the household level, large households with little human capital
tend to be more prone to poverty than others. Data from some countries
show that polygamous households or households headed by widows are often

Table 2.1 Poverty Covariates

	Individual characteristics		Characteristics of household				Economic activity	Geographic location	
	Female	Children or elderly	Female headed	Education of head greater than primary	Number of members or children	Polygamous or widowed	Agriculture or other informal	Rural areas	Access to services
Benin	+	+	−	−	+	+	n.i.	+	−
Botswana	n.i.	+	+	−	+	+	n.i.	+	n.i.
Burkina Faso	+	n.i.	−	−	+	+	+	+	n.i.
Cameroon	n.i.	n.i.	−	−	+	+	+	+	−
Kenya	n.i.	+	+	n.i.	+	n.i.	n.i.	+	−
Lesotho	n.i.	−	+	n.i.	+	n.i.	+	+	n.i.
Liberia	+	+	−	−	n.i.	n.i.	+	+	n.i.
Madagascar	n.i.	+ (children) − (elderly)	+	−	+	n.i.	+	+	−
Mali	+	n.i.	no diff.	−	+	+	+	+	n.i.
Mauritius	n.i.	n.i.	+	n.i.	n.i.	n.i.	n.i.	−	n.i.
Mozambique	n.i.	+	+	−	+	n.i.	+	+	n.i.
Niger	n.i.	n.i.	+	−	+	n.i.	+	+	n.i.
Rwanda	n.i.	n.i.	+	−	+	n.i.	+	+	n.i.
Sierra Leone	n.i.	+	n.i.	−	+	n.i.	+	+	−
Swaziland	n.i.	+	n.i.	−	n.i.	n.i.	n.i.	+	−
Tanzania	n.i.	+	no diff.	n.i.	+	n.i.	+	+	n.i.
Togo	n.i.	+	n.i.	−	+	n.i.	n.i.	+	n.i.
Zambia	no diff.	no diff.	no diff.	n.i.	+	n.i.	+	+	n.i.

Sources: Secondary data; country safety net assessments.

Note: + = positive correlation with poverty; − = negative correlation with poverty; no diff. = no significant difference; n.i. = no information from safety net assessment.

the poorest. In many countries, children and the elderly are particularly vulnerable to poverty. However, in both Lesotho and Madagascar, no evidence indicates that the elderly are poorer than the rest of the population.

Poverty is closely related to underemployment—seasonal or constant—either in low-productivity agriculture or in the informal sector. Not all of the safety net assessments looked into labor market trends in relation to poverty, but in those that did, poverty clearly is not associated with *unemployment* in Africa; it is associated with *underemployment* (which occurs when households do not make enough money from their economic activities to survive). In general, the poor cannot afford to be unemployed, and although formal employment rates are very low for those in the lowest income deciles, poor households are engaged in different kinds of informal activities, mostly related to agriculture (for example, in Benin, Liberia, and Tanzania). In Benin, for example, the rate of invisible underemployment (in activities characterized by low productivity and low earnings) is over 70 percent and mainly affects rural areas. It also affects women to a larger extent than men. In Cameroon, two-thirds of the active population work in agriculture-related activities (this figure rises to 85 percent in rural areas), and over 90 percent of the population is employed in the informal (agriculture and nonagriculture) sector. Almost 40 percent of rural workers earn less than the minimum wage. In 2008, the United Nations estimated that, of 300,000 extremely poor households in Liberia, 250,000 were poor because able-bodied adults had no access to productive employment. Evidence from Tanzania shows long periods when the able-bodied poor do not have enough work to do, and off-farm employment does not expand enough to compensate for the drop in agricultural work on farms during the slack season.

In sum, although poverty in Africa remains widespread, it is concentrated in certain areas and among certain groups of people who are trapped in poverty and have not been able to benefit from Africa's recent economic growth. Given the high level of vulnerability, chronic poverty, and food insecurity in Africa, targeted safety nets are needed. Safety nets not only should focus on the chronically poor, who have not been able to benefit from economic growth, but also should be designed to provide extra support to those who find themselves in temporary poverty when shocks occur so that they do not need to resort to drawing down on their investments to survive. The increasing inequality also suggests that targeted interventions to help the poor invest in productive and capital-forming activities are central elements for helping speed up poverty reduction.

Summary of Main Messages

This chapter has several messages:

- Despite economic growth, high poverty levels persist in Africa, especially in rural areas. In addition to chronic poverty, vulnerability is high. Certain groups are especially vulnerable, including children, the elderly, people living in large households with little human capital, and rural households suffering from low agricultural productivity and underemployment.
- Safety nets are needed in Africa because of its high levels of vulnerability, chronic poverty, and food insecurity. Safety nets can be important instruments for helping those who have been left out of the economic growth process and for reducing inequality and speeding up the pace of poverty reduction.
- Targeted measures such as safety nets should support the chronically poor and provide them with the resources necessary to break the cycle of poverty and help them improve their livelihoods. Safety nets also need to be able to provide extra support when shocks occur and help people build asset buffers and avoid drawing down on investments during hardships.
- Given the extent of poverty and vulnerability, safety nets in Africa cannot reach all of the poor but instead need to focus on the extremely poor and on specific vulnerable groups for maximum influence and affordability.
- The extent and type of poverty and vulnerability vary between and within African countries. Careful analysis of the poverty and vulnerability profiles of each country is needed to tailor the safety net system to address that country's specific needs.

Notes

1. Calculations are based on gross domestic product (GDP) growth reported in the World Bank's World Development Indicators database for the 22 countries.

2. The figures in appendix C compare poverty rates at 2005 purchasing power parity amounts of US$1.25 and US$2.00 per day from the World Bank's PovcalNet database.

3. Nonmonetary poverty usually includes other measures of poverty, such as life expectancy, mortality rates, and literacy rates.

4. Many of these risk factors may not be addressed by safety nets but rather by social legislation and its enforcement.

5. The World Food Programme defines the minimum caloric intake for an adult as 2,100 calories per day.

References

PSNP (Productive Safety Net Program). 2010. *Designing and Implementing a Rural Safety Net in a Low-Income Setting: Lessons Learned from Ethiopia's Productive Safety Net Program 2005–2009.* Addis Ababa: Government of Ethiopia.

World Bank. 2011. *Tanzania: Poverty, Growth, and Public Transfers—Options for a National Productive Safety Net Program.* Washington, DC: World Bank.

CHAPTER 3

Existing Safety Net Policies and Programs

Safety nets are still fairly new in Africa, but since the early 2000s social protection has become a key component of poverty reduction efforts in the region. In 2009, members of the African Union endorsed the Social Policy Framework for Africa.[1] The framework moves away from treating social development as subordinate to economic growth and instead justifies social development and social protection as being essential to growth promotion. This agreement, as well as the increased support provided for social protection by many international agencies and the urgent need to protect the poor that arose because of the economic crisis, has led to a recent expansion of safety nets all over Africa.

Each country has its own approach to safety nets based on its sociopolitical heritage and on the social contract that exists between the state and its citizens. Some countries in Africa, mainly middle-income countries (MICs) in southern Africa, have a rights-based perspective on social protection and commonly provide a relatively generous set of safety net programs to specific groups. In other countries, government-provided safety nets have not been as generous and sometimes do not exist at all. This chapter reviews the policy context and the existing safety net systems and programs in 22 African countries.

The chapter's main findings indicate that the number of safety nets in Africa is growing and the type of safety net support is evolving. Nevertheless, safety net systems generally consist of a large number of small and uncoordinated programs, and because of this fragmentation, political champions for these programs fail to emerge. Because of fragmented programs and uncoordinated donor support, few countries have a well-planned system that is capable of reducing poverty and vulnerability. Hence, harmonizing and consolidating safety net programs into a coherent system to meet each country's specific needs should be a priority for the governments of Africa. Underlying implementation tools such as beneficiary registries, targeting methods, and payment systems are also needed to enable programs to deliver support effectively, efficiently, and transparently to targeted groups.

Policies and Strategies

The aim of social protection policy frameworks is to address the problems of persistent poverty and vulnerability in a systematic way and to guide the harmonization and coordination of fragmented social protection programs. In any given country, social protection policy is shaped by the government's vision for social policy, its preferences for providing resources directly to the poor, and the social contract that exists between the state and the people. For instance, in Tanzania, cash transfers are a main instrument used to protect the poorest and most vulnerable. However, in countries such as Mozambique, providing cash without conditions (except for the elderly and those unable to work) or even with conditions (for example, requiring beneficiaries to keep their children in school or to take them for health checkups) is not considered an acceptable way of supporting vulnerable groups. Instead, much greater emphasis is placed on workfare and social care services. In neighboring Madagascar, the development of a social protection policy and action plan has been halted by several political crises in recent years.

Differences in political economy and the legacy of past regimes strongly influence social protection strategies in Africa.[2] Southern African countries (such as Lesotho, Mauritius, and South Africa), which tend to have nationally driven social protection agendas and popular support for programs that assist those who cannot provide for themselves, value programs that emphasize horizontal equity (equity between like groups) rather than vertical or poverty-based equity (Hickey 2007). Support for social services is also strong. In contrast, this analysis shows that in highly indebted countries (for example, Benin, Burkina Faso, Mali, Niger, and Togo), donor influence on domestic policy is significant.

Despite differences in their political economy, most countries have some plan that outlines how social protection relates to the overall development strategy. This plan might consist of a Poverty Reduction Strategy Paper (PRSP), a social protection strategy, or social legislation. As can be seen in figure 3.1, 82 percent of the 22 countries have some such plan. In about 77 percent of the countries, social protection or safety nets feature in the country's development strategy (such as the PRSP). Interestingly, more low-income countries (LICs) than MICs refer to social protection in their development strategy documents. In Benin, Botswana, Ethiopia, Kenya, Rwanda, Tanzania, Togo, and Zambia, safety nets feature explicitly in the development strategy as a tool for achieving pro-poor growth. However, in Burkina Faso, Liberia, and Mali, social protection has only recently featured in the latest Poverty Reduction Strategy Credits, and in Malawi, safety nets are not specifically mentioned in the development strategy, which instead mentions efforts to provide specific support and services to categorical groups such as those with disabilities. In Sierra Leone, a social protection and labor strategy is one of the pillars of the PRSP for 2013–17.

Roughly half (55 percent) of the 22 countries analyzed have a social protection strategy. Of these, about half (or 32 percent of all 22 countries) have an operational strategy that links safety nets to other forms of social protection over a period of time (Botswana, Kenya, Malawi, Rwanda, Sierra Leone, and Tanzania),

Figure 3.1 Percentage of Countries with a Social Protection Strategy

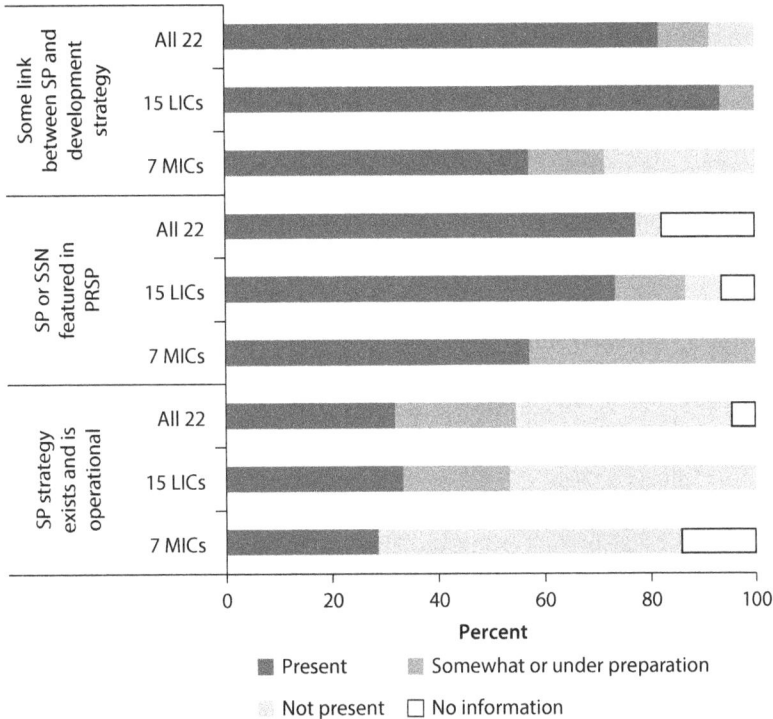

Source: Calculations based on information from safety net assessments.
Note: LIC = low-income country; MIC = middle-income country; PRSP = Poverty Reduction Strategy Paper;
SP = social protection; SSN = social safety net.

and Liberia and Mozambique are in the process of developing an operational and coordinated strategy for safety nets.[3] Madagascar, Mauritania, and Zambia have drafted social protection strategies, but for different reasons, those strategies have never become operational. In Madagascar, a strategy was drafted in 2007 but was not officially adopted, and the dissolution of the ministry responsible for social policies (the Ministry of Health, Family Planning and Social Protection) further weakened the standing of social protection. Once again, the 15 LICs have made more progress on developing social protection strategies than the 7 MICs.

Experience from some African countries shows that clear implementation plans with careful cost estimates are crucial for putting strategies into operation. Many developing countries in Africa have developed sectoral strategies but have never implemented them, even though putting these strategies into operation is crucial for achieving the desired objectives. This is the case in Madagascar and Zambia, as discussed previously. How have some countries been able to put their strategies into practice? Some lessons emerge from the 22 countries analyzed. The countries that have been able to implement their social protection strategies (for example, Rwanda) made realistic cost estimates of their strategies and defined a clear resource envelope that could be justified to and supported by the Ministry of Finance. Even though social protection is coordinated and operated by other ministries, close dialogue with decision-making and coordinating ministries such as the Ministry of Finance and the Ministry of Planning is very important. Box 3.1 highlights lessons from the evolution of Rwanda's social protection sector.

Box 3.1 Evolution of the Social Protection Sector in Rwanda

Rwanda's social protection sector has evolved from a set of fragmented programs into an increasingly coordinated system with strong government ownership. Rwanda's case is unique among developing countries not only for its level of political commitment backed by resources, but also for the increasing sophistication of the dialogue and the growing capacity of the line ministry to lead the sector. However, Rwanda also faces a new set of challenges for which no strong international examples are found among developing countries.

The national social protection policy of Rwanda, which was first prepared in 2005, recognizes the risk involved in allowing poverty to continue and the ways in which different groups are vulnerable to shocks. It focuses on different vulnerable groups, such as genocide survivors, orphans and vulnerable children, widows, demobilized soldiers and repatriates, elderly people, and other destitute people. The policy outlines strategic objectives for supporting these groups in the short, medium, and long terms. In the medium term, which is where the policy developments currently stand, the objective was to establish a coordinated system of social protection interventions.

The most recent poverty reduction strategy, known as the Economic Development and Poverty Reduction Strategy (EDPRS), 2008–12, concluded that it was imperative for Rwanda to achieve more efficient poverty reduction and better progress toward the Millennium Development Goals while maintaining robust growth. The EDPRS outlined the policy and institutional arrangements, which are now being implemented through the flagship Vision 2020 Umurenge Program (VUP). The poverty reduction strategy is consistent with the risk assessment approach that underpins Rwanda's social protection policy. However, rather than target safety net programs solely on the basis of vulnerability, the EDPRS uses households' poverty status and criteria such as their asset profile, income sources, employment status, and human development conditions.

In 2011, building on lessons from the VUP, the National Social Protection Strategy (NSPS) was developed and approved by the Rwandan cabinet. The objective of the NSPS is to "build a social protection system that tackles poverty and inequality, enables the poor to move out of poverty, helps reduce vulnerability and protect people from shocks, helps improve health and education among all Rwandans, and contributes to economic growth" (MINALOC 2011, 3). Achieving this objective involves three dimensions: (a) a set of core activities, which comprise social assistance programs and the expansion of social insurance and labor standards to those living in poverty; (b) a set of broader activities to ensure access to other public services; and (c) a set of complementary social development interventions.

On the basis of the definition of poverty and risk, interventions are targeted appropriately, most notably through the flagship VUP. For example, landowners are the target of

box continues next page

Box 3.1 Evolution of the Social Protection Sector in Rwanda *(continued)*

interventions aimed at improving productivity and welfare, including activities conducted through public works and access to microfinance. The landless who are able to work are targeted with public works, microfinance services, vocational skills training, and direct support, with conditions related to the use of health and education services. Those who are unable to work receive social assistance in the form of direct support and microfinance services, including skills development. Those who are above the poverty line also receive some support because of their potential role in employment generation and supply-chain management.

The NSPS and the implementation plan spelled out a vision for consolidating the sector, but further feasibility studies are needed to explore ways to put this vision into practice. In particular, finding options for harmonizing the two main safety net programs—the VUP and the Assistance Fund for Genocide Survivors, which provides direct cash and in-kind support to genocide survivors—is an important priority.

Source: World Bank 2012d.

Institutions and Implementation Arrangements

Institutional and implementation arrangements for safety nets in Africa are characterized by a mix of government and donor programs with large involvement of nongovernmental organizations (NGOs) for implementation at the local level. Programs range from being fully government owned and operated to being managed by the government with the support of donors, managed by donors together with the government, and run by donors or NGOs alone (these programs tend to be smaller). Ethiopia's Productive Safety Net Program (PSNP) is a federal government program implemented largely through government systems. Donor agencies have pooled financing and have formulated a unified stream of technical advice in support of a single program led by the government. In Madagascar, where there have been frequent political changes and a lack of stable governments in the past decade, social protection programs are almost completely donor driven. The World Food Programme (WFP) plays a large role in many countries in managing, funding, and partially implementing school feeding and other food emergency programs. Figure 3.2 shows that, as expected, donors are much more involved in safety nets in LICs than in MICs. Donor-government relationships for funding and coordinating safety nets are discussed further in chapter 5.

African countries evidence no clear institutional consistent coordinator or leader for safety nets. Strong coordination is especially important in social protection because of its inherently cross-cutting, multisectoral nature and because of the involvement of various government bodies as well as many NGOs and donors. In most countries, because of weak coordinating mechanisms, a range of different government agencies manages safety net programs. These agencies include the president's office; the prime minister's office; the ministry of finance; or the ministries of social affairs, social security, food security, agriculture, employment, health and education, youth, and women and family, each with its

Figure 3.2 Donor Involvement in Safety Nets

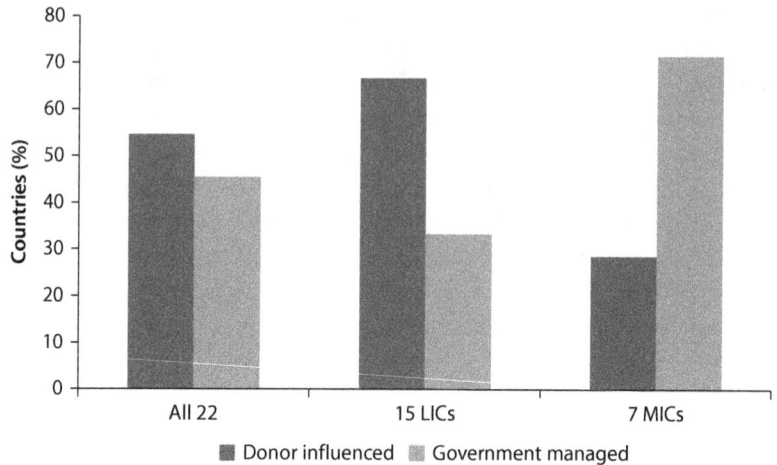

Source: Calculations based on information from safety net assessments.
Note: LIC = low-income country; MIC = middle-income country.

own mandates. This scattering of the responsibility for social protection among many government agencies has meant that the sector has not had a strong institutional champion within the government to propel social protection into the forefront of long-term social policy. In addition, in some countries, programs are run by semiautonomous funds such as the public works program run by the Tanzania Social Action Fund (TASAF) and various solidarity funds in several francophone countries.[4] Even in the absence of a single institutional base for social protection, a steering committee that includes representatives of all relevant ministries, donors, and nonstate actors should oversee and coordinate the safety net system.

The responsibility for social protection is commonly given to ministries that have little political leverage in the government's decision-making process. The mandate of whichever institution is responsible for safety nets affects how they operate and achieve their objectives. For instance, ministries of employment that are used to implementing public works may be well equipped to organize short-term work on building or maintaining public assets but may not be as capable of providing a safety net for the poorest and carefully ensuring that they benefit from employment opportunities. Meanwhile, social welfare ministries that are used to assisting people with disabilities and elderly people who are not able to provide for themselves may not be best suited for delivering programs aimed at reducing extreme poverty for populations without special needs. In both Burkina Faso and Mali, the key ministries in charge of safety nets do not operate any major antipoverty transfer programs. In Burkina Faso, even though the Ministry of Social Action and National Solidarity has a strategic focus on social safety nets (SSN) and social action, it runs no significant SSN program. The same is true of the Ministry of Social Development, Solidarity, and the Elderly and the National

Solidarity Fund in Mali. Most of Mali's programs, which are very small in both scope and coverage, are directed at communities or associations, and they mostly provide social services to categories of poor people such as orphans and people with disabilities. Instead, line ministries, whose main concern is basic service delivery, appear to be the most active in implementing safety nets. For example, the Ministry of Education is responsible for school feeding programs, and the Commissariat of Food Security is responsible for distributing food at subsidized prices or at no cost during periods of crisis.

In some countries, decision-making ministries with strong mandates for poverty reduction and with the capacity to target and deliver benefits to the most vulnerable have emerged as the lead ministries for social protection. In Rwanda, the Ministry of Local Government manages the main social protection programs (the Assistance Fund for Genocide Survivors and the Vision 2020 Umurenge Program, or VUP) and coordinates with the other ministries (the Ministry of Women and Family, the Ministry of Health, and the Ministry of Education) that manage smaller programs. An important aspect of the Rwandan program is that it also benefits from strong backing from the Ministry of Finance. In Cameroon, where the Ministry of Social Affairs traditionally provides social assistance to excluded groups, the Ministry of Economy, Planning, and Regional Development is now taking the lead in establishing safety net programs targeting the poorest through its intersectoral Technical Committee for Monitoring of Economic Programs. In Madagascar, in contrast, because no ministry is capable of leading the social protection agenda, the president's office is currently responsible for the main safety net program, Tsena Mora, which sells food items at subsidized prices to poor households in urban areas.

Of the 22 countries reviewed, 86 percent have no SSN system but instead have many ad hoc safety net programs that are not coordinated in any way (figure 3.3). This problem is a result of several factors, including the lack of operational social protection strategies, the strong influence of several donors, and the lack of strong government champions for safety nets who can effectively coordinate donors. However, although only 1 of the 15 LICs analyzed has a developed safety net system (the PSNP and other programs that together aim at reducing food insecurity in Ethiopia), almost half of them (40 percent) are in the process of developing one. In the MICs that this study looked at, almost one-third have a safety net system in place, and another 43 percent are moving toward a more coordinated system. Only Botswana has a comprehensive system of safety net programs, while Mauritius has all the necessary elements but no systematic coordination. Kenya, Malawi, Mozambique, Rwanda, and Tanzania are in the process of establishing safety net systems or consolidating and reforming their existing programs. In addition, Ghana, Liberia, and Mali have shown an interest in reforming their existing programs and in building national safety net systems.

As more countries develop strategies or systems for safety nets and social protection, increasing interministerial and agency coordination, oversight, and planning become more essential. Such coordination can reduce duplication and

Figure 3.3 Percentage of Countries with a Coordinated Safety Net System
Percent

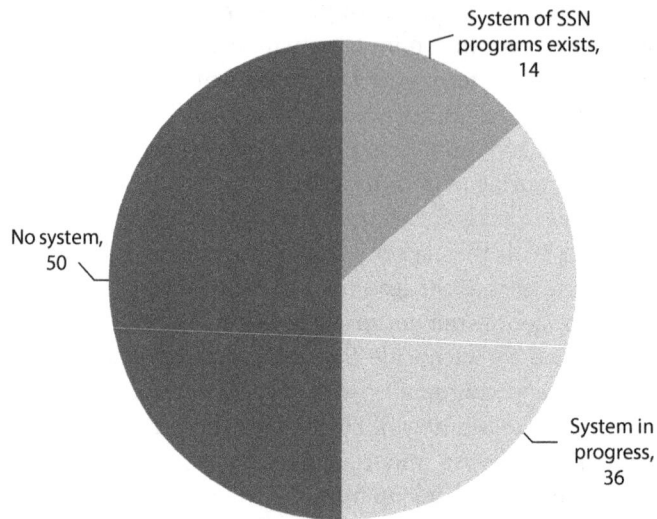

Sources: Calculations based on information from safety net assessments and World Bank's World Development Indicators database.
Note: SSN = social safety net.

overlap between programs and can help overcome challenges related to the scope and scalability of programs. In Kenya, for instance, the new National Social Protection Council will set standards for the implementation of social protection initiatives at both the national and local government levels and is likely to increase coordination among social protection programs, which will ensure that beneficiaries have access to the range and combination of programs and services that they need.

In Ethiopia, the objectives of the flagship PSNP span the mandates of two ministries and multiple departments within each ministry. The program is implemented jointly by the Food Security Coordination Directorate and the Natural Resources Management Directorate at the Ministry of Agriculture and Rural Development. The roles and responsibilities of the different agencies for the PSNP are described in box 3.2. The program is unique in that all donors pool their funds and provide a unified stream of technical assistance to a single government-led program. The donors are all represented on the government-chaired Joint Coordination Committee, which meets biweekly. Thematic working groups have been established with both donor and government members. Rwanda and Zambia have also established social protection working groups to coordinate ministries, partners, and donors. In Sierra Leone, the president recently decided that all of the country's social protection programs would be managed under the institutional framework created by the PRSP, which will strengthen the coordination and oversight of safety nets.

Box 3.2 Ethiopia's PSNP: Multiministerial Institutional Framework

The Productive Safety Net Program (PSNP) is a government program guided by a single program document. The institutional framework of the PSNP is predicated on the federal administrative structure of the Ethiopian government and is implemented largely through government systems. The nature of the program does not fit neatly into the mandate of a single government agency. Rather the objectives span the mandates of two ministries and multiple departments. The roles and responsibilities of these ministries and departments are as follows:

- The Ministry of Agriculture and Rural Development (MOARD) is responsible for management of the PSNP, with the Disaster Risk Management and Food Security Sector (DRMFSS) responsible for overall program coordination. Within the DRMFSS, the Food Security Coordination Directorate (previously called the Food Security Coordination Bureau) facilitates the day-to-day management and coordination of the PSNP. It is directly responsible for the timely delivery of transfers to beneficiaries and supports the implementation of public works.
- The Early Warning and Response Directorate (previously called the Disaster Prevention and Preparedness Agency), which is under the DRMFSS, provides accurate and timely early warning information for the PSNP Risk Financing Mechanism and ensures adequate links between PSNP risk financing and other humanitarian response activities. The Early Warning and Response Directorate is responsible for the timely delivery of food resources.
- The Natural Resources Management Directorate within MOARD is responsible for coordination and oversight of public works. This responsibility includes capacity building and technical support, supervision of environmental guidelines, liaison with the Food Security Coordination Directorate and other PSNP partner institutions on coordination and management of public works, and participation in PSNP design and management forums, including policy issues and the rollout of the pastoral PSNP.
- The Ministry of Finance and Economic Development oversees financial management of the program and disburses cash resources to implementing federal ministries and to the regions on the basis of the annual plan submitted by MOARD.

These federal implementation arrangements are replicated by regions and subregions (*woredas*). Within the regions, the ultimate authority for the PSNP resides in the regional council, which is the highest regional-level decision-making body. In addition to program implementation, regional and woreda bodies are responsible for ensuring sound multisectoral coordination of public works. Public works planning and selection of PSNP beneficiaries occur within communities and *kebeles* (groups of communities).

Moreover, within the overall framework, nongovernmental organizations (NGOs) and the World Food Programme (WFP) play an important role in implementation because of their experience in delivering food aid and the institutional requirements of some donor agencies to channel resources through NGOs and the WFP.

Source: PSNP 2010.

The most common weaknesses associated with the implementation of safety net programs in Africa are lack of monitoring and evaluation, absence of information systems, and limited human and technical capacity. Because public opinion often regards transfers as handouts rather than as investments in human capital, monitoring and evaluation arrangements are largely absent. In addition, complicated arrangements for procuring food and goods and for disbursing funds often cause delays in getting transfers to beneficiaries. In several countries in West and Central Africa, particularly in Madagascar, both government and donor programs are created in response to emergencies such as spells of food insecurity. As a result, they are not designed with long-term sustainability and productivity objectives in mind. However, many safety net programs, particularly cash transfers, have been subject to robust impact evaluations, and this evidence base has been critical in advancing the provision of effective safety nets in these countries.[5]

Information systems tend to be weak but are improving with new information technology. Many African countries could benefit from building stronger management information systems (MISs), payment mechanisms, and beneficiary identification systems to support social protection programs. Some countries, such as Ethiopia, have made significant investments in building the capacity of the public financial management system to deliver timely, predictable transfers to beneficiaries. Other countries, such as Kenya, are harnessing information and communication technology (ICT) to increase the efficiency of payments. In Kenya, the Hunger Safety Net Programme (HSNP) in northern Kenya makes payments through Equity Bank using smart cards and biometrics. This approach is being adopted for the Cash Transfer for Orphans and Vulnerable Children (CT-OVC) program. In phase 2 of the HSNP, which starts in late 2013, the payments will be made into beneficiaries' bank accounts to promote financial inclusion. Box 3.3 describes how Niger is adopting ICT to improve the efficiency of its payment system. Regardless of the approach adopted, in developing and strengthening these systems, policy makers need to ensure that the systems are not only simple enough so that they can be put to use quickly but also sophisticated enough to be capable of covering several programs. Policy makers also need to ensure that sufficient upfront investment is made to cover the costs of developing these crucial systems.

Unique beneficiary registries (single registries) have been used in several countries in Latin America and are now being developed in a number of African countries. Unique registries, which keep all relevant information about beneficiaries and other vulnerable groups in one database and can be used to target all safety net programs, enhance coordination and reduce duplication. Of the 22 countries reviewed, only Mauritius had a unique registry used by more than one program, although several other countries were in the process of developing one. Nevertheless, the registry in Mauritius has suffered from several operational challenges, and overlaps still exist in the country's multitude of social protection programs. Kenya and the Seychelles are in the process of implementing unique registries. In addition, Lesotho is in the process of developing the National

Box 3.3 Harnessing Information and Communication Technology for an Accountable Payment System in Niger

In 2011, the government of Niger established a safety net project, with World Bank support, to address the finding of the safety net assessment that most safety net support to poor and vulnerable households was through ad hoc emergency initiatives that had little effect on chronic poverty. The project aimed to create a predictable safety net for an estimated 140,000 poor, food-insecure households. This aim is particularly noteworthy because Niger is a low-income country with limited banking and telecommunication infrastructure.

To build the payment system, the project considered international best practice with regard to payment mechanisms and management information systems (MISs) and assessed the policy and institutional context of Niger that would enable the use of various technological solutions. The project has adopted a payment system using field-based payment verification and recording with smart cards and information from the database. More specifically, the payment system is fully integrated with the MIS. The system generates the list of the beneficiaries and gives it to the payment service providers, which are either microfinance institutions or a local bank. Mobile teams equipped with a laptop that reads the smart cards make the payments. The beneficiary collects the payment after verifying his or her identity by swiping a smart card in the terminal, which matches the information on the card with the data in the system (see figure B3.3.1). Payments are recorded electronically and transmitted either in real time or at the end of the day, depending on availability of Internet access. International experience has shown that this system minimizes the time of the transaction process and maximizes the transparency and security of the payments to beneficiaries.

Figure B3.3.1 Verification of Beneficiary Identity

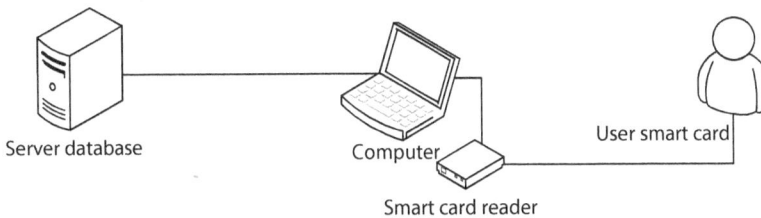

Server database

Computer

Smart card reader

User smart card

Sources: del Ninno *et al.* 2012; Government of Niger 2013.

Information System for Social Assistance (NISSA), which would form the basis for a more coordinated safety net in the county. Improving NISSA is an important first step in consolidating and rationalizing safety net programs. The system is designed to capture a number of key safety net programs, including the child grants program, the old-age pension program, the public assistance program, and the orphans and vulnerable children (OVC) bursary program. The initial step has been to launch NISSA under the targeting process of the pilot child grants program. In South Africa, the social protection MIS is linked to other government databases, such as that for the tax system.

Existing Safety Net Programs

This section analyzes the existing safety net programs in the 22 countries by program type. It reviews the most predominant types of safety nets, their beneficiaries, and their objectives. To present a complete picture, it discusses other complementary programs, such as general subsidies and microcredit and grant programs, even though they are outside the definition of targeted and noncontributory safety nets used by the World Bank. However, social programs such as support to schools in disadvantaged areas, universal free primary education, and health services are excluded.

The typical safety net in an African country consists of many small and fragmented programs. Few programs in the 22 countries provide regular and predictable support to the millions of households that remain below the poverty line, even in "good" years. In LICs, safety nets tend to be emergency responses to food-related shortages. Poverty-focused cash transfer programs, although not frequent overall, are more prevalent in LICs, but most are only small donor-supported pilots rather than large-scale, government-run programs. However, this situation is beginning to change, with governments increasingly financing safety net programs as long-term investments. In MICs such as Botswana and Mauritius, in contrast, the safety net is characterized by long-term programs providing continuous support to vulnerable groups such as OVC, the elderly, and persons with disabilities. Although Cameroon and Zambia are technically MICs, they are exceptions in that their safety nets are dominated by subsidies for income redistribution rather than programs aimed at vulnerable groups. On average, each country has about eight different program types, such as school feeding, other in-kind transfers, categorical transfers, public works programs, emergency programs, fee waivers, social care services, subsidies, and microcredit programs.

The most common types of safety net programs in the 22 countries are school feeding programs, public works programs, categorical transfer programs, and other in-kind transfer programs (figure 3.4 and table 3.1). Of the 22 countries, 21 have well-established school feeding programs (Rwanda is the exception), while 18 countries have other non-emergency-related in-kind transfer programs such as nutrition and food programs for special groups or programs providing school supplies. Twenty countries have cash-for-work, food-for-work, or cash-for-training programs. Thirteen countries, mainly those countries that struggle with food insecurity, undertake various kinds of emergency support programs in areas affected by drought, floods, or other emergencies. These programs hand out not only food but also other supplies. About 82 percent of the countries (18) have categorical programs targeting cash or other in-kind support to special vulnerable groups such as OVC, people affected by HIV/AIDS, the elderly, the indigent, and people with disabilities. About 77 percent of the countries (17) have some sort

Figure 3.4 Types of Safety Net Programs

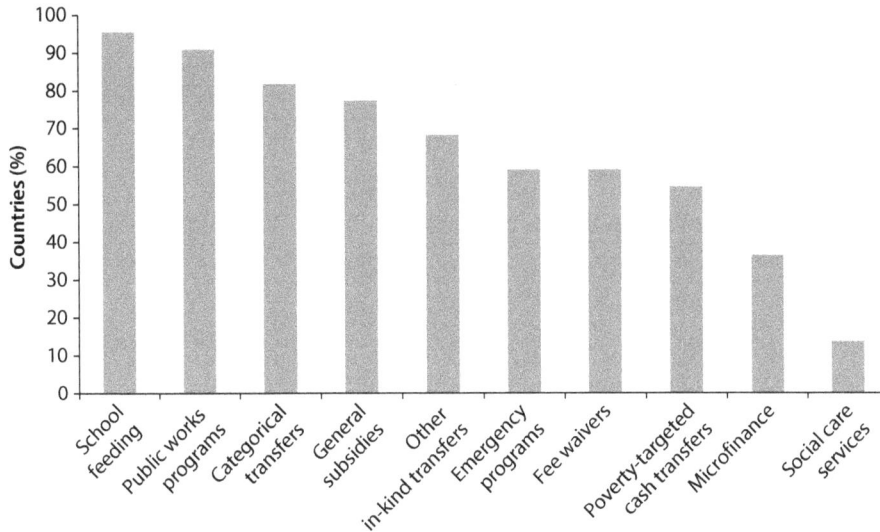

Source: Calculations based on information from safety net assessments.
Note: Programs are classified into groups according to the categories in table 3.1.

Figure 3.5 Short- or Long-Term Focus of Safety Nets

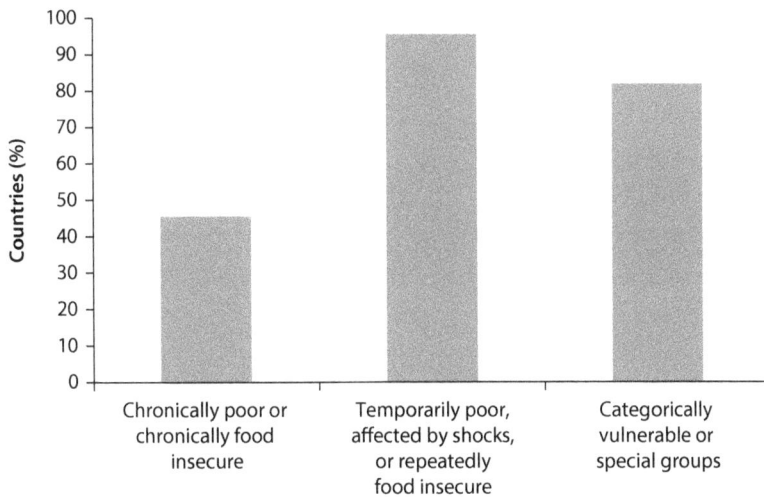

Source: Calculations based on information from safety net assessments.

of general subsidies (on food, fuel, or inputs), which are mostly untargeted. Each program group is discussed in more detail in the sections that follow.

In the African countries studied, safety nets focus on short-term support in response to shocks and on special or categorically vulnerable groups. In 95 percent of the countries analyzed, the main safety nets consist of short-term emergency responses aimed at supporting people who have been affected by a shock or who have temporarily fallen into poverty or food insecurity (figure 3.5).

Table 3.1 Types of Safety Net Programs in 22 Countries

| Program group | Poverty-targeted cash transfers | | Categorical cash and near-cash transfers | | | | | In-kind transfers | | | | |
Program type	Unconditional cash transfer	Conditional cash transfer (including soft)	Elderly	Indigent	OVC	HIV/ AIDS	Disabled	School feeding	Regular food handouts or feeding	Training	School supplies	Other
Benin				x			x	x	x	x	x	x
Botswana			x	x	x			x	x			x
Burkina Faso	Pilot	Pilot	x		x	x	x	x	x			
Cameroon			x	x	x		x	x				
Ethiopia	x					x		x	x			
Ghana	x							x			x	
Kenya	x		x	x	x		x	x	x			x
Lesotho			x	x	x			x	x		x	
Liberia	Pilot				x			x	x	x		
Madagascar		Pilot	x				x	x	x			
Malawi	Pilot							x	x			
Mali								x	x		x	
Mauritania	Pilot			x	x	x	x	x	x			
Mauritius	x		x				x	x			x	x
Mozambique			x		x	x	x	x	x		x	
Niger	Pilot							x				
Rwanda	x		x		x		x					
Sierra Leone			x	x	x	x	x	x	x			
Swaziland			x	x	x		x	x	x			
Tanzania	Pilot	Pilot	Pilot		x			x			x	
Togo		Pilot		x	x			x				x
Zambia	x		x		x	x		x	x			x

Source: Country safety net assessments.   *table continues next page*

Note: OVC = orphans and vulnerable children. "All" means that health and education is universally free.

This is the case in both LICs and MICs. These programs tend to consist of short-term public works programs, emergency food handouts, or temporary subsidies—all mainly in rural areas. In 82 percent of the countries, more regular or longer-term support (in the form of cash or in-kind transfers) is also provided to groups with special needs (OVC, people affected by HIV/AIDS, the elderly, the indigent, and persons with disabilities).

Regular or longer-term poverty-targeted cash transfer programs were less common and are underused as mechanisms to reduce poverty. Only 10 countries in the group (mainly LICs) have programs that aim to provide regular transfers over an extended period to households identified as being poor (figure 3.5). Most of these programs are small pilots financed by external sources (in Burkina Faso, Liberia, Madagascar, Malawi, and Tanzania). Only Ghana (Livelihood Empowerment against Poverty, or LEAP); Kenya (HSNP, the CT-OVC program,

Table 3.1 Types of Safety Net Programs in 22 Countries (continued)

Public works			Social care services		Fee waivers			Emergency programs			Microfinance	Subsidies		
Cash for work	Food for work	Cash or food for training	Orphan centers	Community home-based care	Health	Education	Other free	Emergency food handouts	Emergency kits	Other	Microfinance	Targeted (commodities)	Untargeted (price)	Other
x		x			x	All		x	x				x	
x			x	x	All	All					x			
x	x	x			Pilot			x				x		
x	x				x	x		x			x		x	
x	x				x							x		
					x	All							x	
	x			x	x	x		x			x			
x												x		
x	x				All			x			x		x	
x	x				x	All	x					x		
x	x							x			x			x
x	x	x				x		x	x				x	
x	x				x			x	x		x		x	
					x	x				x	x		x	x
			x	x									x	
x	x							x						
x					x						x			
x	x	x	x							x			x	
x	x				x			x				x		
x	x				x						x	x		x
Pilot					x	All		x					x	
x													x	

and the Older Persons' Cash Transfer program); Mauritius (the Social Aid and Income Support programs); and Rwanda (VUP) have poverty-targeted cash transfer programs operating at scale or in the process of being rapidly expanded nationwide. In addition, Ethiopia's PSNP provides regular and predictable support to a large number of the poorest households nationwide but is to a very large extent financed by broad-based donor support. South Africa's social grants program is the largest cash transfer program in Africa and includes several types of means-tested benefits for different categorical groups. Some examples of Africa's staple safety net programs are described in box 3.4. Social pensions to all elderly people (usually those over 60 years of age) and persons with disabilities exist in several southern African MICs, such as Botswana, Lesotho, Mauritius, the Seychelles, and Swaziland. However, these programs are part of the regular pension architecture, are universally provided to all those who no longer take part in

Box 3.4 Examples of African Safety Net Programs

Ethiopia's Productive Safety Net Program (PSNP) was launched in 2005 to transform the his-
toric food aid–based system into a more predictable safety net that produces productive
assets in poor communities. The PSNP provides cash and food transfers to food-insecure
households through labor-intensive public works for households with able-bodied members
(80 percent) and direct transfers to households that are unable to fulfill a work requirement
(20 percent). Estimated annual transfers per household are equivalent to about 40 percent of
their annual food needs. The PSNP reaches more than 7 million people, or about 10 percent of
the population, and implements about 34,000 small works projects per year. The PSNP's public
works have rehabilitated more than 167,000 hectares of land and 275,000 kilometers of stone
and soil bund embankments and have planted almost 900 million seedlings, all of which will
help mitigate the effects of future droughts. Rigorous evaluations of this program have con-
firmed that it has made significant transfers to the poor in times of need.

Ghana's Livelihood Empowerment against Poverty (LEAP) program is a social cash transfer program that provides cash and health insurance to extremely poor households across
Ghana to alleviate short-term poverty and encourage long-term human capital development. Eligibility is based on poverty and having a household member in at least one of
three demographic categories: a single parent with an orphan or vulnerable child, an
elderly poor person, or a person with an extreme disability who is unable to work. LEAP
started in a trial phase in March 2008, and as of June 2013, 71,000 households were enrolled.
Beneficiaries receive cash transfers of between US$4 and US$8 per month. An impact evaluation is currently ongoing. The objective is to scale up LEAP to 1 million households over
the next three years.

Kenya's Cash Transfer for Orphans and Vulnerable Children (CT-OVC) program was initi-
ated in response to concerns about the well-being of orphans and vulnerable children
(OVC), particularly AIDS orphans. The objectives of the program are to encourage the foster-
ing and family retention of children and to promote their human capital development.
Eligible households, which are those who are poor and contain an orphan or vulnerable
child, receive a flat monthly transfer of US$21. As of June 2012, the program reached 150,000
households, including 495,000 OVC across the country, about 24 percent of the estimated
number of households with OVC. Impact evaluations have found significantly higher expenditures on food and health services among beneficiary households. The effect of the program on schooling is concentrated on the secondary level, where enrollment was increased
by 9 percentage points and children from beneficiary households were less likely to be
behind a grade and more likely to progress to the next grade.

Rwanda's Vision 2020 Umurenge Program (VUP) combines public works (50 percent), cash
transfers (20 percent), and microfinance loans (30 percent) to targeted poor households in the
poorest subdistricts. Managed by the Ministry of Local Government, the public works encom-
pass land productivity and irrigation, mainly terracing, ditches, small dams, and forestry, as
well as construction of roads, school classrooms, and health centers. Wages are set at the district level and vary by project type but with a guideline that they should be less than or equal
to the market rate for similar work. As of 2009, wages averaged about US$1.50 per day. As of

box continues next page

Box 3.4 Examples of African Safety Net Programs *(continued)*

fiscal year 2010/11, the government spent about 0.7 percent of the national budget on VUP public works and employed 522,856 people, half of whom were women. This number is equivalent to about 5 percent of the national population. VUP public works were found to have reduced extreme poverty in the areas covered by the program.

South Africa's social grants program is the largest cash transfer program in Sub-Saharan Africa. It includes several types of means-tested grants targeted to older people, poor families with children, foster families, people with disabilities, and war veterans. Roughly 15 million people, or about 30 percent of the national population, receive a social grant. The child support grant (CSG) reaches about 10 million people, whereas the old-age grant, which applies to poor people over 60 years of age, reaches about 2 million people. According to household survey data, social grants make up over 60 percent of the income of the poorest 20 percent of recipient households, with CSGs being the largest contributor. Children who were enrolled in the CSG program at birth completed significantly more grades of schooling and achieved higher scores on a math test than did children who were enrolled at six years of age. These effects were particularly significant for girls. Enrollment in the CSG program reduced the likelihood of illness among children by 9 percentage points. The main effects on adolescents were reduced sexual activity, fewer teen pregnancies, and less drug and alcohol use.

Source: World Bank 2012c.

the active labor force, and are adapted from the large social pension program in South Africa. Hence, they are usually not poverty targeted.

African safety net programs generally aim to develop human capital and reduce malnutrition through the strong presence of food-based programs. This aim is found in all school feeding programs[6] and other food and in-kind handouts (emergency or regular) as well as in health and education fee waivers and programs focusing on OVC (figure 3.6). Targeted health fee waivers or scholarships exist in 12 countries (excluding countries where primary health care or education is free for all), but they are rarely well enforced or fully operational. In eight countries, various types of microcredit or small grant programs exist to provide poor and vulnerable groups with the means to undertake income-generating activities, thus making the lives of the beneficiaries more productive.

Although informal safety nets are not analyzed in this review, they are also important first-resort safety nets in Africa. A recent study showed that *informal safety nets*, defined as coordinated strategies used by social groupings of individuals to protect themselves against the adverse effects of different risks, are widespread in African countries (World Bank 2012a).[7] Although they generally have much lower information, transaction, monitoring, and enforcement costs than formal safety net arrangements, they may not reach the poorest and most vulnerable who are not included in social groups. In addition, they often break down when a covariate shock occurs because the risk-sharing arrangements do not extend beyond the immediate community or municipality.

Figure 3.6 Safety Nets, by Objective

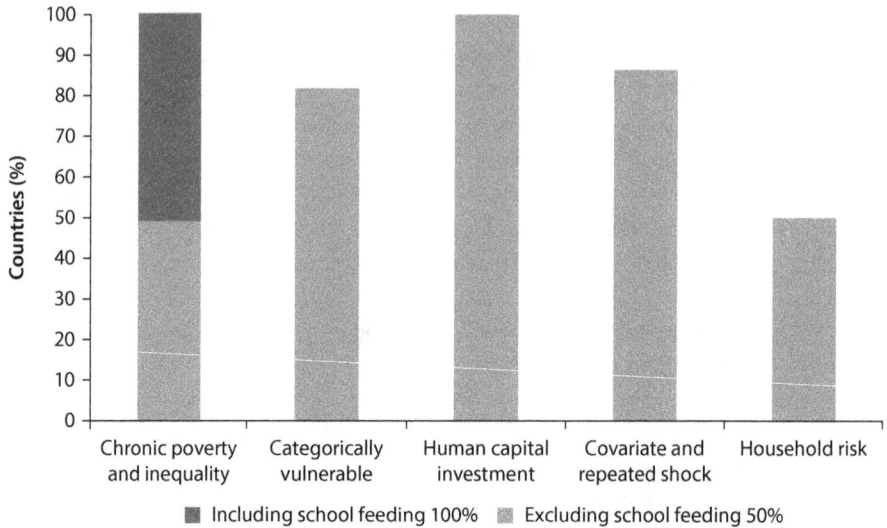

Source: Calculations based on information from safety net assessments.

A Look at Each Program Type

This section takes a deeper look at each type of program and attempts to analyze the main features and objectives of the various safety nets. The chapter also draws on separate analyses that have been done of cash transfer programs (Garcia and Moore 2012), public works programs (McCord and Slater 2009; Milazzo and del Ninno 2012), and school feeding programs (World Bank 2009) in Africa. The section is broken down as follows:

- School feeding programs
- Cash and in-kind transfer programs
  - Cash and near-cash transfer programs
  - In-kind transfer programs
- Public works programs
- Fee waiver programs
- Complementary social protection programs
- General price subsidies

School Feeding Programs

School feeding programs are the most common safety net program and exist in 21 of the 22 reviewed countries (Rwanda is the exception). The WFP is the most common implementer and funder of these programs, together with ministries of education.[8] School feeding usually consists of a hot lunch, often complemented by a snack or take-home rations for girls, provided that they have a regular attendance record. School feeding programs tend to be focused on children of primary school age, but some secondary and boarding school children also benefit from feeding in countries such as Botswana and Mozambique. Government-provided school feeding programs are most common in southern African countries.

School feeding programs mostly have education- and nutrition-related objectives, but their targeting to disadvantaged areas makes them important safety net instruments. Because these programs promote human development by increasing the nutritional intake of school-age children and by encouraging enrollment, especially of disadvantaged girls, they are a crucial safety net intervention in LICs. Compared with many MICs in other regions that, in addition to school feeding programs use household-targeted conditional cash transfer (CCT) programs to encourage school participation of the poorest, in African countries school feeding programs are the main vehicle for increasing the human capital investment of the poor. Most school feeding programs in Africa are implemented in areas with high poverty, extensive food insecurity, and low educational attainment; these areas are identified by geographic targeting. However, within these areas, such programs usually provide benefits to all schoolchildren rather than just targeting the most disadvantaged, which results in significant errors of both inclusion and exclusion. In addition, in areas where enrollment is low, school feeding programs will not benefit the poorest children because they are unlikely to attend school. The targeting of take-home rations may be more precise than in-school meals because children from particularly disadvantaged households—most often girls—are selected to receive support.

Despite the existence of school feeding programs in almost all of the reviewed countries, their coverage as a share of the nationwide primary school population is rather low, and their costs are high. Spending on school feeding programs in Africa accounts for a large share of total safety net spending. In Burkina Faso and Mali, school feeding accounts for over 20 percent of total government spending on safety nets, as well as a large share of total donor contributions. Despite significant resource allocations, the coverage of school-age children is low. For instance, in Cameroon, school feeding programs reach only 5.3 percent of all primary school children in the northernmost (and poorest) four regions. In Tanzania, the program is currently being expanded but is expected to cover only 7 percent of all primary students nationwide. In Ghana, targeting analysis has shown that the poor receive only 21.3 percent of school feeding benefits. In several of the countries reviewed, the administrative costs of school feeding programs are high, which makes them an inefficient way of transferring funds to the poor. The costs of transporting and storing food are generally a challenge, especially in the most disadvantaged areas. The universal school feeding programs in Lesotho and Swaziland clearly provide benefits to many nonpoor students, although no rigorous impact evaluations of the programs have yet been done. More work is needed to identify the role that school feeding and other food-based programs can and should play in safety net systems.

Cash and In-Kind Transfer Programs
Cash and Near-Cash Transfer Programs

Across Africa, poverty-targeted cash transfer programs tend to be small and are often implemented on a pilot or experimental basis. Of the countries reviewed, small cash transfer programs (in other words, those with low coverage of poor households) have been tried in Benin, Burkina Faso, Kenya, Liberia, Malawi, Mali, and Mauritania. Although not part of this review, South Africa's social grants program is the largest cash transfer program in Sub-Saharan Africa. It includes several types of means-tested grants targeted to older people, poor families with children, foster families, people with disabilities, and war veterans. Roughly 15 million people receive a social grant, or about 30 percent of the national population. Some other larger programs in Africa use means testing or proxy means testing to focus the benefits to the poorest segments of the population. These programs include LEAP in Ghana, the CT-OVC program in Kenya, the Social Aid and Income Support programs in Mauritius, the VUP in Rwanda, the Social Cash Transfer Scheme in Zambia, and the destitution program in Botswana. In Mali, two cash transfer programs have been piloted in the past: the United Nations Children's Fund's Bourse maman in 2006 and Oxfam GB and Save the Children's program in 2010/11. In Burkina Faso, the WFP introduced a pilot cash transfer program in 2009/10. The lessons emerging from these pilot experiences emphasize the need for strong institutional grounding, clear program objectives, regular payments of adequate size that are targeted using clear and consistently applied criteria and that reflect the program's objectives, and a well-built monitoring and evaluation system to ensure that benefits are reaching the intended target groups.

Most cash transfer programs are categorically targeted to particular vulnerable groups. These groups include OVC, young mothers, people with HIV/AIDS, people with disabilities, families with children who have special needs, and indigents. However, these programs often lack clear criteria for establishing the vulnerability level of the household because of limitations in demographic data and weak enforcement. In several African MICs (including Botswana, Lesotho, Mauritius, the Seychelles, and Swaziland), noncontributory old-age and social pensions are universally provided to all citizens over a certain age (usually 60 to 70 years old) to support them as they exit the labor force. Although many poor elderly people who lack any other significant income source benefit from this income support, because the pensions are universal[9] and because they are part of the basic pension architecture, they are very costly, and as safety nets they provide few benefits to the poor. In Botswana, the old-age pension program is the second-largest safety net program and covers 95 percent of the elderly, who represent 5 percent of the whole population. In Mauritius, the cost of the noncontributory basic pension exceeded 3 percent of gross domestic product (GDP) in 2008/09. In Swaziland, the Old-Age Grant accounts for almost 90 percent of all cash transfer payments, and although the benefits are perceived as benefiting poor households, 28 percent of beneficiaries are not poor. Lesotho's old-age pension scheme, as part of the SSNs, is discussed in box 3.5.

Box 3.5 Lesotho's Old-Age Pension: Part of the Safety Net

The Old-Age Pension (OAP) in Lesotho was introduced in 2004. It is a noncontributory, unconditional transfer paid to all Basotho over 70 years of age. This support is particularly important
in Lesotho, because a large number of grandparent-headed households are supporting
orphaned children. Nevertheless, the OAP directly reaches only about 4.4 percent of the population. Indirectly, it reaches perhaps 17 percent. The program is among the most expensive
noncontributory programs in Lesotho (excluding the tertiary bursary scheme). And as the
number of elderly people continues to grow, concerns are increasing about how the program
can be sustained in the long term.

In 2010, the poverty rate among the elderly in Lesotho was estimated to be the same as
among the population as a whole, a fact that implies that almost two-thirds of the OAP payments go to nonpoor households. A universal social pension may be needed, but as a means
of reducing extreme poverty in the country, the M 371 million spent annually on the OAP has
only a limited effect. As such, when evaluating the program as part of the safety net system for
addressing extreme poverty, policy makers need to recognize that most of the transfers are
going to the nonpoor. Given that only 6 percent of the poor are estimated to be older than 64,
any program targeted according to old age is not going to cover many of the poor.

Although no systematic assessment has been done of how the OAP affects consumption
and poverty, two reviews have identified a number of positive poverty-related effects. The
benefits are shared within households, and some evidence indicates that consumption and
educational attainment increased as a result of the pension. The same evaluation found that
the proportion of beneficiaries reporting that they never or rarely had enough food to satisfy
their hunger fell from 80 percent to 40 percent after receiving the pension. Another assessment noted increases in self-esteem among the elderly and indicated that a large proportion
of the pension (60 percent) is being spent on food. The same assessment estimated that about
20 percent is spent on dependent orphan children.

Source: World Bank 2012b.

Placing conditions on cash transfers to improve human capital outcomes is
being explored in Africa, and such programs are subject to experimentation and
impact evaluations. In general, cash transfer programs in Africa rarely include
conditions (or coresponsibilities) requiring the recipient households to invest in
their human capital. CCT programs have thus far been implemented only as
donor pilot programs in Burkina Faso, Liberia, Madagascar, and Malawi to test the
feasibility of placing conditions, such as regular school attendance of school-age
children or frequent health center checkups for children under two years of age,
on the receipt of transfers. In Tanzania, the TASAF CCT pilot is experimenting
with providing transfers to families with children and elderly people on the condi-
tion that the families ensure that their children enroll in and attend school and
that they receive regular checkups from health providers. In Niger, the recent cash
transfer program financed by the World Bank is supporting poor families in return
for "soft" conditions that provide training for mothers in essential practices in

health, nutrition, and sanitation. The World Bank is currently exploring whether CCT programs can be used to improve human capital outcomes in Guinea and the Republic of Congo. These CCT programs are benefiting from rigorous impact evaluations, the results of which are discussed further in chapter 4.

Near-cash programs are not very common. Only in Botswana, Burkina Faso, Ethiopia, Lesotho, Mauritania, and Zambia have programs been introduced that provide coupons or food vouchers as an alternative to cash. In Botswana, OVC can receive coupons with which they can buy food, shelter, clothing, schooling, and care services, but uptake is low. Programs in Burkina Faso, Ethiopia, Mauritania, and Zambia provided food vouchers in urban areas during periods of food price increases. Some of these programs were implemented by the WFP during the 2009–10 economic crisis.

Food and In-Kind Transfer Programs, Regular and Emergency

Given the strong focus on food security and nutrition in the countries reviewed, almost all have some form of program providing access to food. These programs are particularly common in countries that have historically suffered from droughts. For instance, in Burkina Faso, programs that hand out food and respond to short-term shocks account for 69 percent of total safety net spending and for 80 percent of all safety net beneficiaries. In Mali, cereal banks account for 25 percent of total safety net spending. The largest PSNPs in Zambia are all related to increasing the food production of small farmers, particularly the farm-input subsidy program and free seed and fertilizer starter packs. In Mauritania, the Emel ("hope") program aimed to protect vulnerable groups from rising food prices and food insecurity by providing support to the national network of village cereal banks, or SAVS (Stock Alimentaire Villageois de Sécurité); by distributing free food; and by subsidizing basic goods through special food-based boutiques. Ethiopia is the only country that has successfully turned a food emergency relief system into a more effective safety net program. The next chapter discusses the scarce evidence on cash versus food transfers. In general, three types of food-based programs exist:

- *Subsidized food sales or cereal banks.* These programs exist in countries in the Sahel region (Benin, Burkina Faso, Cameroon, Mali, Mauritania, and Niger) and are often the main safety net in such countries.
- *Food distribution programs and supplement and feeding programs.* These programs focus on particular vulnerable groups, such as malnourished children under five years of age, pregnant or breastfeeding mothers in food-insecure areas, refugees, and people suffering from HIV/AIDS. Food and other vitamin supplements are provided to these groups either on an emergency basis (for example, during a couple of months of acute food insecurity) or on a more regular basis (for groups with long-term care needs).
- *Other in-kind transfer programs.* These programs provide school supplies (Benin, Kenya, Lesotho, Mali, Mauritius, Mozambique, and Togo) or small farm inputs (Liberia, Mauritius, and Zambia).

Public Works Programs

Table 3.2 summarizes the main features of the public works programs in the countries reviewed. Nineteen (86 percent) of the 22 countries reviewed have cash-for-work programs, and 13 countries (59 percent) have food-for-work programs. Cash- or food-for-training programs have been started in Benin, Burkina Faso, Mali, and Sierra Leone. Moreover, Burkina Faso, Liberia, Madagascar, Malawi, Mali, and Sierra Leone each have several different public works programs operated by the government and by various development partners with different target groups (such as urban youths, rural women, ex-combatants, or food-insecure populations) and objectives (mainly focused on providing short-term employment and on building or rehabilitating infrastructure). A recent report (Milazzo and del Ninno 2012) showed that public works programs in Africa have been mostly used as short-term safety net instruments in the aftermath of natural disasters or in postconflict settings. A few recent programs adopted a longer-term approach to reducing chronic poverty by providing a reliable source of income to poor participants in a more predictable manner and for a longer period. Examples are the PSNP in Ethiopia (the largest public works program in Africa, benefiting about 7 million people), the Expanded Public Works Programme in South Africa, and the Malawi Social Action Fund (MASAF).

The way these public works programs are designed does not always allow them to meet these safety net objectives effectively. Most of the public works safety net programs reviewed pay wages in cash (70 percent), whereas fewer (33 percent) pay participants with food (table 3.2).[10] Most programs combine several different targeting methods to select the beneficiaries, the most common being geographic (42 percent) and community-based (29 percent) targeting (Milazzo and del Ninno 2012). The wage level is also used as a targeting tool. However, in many programs that provide cash, the wage rate is set well above the local minimum wage level and therefore does not work well in encouraging self-targeting to the poor. In fact, McCord and Slater (2009) found that only 39 percent of public works programs in Africa set the wage rate below minimum wage. Only Botswana's Ipelegeng program, MASAF in Malawi, the PSNP in Ethiopia, and the Tanzania food-insecurity project (operated by TASAF) have set their wage rates low enough to attract low-skilled poor labor.

In addition, many public works programs in Africa serve objectives other than safety net objectives. McCord and Slater (2009) reviewed 167 public works programs in 29 African countries and found that only about half (47 percent) have safety net objectives (defined as offering a wage transfer for a single short-term episode of employment for basic risk coping). The other half aim to provide short-term employment opportunities (not necessarily targeted to the poorest) and to create and maintain infrastructure and services (figure 3.7). Almost all public works programs are providing employment for a short duration (mainly during the agricultural slack season) to absorb the temporary labor surplus and to reduce seasonal poverty and food insecurity. However, because of the temporary nature of most public works programs in Africa, they are not sufficient to address the needs of the chronically poor.

Table 3.2 Core Features of Public Works Programs, Selected Countries and Programs

Program name	Agency	Main objectives	Payment type	Location	Targeting	Wage setting for cash programs	Duration or frequency of employment	Gender of participants	Poverty targeting
Benin									
Projet de Gestion Urbaine Décentralisée (Decentralized City Management Project)	Agetur	Creation of jobs, know-how development of workers, and creation of assets	Cash	Urban	Geographic; self-targeting to unemployed graduates using wage rate	CFAF 2,000, 100–200% of minimum wage	4–5 months, 8 hours per day	—	—
Programme d'Appui aux Secteurs Routiers (Road Sector Assistance Program)	Danish International Development Agency	Improvement of rural road transportation and increased accessibility	Cash	Rural	Geographic; food-insecure communities targeted; self-targeting using wage rate	CFAF 2,000, about 150% of average local wage	During agricultural slack seasons	35% women	55% poor
Botswana									
Ipelegeng (self-reliance)	Government	Launched during global crisis as a permanent, non-drought-related SSN to replace a series of emergency programs	Cash	Rural and urban	Self-targeting using wage rate (rationed because of excess demand)	P 18 per day for casual labor; P 24 per day for supervisors; deemed low enough to encourage self-selection by the poor	Maximum 30 days per year	80% women	—
Burkina Faso									
Programme Pistes Rurales: Désenclavement à l'Est (Rural Access Roads Program)	Helvetas, supervised by Ministry of Infrastructure	Asset creation and labor intensity; not designed as SSN	Cash	Rural	Self-targeting using wage rate	CFAF 130,950 per year on average, slightly below minimum wage	6 months	16% women	Reduced poverty among direct beneficiaries
Food for Assets	World Food Programme (WFP)	Asset creation and labor intensity	Food	Rural	Self-targeting using wage rate	—	—	About 50% women	—

table continues next page

Table 3.2 Core Features of Public Works Programs, Selected Countries and Programs (continued)

Program name	Agency	Main objectives	Payment type	Location	Targeting	Wage setting for cash programs	Duration or frequency of employment	Gender of participants	Poverty targeting
Cameroon									
Projet d'Assainissement de Yaoundé (Yaoundé Sanitation Project)	Government, African Development Bank	Temporary employment to clean up infrastructure	Cash	Urban	Geographic; self-targeting using wage rate	CFAF 300 per hour, almost 200% of regular pay	—	—	—
Food for work	WFP	Reduction of food insecurity and building of rural assets	Food	Rural	Self-targeting using wage rate	—	—	—	—
Ethiopia									
Productive Safety Net Program	Government, supported by a number of donors	Assurance of food consumption and prevention of asset depletion for rural food-insecure households in a way that stimulates markets, improves access to services and natural resources, and rehabilitates and enhances the natural environment	Food, cash, or a mix	Rural	Geographic, community based; self-targeting using wage rate	Br 10 or 3 kilograms of cereals per day (US$0.80 per day), estimated at about 40% of annual food needs (set to be about 10% of the basket represented by the national poverty line in 2007/08)	6 months during the lean season, repeated over a number of years	Women account for 44% of total person-days	87% of participants food insecure

table continues next page

Table 3.2 Core Features of Public Works Programs, Selected Countries and Programs (continued)

Liberia

Program name	Agency	Main objectives	Payment type	Location	Targeting	Wage setting for cash programs	Duration or frequency of employment	Gender of participants	Poverty targeting
Liberia Emergency Employment Programme and Liberia Employment Action Programme	Ministry of Labor	Provision of emergency employment, mainly to former combatants	Cash	Rural and urban	Communities apply to their local governments to begin the process	US$3 for unskilled workers; US$5 for skilled workers	8-hour working day; short term	—	Little is known on the actual capability of beneficiaries to leverage the short-term employment, through savings or investments, to reduce their vulnerability
Vacation Job	Ministry of Labor and Interministerial Committee on Youth Employment	Provision of emergency employment, internships, and community service jobs for students	Cash	Urban	Nomination of students by their principals or community leaders	US$100 (US$150 in the private sector)	8-hour working day; short term	—	—
National Beautification Days	Ministry of Labor	Emergency employment	Cash	Rural and urban	Selection by county authorities and local town chiefs	US$3 for unskilled workers; US$5 for skilled workers	8-hour working day; short term	—	—
YES (Youth Employment Skills)	Liberia Agency for Community Empowerment, Ministry of Youth and Sports, and World Bank	Expansion of access of poor and young Liberians to temporary employment programs in an effort to increase their employability	Cash	Rural and urban	Selected based on at-risk, unemployment, vulnerability status	US$3 for unskilled workers; US$5 for skilled workers	8-hour working day; 32 days employment and 8 days training	Currently 50% female	80% of participants in the lowest 3 quintiles, but only 14.5% were from the first (lowest) quintile

table continues next page

Table 3.2 Core Features of Public Works Programs, Selected Countries and Programs *(continued)*

Program name	Agency	Main objectives	Payment type	Location	Targeting	Wage setting for cash programs	Duration or frequency of employment	Gender of participants	Poverty targeting
Livelihood Asset Rehabilitation	WFP	Food security	Food	Rural	Households chosen by communities on the basis of access to food markets or ability to produce food	—	—	—	—
Madagascar									
Cash-for-work (Emergency Food Security and Reconstruction Project)	World Bank, Madagascar government, and Fonds d'Intervention pour le Développement (Development Intervention Fund)	Increased access to short-term employment in targeted food-insecure areas; raising of disposable income; increased food consumption	Cash	Rural	Geographic; self-targeting by wage rate, and then community selection (if demand is high)	Ar 2,000 (about US$1) for 5 hours of work, above the Ar 1,500 daily rate for unskilled rural workers	Mainly during lean season (average 25 days)	Expected 50% women	Wage (about 25 days of labor employment) estimated to be largely insufficient to lift people out of poverty
Country program food for work and protracted relief and recovery operations	WFP	Provision of temporary employment during lean seasons and building of sustainable livelihoods; disaster risk management in the aftermath of shocks	Food	—	Geographic, southern regions; female heads of households, large households, and households cultivating less than 1 hectare favored	—	During the lean season (October–April) and after natural disasters (average 25 days)	—	

table continues next page

Table 3.2 Core Features of Public Works Programs, Selected Countries and Programs *(continued)*

Program name	Agency	Main objectives	Payment type	Location	Targeting	Wage setting for cash programs	Duration or frequency of employment	Gender of participants	Poverty targeting
Food-for-work component of SALOHI (Strengthening and Accessing Livelihood Opportunities for Household Impact) program	U.S. Agency for International Development	Strengthening of resilience to shocks	Food	—	Geographic, eastern and southern districts regularly affected by disasters	—	—	Participation of women emphasized	—
Cash-, food-, or seeds-for-work program	National Office of Nutrition	Improvement of the lives of the most vulnerable, increased productive capacity and improved health of communities, and mitigation of the effects of disasters on nutrition	Cash, food, and seeds	—	Priority given to households with children younger than 5 years of age, large households, households with people with disabilities or old people, very poor households, and low-paid casual workers	—	—	—	—
Malawi									
Livelihoods through Public Works Programme	MASAF	Employment creation and promotion of livelihoods	Cash	—	Geographic; vulnerable households able to engage in productive activities	—	Guaranteed 2.5 months of employment	—	—

table continues next page

Table 3.2 Core Features of Public Works Programs, Selected Countries and Programs *(continued)*

Program name	Agency	Main objectives	Payment type	Location	Targeting	Wage setting for cash programs	Duration or frequency of employment	Gender of participants	Poverty targeting
Emergency Drought Recovery Project	MASAF	Emergency response to drought	Cash	—	Geographic; self-targeting by wage rate and then community selection	MK 43 per 4-hour task in rural areas, 12.4% above rural minimum wage and 88% of the urban minimum wage	Guaranteed 2.5 months of employment	—	—
Public Works Programme–CCT	MASAF	Emergency response to drought, providing cash relief to poor, vulnerable households so they can purchase food and agricultural inputs	Cash	Rural	Geographic; self-targeting by wage rate and then community selection	MK 200 per 8-hour day deemed sufficient to access subsidized fertilizer and purchase some food	Guaranteed 10 days of employment	—	93% accurately targeted to poor and vulnerable households
Government and EU Public Works Programme	Government and EU	Improved rural development and replacement of food handouts with activities that promote longer-term food security	Cash	Rural	Selection by local contractors	Varies from contractor to contractor but with a minimum guide of MK 64 per 6-hour task	—	—	—
Government and EU Food Security Programme	Government and EU	Employment creation and increased food security	Cash	Rural	Selection by local leaders with guidance from district assembly	MK 147 per 5-hour task	—	—	—

table continues next page

Table 3.2 Core Features of Public Works Programs, Selected Countries and Programs *(continued)*

Program name	Agency	Main objectives	Payment type	Location	Targeting	Wage setting for cash programs	Duration or frequency of employment	Gender of participants	Poverty targeting
Government and EU income-generating public works	Government and EU	Cash for food, promotion of productive activities, and facilitation of access to subsidized agricultural inputs	Cash	Rural	Selection by local contractors and local leaders	Special injection of MK 150 per day for an average period of 20 days during hungry season	—	—	—
Mali									
State-supported public works	Agency for Youth Employment Promotion	Reorienting of investment to infrastructure using a labor-intensive approach and stimulating the local economy	Cash	—	No clear targeting criteria	Wage level set much higher than both the minimum and the market wages	—	—	—
Programme d'Emploi des Jeunes par l'Approche Haute Intensité de Main d'Œuvre (Employment Program for Youth by High Labor Force Intensity)	Agency for Youth Employment Promotion, International Labour Organization, Luxembourg	Bridge to employment	Cash	—	Local authorities select beneficiaries; self-targeting	CFAF 3,000–CFAF 5,000 per day, much higher than minimum and market wages	90 days, long enough to learn the job	—	There has been no attempt to enroll the poorest individuals
Food-for-work and food-for-skills programs	WFP	Mitigation of soil degradation and development of agriculture lands in food-insecure areas	Food	Rural	—	—	—	50–70% women	—

table continues next page

Table 3.2 Core Features of Public Works Programs, Selected Countries and Programs *(continued)*

Program name	Agency	Main objectives	Payment type	Location	Targeting	Wage setting for cash programs	Duration or frequency of employment	Gender of participants	Poverty targeting
Food for Peace Program ("Nema" Program)	U.S. Agency for International Development	Prevention of food insecurity	Food	Rural	—	—	—	—	—
Rwanda									
Vision 2020 Umurenge Program–Public Works	Government-led with multidonor support	Increased rate of poverty reduction	Cash	Rural and urban	Geographic and *Ubudehe* targeting method (based on access to land, livestock, and assets) for households with able-bodied adults	Average US$1.50 per day, wages about 10% on average higher than the market rate in 14 of 30 sectors	—	—	Only small benefits provided to individual households, thereby undermining the protective objectives
Sierra Leone									
Youth Employment Support Project	World Bank, government of Sierra Leone, and National Commission for Social Action	Increased short-term employment opportunities and increased employability of targeted youths	Cash	Rural and urban	Geographic; self-targeting by wage rate	Le 6,000–Le 8,000 per day (varies by locality)	50–70 days	Expected 30% female	—

table continues next page

Table 3.2 Core Features of Public Works Programs, Selected Countries and Programs *(continued)*

Program name	Agency	Main objectives	Payment type	Location	Targeting	Wage setting for cash programs	Duration or frequency of employment	Gender of participants	Poverty targeting
Food for work and food for training	Ministry of Agriculture, Forestry, and Food Security; World Bank; and other partners	Augmentation of food security through food (and cash) transfers while creating assets that increase the commercialization of smallholder farmers	Mainly food	—	Selection by district councils and chiefdoms	—	—	—	—
Tanzania									
Food-insecurity project	TASAF	Raised consumption of the poor and food insecure while assets are built to contribute to longer-term growth	Cash	Rural	Geographic; community targeting of poor and food-insecure households; self-selection using wage rate	T Sh 3,000–T Sh 5,000 per day, 10% below local wage, but substantial local discretion exists in setting wages	20–30 days, during the agricultural slack season, but in practice there have been delays	—	T Sh 3,000 is in line with current unskilled wages; T Sh 5,000 is above the normal wage for unskilled labor
Food-for-asset creation program	TASAF	Reduced pressure on families by provision of food when stocks are low and prices are high	Food	Rural	Food-insecure districts selected; community decides which households to benefit	—	About 30 days during agricultural lean season	—	—

table continues next page

Table 3.2 Core Features of Public Works Programs, Selected Countries and Programs *(continued)*

Program name	Agency	Main objectives	Payment type	Location	Targeting	Wage setting for cash programs	Duration or frequency of employment	Gender of participants	Poverty targeting
Togo									
Cash-for-work program	World Bank, Ministry of Local Development, Youth Artisans, Youth and Youth Employment	Provision of a complementary source of revenue to 25,000 disadvantaged youths	Cash	Rural	Geographic; self-targeting using wage rate	US$3 per day, equal to official minimum wage and 30% of consumption per person living in rural areas	40 days	Estimated to be 50% women and 75% youths	At least 75% of workers living below the poverty line
Zambia									
Peri-Urban Community Self-Help	Government of Zambia		Cash and food	Rural and urban	Varies from operation to operation, including geographic, proxy means testing, and self-targeting, depending on extent of vulnerability in the areas concerned	Required to pay minimum wage of K 20,000 (US$4) per day but pays only K 10,000 (about US$2) for half a day; much higher than daily wage rate for unskilled rural agricultural workers (K 6,000)	3–24 months (average 4 months) in the dry season	About 60% women	—

Source: Country safety net assessments.

Note: CCT = conditional cash transfer; EU = European Union; MASAF = Malawi Social Action Fund; SSN = social safety net; TASAF = Tanzania Social Action Fund; — = not available.

Figure 3.7 Objectives of Africa's Public Works Programs
Percent

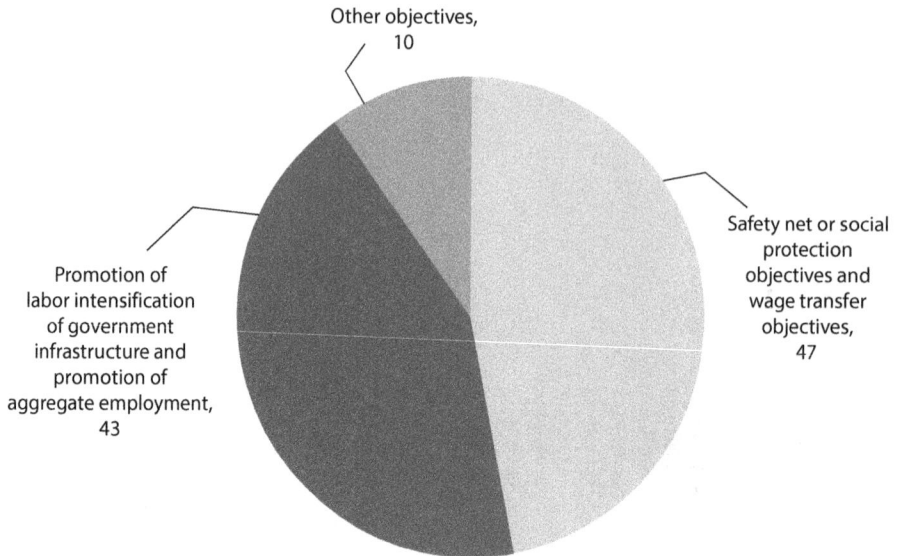

Source: McCord and Slater 2009.
Note: Based on a review of 167 public works programs in 29 African countries.

Public works can encourage social cohesiveness in postconflict settings. Experiences from Liberia and Sierra Leone show that safety nets, particularly public works, can have a positive effect on social cohesion (Andrews *et al.* 2012). In postconflict countries, this effect can be an important outcome, which could have the potential to help overcome societal divisions that may have contributed to the outbreak of the conflict.

Fee Waiver Programs

In line with the focus on human development, many African countries have health care fee waivers for the poorest. In several LICs (Benin, Burkina Faso, Cameroon, Madagascar, Mali, and Mauritania), health care is free for indigents and for other categorically targeted groups. In Burkina Faso, children, women, and the at-risk elderly are entitled to both preventive and curative care at no cost. In Cameroon, the poor are exempt from any fees for urgent hospital care or medical evacuations. However, the criteria for who is eligible are generally poorly defined, and in reality fee waiver programs are poorly targeted and enforced. Nevertheless, a pilot program in Burkina Faso provides some evidence that abolishing fees for poor women and children can increase their use of health care. However, appropriate evaluations are still needed to confirm this outcome and to establish whether health care waivers reduce poverty and increase the use of health care services. In several of the anglophone countries, fee waiver and voucher systems for health care are better enforced and targeted. In Ghana, the poor may register free of charge for the National Health Insurance Scheme

(NHIS), whereas in Tanzania, the poor are issued with health cards entitling them to free health care. In Botswana, Liberia, and Swaziland, primary health care is free for all, and in Mauritius the government pays for all necessary medical evacuations. In Swaziland, general maternal and child health services are also free, and people over 60 years of age, people with disabilities, and OVC are exempt from medical fees. Box 3.6 describes Ghana's NHIS, which is unique in Africa.

Primary education is commonly free for all children. When primary schools do charge fees, poor and disadvantaged children often receive tuition waivers (as happens in Cameroon even though primary school is generally free). However, data from some countries (Liberia, for instance) indicate that, even though primary education is free, one of the most frequent explanations given by parents for why their children are not attending school is cost (of school fees, transport, and uniforms). In Kenya, the Secondary Education Bursary Fund provides support to the most needy, and in Mozambique, the Institute for Study Grants provides university scholarships. In Mauritius, school fee waivers are available for preprimary schooling.

Complementary Social Protection Programs

Microcredit or grant programs targeted to poor individuals and groups are common in Africa and serve to increase the productivity of the recipients. Burkina Faso,

---

Box 3.6 Ghana's National Health Insurance Scheme Indigent Exemption

One program that appears to be very well targeted is the indigent exemption for the registration and coverage of very poor households under Ghana's National Health Insurance Scheme (NHIS). The NHIS was created in 2003 in an effort to increase access to and affordability of health care. The scheme is funded by premiums paid by participants, but it is also heavily subsidized through indirect taxation (a special levy on value added tax and import duties). Currently, the scheme has managed to enroll about 60 percent of the population, according to NHIS data. Indigent people benefit from exemptions, but there are strict controls on the registration of indigents at the district level.

According to limited district-level data, the share of NHIS benefits accruing to the poor is 38.5 percent. However, the actual targeting performance of the exemption is likely to be much better because of the relatively strict targeting within each district. Although the scheme does reach some of the poor, it continues to benefit far more of the better-off segments of the population, and the premiums are often too high to be affordable for the very poor.

Given low levels of enrollment under this exemption compared to the share of the population in extreme poverty, districts should be encouraged to make more extensive use of the indigent exemption. A first step could be to allow most beneficiaries of the Livelihood Empowerment against Poverty (LEAP) cash transfer program to benefit from the exemption. The goal of LEAP is to scale up to reach 1 million households.

Source: World Bank 2011.

Cameroon, Kenya, and Rwanda all have a plethora of microcredits or grants. Although they are not necessarily safety net programs, they complement safety nets by providing small amounts of financing to individuals or groups (usually of women, youths, or farmers) in marginalized communities to enable them to undertake income-generating activities. However, how these programs have affected poverty has not been evaluated, and no evidence exists of their cost-effectiveness. In Rwanda, microcredit programs and other programs that promote income generation and productive activities play a large role in the social protection strategy.

Agricultural input vouchers and schemes are also important risk reduction programs. They provide smallholder farmers or farmers' groups either with agricultural inputs or with vouchers and subsidies to purchase inputs at a reduced cost. The National Agriculture Input Voucher Scheme in Tanzania provides vouchers to be used to buy fertilizer and improved seeds at reduced prices for 1.5 million households that engage in rice or maize farming. In Ethiopia, the Household Asset Building Program provides agricultural households a one-time highly subsidized credit to rebuild their asset base or to purchase "household extension packages." Similarly, the Malawi Farm Input Subsidy Program subsidizes the prices of fertilizer and seeds. The large Food Security Pack program and Farmer Input Support Program in Zambia are meant to reduce food insecurity among small farmers. This strong focus on providing inputs for agricultural production in Zambia makes sense because the consumption levels of most of the poor depend largely on how much food they are able to produce on their own small plots of land. However, providing in-kind supplies generally involves high administrative costs, and price subsidies tend to be regressive. In Lesotho, selected farmers are provided input vouchers to use at agriculture fairs.

Other innovative approaches that complement safety nets exist in several countries, ranging from giving small grants to nomadic populations to providing backyard gardens. A few countries, including Botswana and Mozambique, have small social care services, such as community homes or home-based care for the elderly and terminally ill.

General Price Subsidies

In addition to targeted safety nets, general price subsidies are purported to play a safety net role in many countries. The most common subsidies consist of price reductions on energy products such as petrol, liquefied petroleum gas, butane, and kerosene and of lower value added tax and export tariffs or import bans on certain food staples such as maize and rice.

Fuel subsidies have been in place in several countries since the early 2000s and account for a substantial portion of government spending. In 2011, energy subsidies amounted to 1.5 percent of regional GDP, or 5.5 percent of total government revenues in Sub-Saharan Africa (IMF 2013). Total subsidies exceeded 4 percent of GDP in three countries (Mozambique, Zambia, and Zimbabwe). Fuel subsidies in Burkina Faso and Cameroon cost 0.8 and 2.6 percent of GDP, respectively. Food subsidies are substantially less costly and were put in place in response to the rising food prices in 2007 and 2008 in Benin, Burkina Faso,

Cameroon, Ghana, Mali, Swaziland, Togo, and Zambia. In Cameroon, spending on subsidies accounts for 88 percent of total safety net spending. To minimize the adverse impact of the crisis, particularly on the most vulnerable groups, Sierra Leone reduced import duties on rice, wheat, flour, and sugar. In addition, it provided 71,000 bushels of seed rice to farmers to increase domestic production of the staple. The government also decided not to pass on to the domestic market the higher price of import fuel, thus introducing fuel subsidies. According to the Ministry of Finance in Sierra Leone, the cost of the fuel subsidy increased gradually from 0.3 percent to 2.1 percent of GDP from 2008 to 2011. The fiscal cost of general subsidies is discussed in more detail in chapter 5.

Food and fuel subsidies have been shown to be regressive and ineffective in terms of protecting the poorest. Studies from several countries have shown that a very small share of subsidy benefits accrues to the poorest segments of the population because their consumption of exempt products is usually low. For instance, only 10 percent of the food staple subsidy introduced in Burkina Faso in 2008 benefited those in the poorest quintile, yet this group was hit the hardest by increased global food prices. Also, only 16 percent of the long-term fuel subsidy has been shown to benefit the poor. In Cameroon, about 80 percent of the fuel subsidy benefits the richest 20 percent of the population. Moreover, most of the food products that are subsidized (rice, frozen fish, and wheat) are not usually consumed by the poor. In Ghana, only 8.3 percent of the subsidy on rice and 2.3 percent of the petrol and diesel subsidies are estimated to benefit the poor, whereas the nonpoor benefited most from tax cuts on imported foods.

Summary of Main Messages

Main messages of the chapter are the following:

- Safety net development in Africa differs depending on the country context and is driven by the political economy and sociocultural background of each country. Hence, the policies and approaches taken to safety nets are not homogeneous across the continent, nor are the institutions chosen to manage them. For instance, MICs in southern African countries have strong government-led safety net systems that are based on horizontal equity, whereas in LICs and fragile states, the social protection agenda tends to be heavily donor influenced and to focus on emergency relief. Therefore, any attempts to strengthen safety nets need to take these context-specific factors into account.

- Despite intraregional differences, safety nets, as core instruments for development and poverty reduction, are solidifying in Africa as more and more countries are preparing social protection strategies to anchor objectives and policies and to serve as the basis on which to build effective safety net systems. Governments should continue to prepare these strategies and put them into operation in the context of the country's broader poverty reduction strategy.

- Coordinating mechanisms for safety nets in most African countries need to be strengthened. Within governments, the responsibility for safety net programs is generally spread over a number of junior ministries that tend to lack significant political decision-making power. Fragmented donor support has also left LICs with a host of small and separate programs. Steering committees or similar mechanisms are needed to organize and coordinate the work of all safety net programs in any given country, to champion the safety net agenda in the political sphere, and to leverage adequate resources from donors and financing ministries.

- Few countries have safety net systems that are capable of addressing the core issues of poverty and vulnerability. Safety nets now consist of a large number of small and fragmented programs focused on providing emergency relief and mitigating food insecurity. Few provide predictable support to the chronically poor to help them move out of poverty. A handful of countries have created sustainable and more institutionalized programs of longer-term support overseen by influential ministries such as the ministry of finance and the ministry of economy and planning.

- The most common safety net programs in Africa are school feeding programs, public works programs, in-kind emergency and nonemergency programs, categorical programs, and general subsidies. Poverty-targeted cash transfer programs are now growing at a dramatic pace, and some larger programs are developing in, for example, Kenya and Rwanda.

- A small number of well-coordinated and well-functioning programs could form the basis of a safety net that could effectively and feasibly meet the needs of the poorest. These programs' efficient operation would be greatly enhanced by the development of joint systems (such as a single beneficiary register; a joint MIS; and common monitoring and evaluation, targeting, and payment systems) to support the implementation and monitoring of all safety net programs. Such operational systems, based on which programs can effectively deliver support to targeted groups, are the platform for a safety net system.

- Hence, the agenda of harmonizing and coordinating safety net programs into a system of instruments that can be used to address the country-specific needs should be an integral part of building safety nets in Africa.

Notes

1. The text of the framework is available at http://sa.au.int/en/content/social-policy-framework-africa.
2. The political economy of safety nets and social protection policy is discussed further in chapter 5.
3. Since 2003, Ethiopia has a National Food Security Strategy that sets out how the Productive Safety Net Program and other programs are used to increase food security.

4. For a review of 167 public works programs in 29 African countries, see McCord and Slater (2009).

5. The results of these impact evaluations are discussed in chapter 4.

6. School feeding programs generally aim to increase school attendance and to provide nutrition to school-age children but do not tackle permanent malnutrition issues, which are more effectively tackled by targeting pregnant and lactating women and children under two years of age.

7. The study (World Bank 2012a) identifies four groups of informal safety nets: informal mutual insurance arrangements, insurance for major life events, informal savings and credit mechanisms, and traditional social assistance facilities.

8. Catholic Relief Services, the United Nations Children's Fund, and several bilateral donors such as the Danish International Development Agency and the U.S. Agency for International Development are also partners. However, in several countries (Kenya, Mali, and Tanzania), efforts are being made to move away from donor-funded programs to full government or local community operation of school meal programs.

9. In Swaziland, recipients of employment pensions are not eligible for the Old-Age Grant, but because this rule is not enforced, the program is de facto universal.

10. McCord and Slater (2009) found that 44 percent of the 167 programs provide cash and 52 percent provide food. Some programs provide a combination of cash and food.

References

Andrews, Colin, Mirey Ovadiya, Christophe Ribes Ros, and Quentin Wodon. 2012. "Cash for Work in Sierra Leone: A Case Study on the Design and Implementation of a Safety Net in Response to a Crisis." Social Protection Discussion Paper 1216, World Bank, Washington, DC.

del Ninno, Carlo, Kalanidhi Subbarao, Annika Kjellgren, and Rodrigo Quintana. 2012. "Improving Payment Mechanisms in Cash-Based Safety Net Programs." World Bank, Washington, DC.

Garcia, Marito, and Charity M. T. Moore. 2012. *The Cash Dividend: The Rise of Cash Transfer Programs in Sub-Saharan Africa.* Washington, DC: World Bank.

Government of Niger. 2013. *Safety Net Project Implementation Manual.* Niamey: Government of Niger.

Hickey, Sam. 2007. "Conceptualizing the Politics of Social Protection in Africa." BWPI Working Paper 4, Brooks World Poverty Institute, University of Manchester, Manchester, U.K.

IMF (International Monetary Fund). 2013. *Case Studies on Energy Subsidy Reform: Lessons and Implications.* Washington, DC.

McCord, Anna, and Rachel Slater. 2009. *Overview of Public Works Programmes in Sub-Saharan Africa.* London: Overseas Development Institute.

Milazzo, Annamaria, and Carlo del Ninno. 2012. *The Role of Public Works Programs in Sub-Saharan Africa.* Washington, DC: World Bank.

MINALOC (Ministry of Local Government). 2011. "National Social Protection Strategy, Rwanda." http://www.ilo.org/gimi/gess/RessShowRessource.do?ressourceId=23208.

PSNP (Productive Safety Net Program). 2010. *Designing and Implementing a Rural Safety Net in a Low-Income Setting: Lessons Learned from Ethiopia's Productive Safety Net Program 2005–2009*. Addis Ababa: Government of Ethiopia.

World Bank. 2009. *Niger: Food Security and Safety Nets*. Washington, DC: World Bank.

———. 2011. *Republic of Ghana: Improving the Targeting of Social Programs*. Washington, DC: World Bank.

———. 2012a. "Informal Safety Nets: A Literature Review of the Evidence in Africa." World Bank, Washington, DC.

———. 2012b. *Lesotho: A Safety Net to End Extreme Poverty*. Washington, DC: World Bank.

———. 2012c. *Managing Risk, Promoting Growth: Developing Systems for Social Protection in Africa—The World Bank's Africa Social Protection Strategy, 2012–2022*. Washington, DC: World Bank.

———. 2012d. *Rwanda Social Safety Net Assessment: Draft Report*. Washington, DC: World Bank.

CHAPTER 4

Effectiveness of Existing Safety Net Programs: An Analysis

In assessing the effectiveness of safety net programs, three design features are key: coverage, targeting, and generosity (benefit level). For safety net programs to meaningfully reduce a country's poverty and improve the country's development indicators, they have to reach a certain number of people, they have to reach those people who are most in need of support, and they have to provide beneficiaries with adequate benefits that enable those beneficiaries to better manage risks and move into higher-return activities. However, given that most safety net programs have budgetary restrictions, trade-offs exist between how much can be transferred, to how many, and for how long. Maximizing the influence of any safety net program requires reaching a careful balance between coverage, targeting, and generosity.

Other factors that influence the effectiveness of a safety net program include how well it can adapt to the changing needs of the existing beneficiaries and how quickly it can absorb new beneficiaries who have been affected by negative shocks. Hence, the flexibility, predictability, and capacity to respond to crises are also important measures of how effective safety nets are in meeting their objectives. Finally, the ultimate indicator of program effectiveness is its impact on a set of outcomes, such as short- and long-term poverty status of beneficiaries, their health and education indicators, and the extent to which they have been able to build their assets.

Among its main findings, this chapter presents the evidence regarding the effectiveness of safety net programs in the 22 African countries reviewed. In general, a great deal of uncertainty exists about the effectiveness and impact of safety nets in Africa because of the weaknesses in data collection and monitoring and evaluation (M&E) in the programs in the countries studied. The coverage by safety net programs of the poor and vulnerable is very low. However, several countries, including Ghana, Kenya, and Rwanda, are beginning to expand some programs that have proven to be relatively effective in an effort to reduce poverty on a national scale, and other countries are following suit. Nevertheless, poverty-targeted safety nets are still not common in Africa, although the World Bank is now moving to support them in over a dozen African countries. Also, the safety nets reviewed tended to lack flexibility and predictability, although more countries are starting to build safety net systems and programs that provide benefits on a more predictable schedule and that are capable of responding flexibly to crises. Because these systems take time to establish, they need to be built up gradually during stable times. The lack of consistent M&E of the implementation and impact of these programs is a crucial weakness to be addressed. Therefore, more effort is needed to collect basic data on the number and type of beneficiaries being reached as well as information on program outcomes and impact.

Coverage

One factor to consider in determining the effectiveness of safety net programs is what share of the poor and vulnerable they cover. Ideally, coverage should be calculated as a share of a given target population. This target group varies depending on the objective of the program. It may be the population in a certain geographic area (for example, where food insecurity is high); the population consisting of certain vulnerable groups, such as orphans or elderly; or the population of those classified as being poor or extremely poor. In countries where government-driven approaches to safety nets are dominant, mainly in middle-income countries (MICs), programs generally focus on categorical groups. In lower-income countries (LICs), where food insecurity or climatic shocks are common, programs are often targeted to specific geographic areas. Information about whom each program is covering and how many is essential not only to guide the expansion of already efficient programs but also to reduce overlaps and duplication of coverage between programs.

Although information is scarce, very few poor and vulnerable households in Africa appear to have access to safety nets; however, coverage is growing. Whereas some programs have widespread coverage, especially universal old-age pension programs in MICs and programs targeted to small groups, such as the emergency feeding program in Benin (first column in table 4.1), national coverage of individual programs in relation to those who could be eligible for benefits if the program were available countrywide is much lower (second column in table 4.1). Taken together, each country's safety net programs cover only a very small share of the total number of its poor and vulnerable people (third column in table 4.1). As many as 77 percent and 84 percent of social protection programs in Sierra Leone and Mozambique, respectively, can be classified as having low coverage of the at-risk population.[1] These rates are comparable to the coverage of the poor in other LICs such as Cambodia but much lower than the coverage in many MICs, where conditional cash transfer (CCT) programs reach up to 60 percent of the poorest decile (Fiszbein and Schady 2009). The average coverage rate of the poorest decile is 31 percent in the World Bank's Europe and

Table 4.1 Coverage of Safety Net Programs, Selected Countries and Programs

Program type	Percentage of specific locally eligible group covered by each program	Percentage of total population potentially eligible nationwide covered by each program	Percentage of total poor and vulnerable covered by all safety nets
Benin			
Cash transfers	—	0	—
Emergency feeding	100.0	49.0	—
School feeding	37.0	2.6–15.1	—
Public works	90.0	0.6–3.8	—
All programs	—	—	5.0–6.0
Botswana			
School feeding	—	33.0	—
Destitution benefits	—	<33.0	<1.0
Old-age grants (universal, 65+)	—	95.0	85.0
Cameroon			
School feeding	5.3	—	—
All programs	—	<1.0	—
Ethiopia			
Productive Safety Net Program (public works and direct support)	—	10.0[a]	—
Kenya			
All programs	—	<1.0	0.1–9.0
Lesotho			
Child grants program (orphans)	—	15.0	3.9
Social pensions (universal, 70+)	—	53.0	4.4
Liberia			
All programs	—	—	7.0–10.0[b]
Malawi			
School feeding	—	21.3	—
Food and cash transfers	—	0.2	—
Mali			
Cash transfers	30.0	—	—
Health insurance fund (elderly)	—	5.0 (planned)	—
Mauritius			
Social Aid Program	—	8.0	—
Social pensions (universal, 60+)	—	100.0	—
Sierra Leone			
Social pension programs (60+)	—	7.0	—
School feeding	—	21.0	—
Public works	—	3.0	—
Refugee program	100.0	—	—
Swaziland			
Old-Age Grant (universal, 60+)	91.0	91.0	—
Tanzania			
Food for work	—	1.0	0.7
School feeding	—	7.0	5.9

table continues next page

Table 4.1 Coverage of Safety Net Programs, Selected Countries and Programs (continued)

Program type	Percentage of specific locally eligible group covered by each program	Percentage of total population potentially eligible nationwide covered by each program	Percentage of total poor and vulnerable covered by all safety nets
Subsidized food distribution	—	20.0	20.6
Pilot cash transfer	—	<0.1	—
Most vulnerable children	—	4.0–5.0	—
Monetary assistance	—	—	4.3
Togo			
School feeding	—	6.0	—
Cash transfers	—	0.0	—
Nutritional support	—	6.0	—
Public works	—	4.0	—
All programs	—	1.0–10.0	13.0–15.0
Zambia			
School feeding	—	22.0	9.3[c]
SPLASH (Sustainable Program for Livelihoods and Solutions for Hunger) food vouchers	—	5.0	1.4[c]
Food Security Pack	—	—	0.9[c]
Farmer Input Support Program	—	—	7.3[c]
Old-age pensions (Katete District)	—	—	0.1[c]
Social cash transfer schemes	—	—	10.0[d]

Source: Country safety net assessments.
Note: — = not available. Table excludes subsidies. School feeding data indicate coverage of all primary school children (poor and nonpoor).
a. Coverage as a share of total national population: poor and nonpoor. Coverage as a share of the chronic poor and food insecure (target population) is likely much higher.
b. Coverage in percentage of the poverty line, adjusting also for generosity and program overlap.
c. Coverage of the extremely poor with reasonable assumption on poverty targeting.
d. Coverage of the extremely poor. Estimate for 2015 assumes perfect targeting.

Central Asia Region (unweighted by population) and 43 percent across 10 countries in Latin America and the Caribbean.[2] Ethiopia's Productive Safety Net Program (PSNP) is the only targeted safety net program in Africa with broad coverage of food-insecure households on a national level.[3] In total, 7.6 million people in 290 chronically food-insecure *woredas* (subregions) in 8 of the country's 10 regions are supported through either public works or direct support. This coverage is equivalent to roughly 10 percent of the national population.

A mismatch in the coverage of specific groups exists in several countries that have universal categorically targeted schemes (mainly MICs with established safety net systems). For instance, in Swaziland, a significant number of poor children do not receive safety net benefits because the majority of programs are targeted to the elderly. Also, many poor children do not go to school and therefore cannot benefit from programs that provide school meals. For example, in Benin, the net coverage rate of all safety net programs is estimated to be only about 5–6 percent of those classified as poor. Similarly, in Zambia, programs that explicitly target the poor cover less than a few percent of the poor (figure 4.1).[4] In Rwanda, social protection programs (both contributory and noncontributory) reach about 4 percent of the population, although 24 percent of the population is classified as extremely poor. In Cameroon, each program covers at most 1 percent of the poor and vulnerable nationwide. For instance, the school feeding program covers 5.3 percent of all primary school children in all prioritized regions. Overall, as a share of poor school-age children nationwide, its coverage is even lower. In Kenya, estimates suggest that cash transfers reached 9 percent of the poor population in 2010. The government is currently planning to expand coverage so that, by 2018, 17 percent of the poor will be reached. Even in Botswana and Mauritius, which have strong and long-standing government-driven social assistance programs, the coverage of poverty-targeted programs is limited. In Mauritius, the Social Aid program covers only 8 percent of the poor (defined as those with incomes that are lower than half the median income). In Botswana, the only poverty-targeted safety net program (destitution benefits) reaches only 0.5 percent of poor households and less than one-third of the targeted group.

Universal old-age pension programs, which are common in southern African MICs, generally have wide coverage of the elderly. As shown in table 4.1, old-age grants in Botswana, Mauritius, and Swaziland are universal (at least de jure) and

Figure 4.1 Coverage of Transfer Programs Relative to Poverty Lines in Zambia

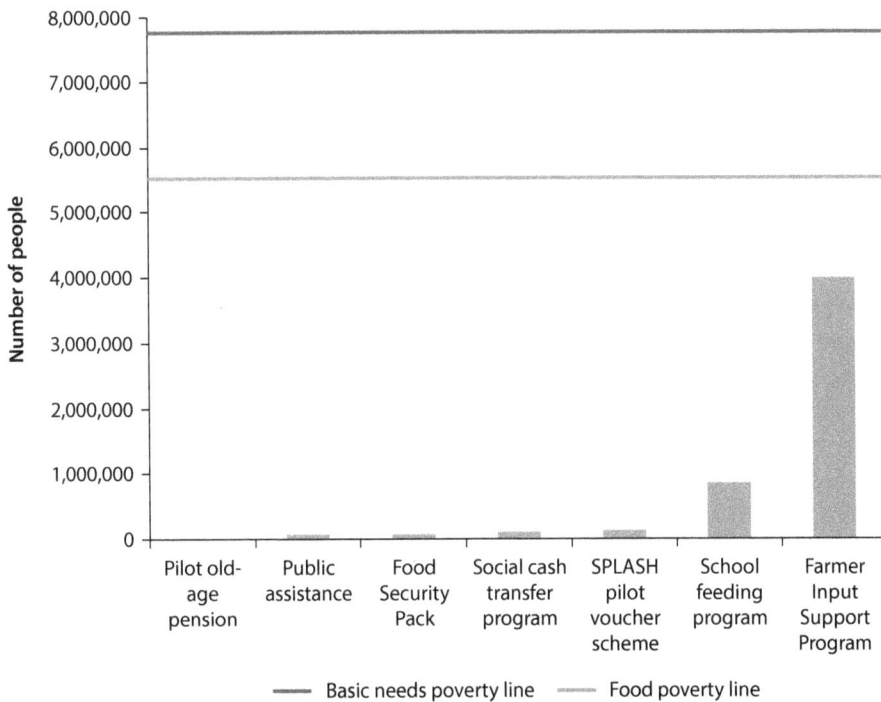

Source: World Bank 2012d.
Note: SPLASH = Sustainable Program for Livelihoods and Solutions for Hunger.

Reducing Poverty and Investing in People • http://dx.doi.org/10.1596/978-1-4648-0094-8

cover 85–100 percent of the eligible elderly. Universal programs come at a cost, however, because many nonpoor elderly people and people who already benefit from other unemployment assistance can receive these social pensions. For these groups of nonpoor people, social pensions form part of the state-supplied pensions provided to all those considered outside the labor force. Means-tested old-age social pensions in South Africa reach 60 percent of the elderly, but coverage of means-tested social pension programs in other MICs is much lower.[5] In contrast, social pension programs in Sierra Leone and Zambia largely fail to cover most elderly people, who receive no other subsistence income or benefits from other safety nets. Interestingly, social pensions were introduced in some countries (Swaziland, for example) to lighten the burden on elderly people caring for orphans, and they have provided some support to orphans who live with an elderly person. However, because 55 percent of poor children in Zambia do not live with an elderly person, 25 percent of orphans are not poor, and 85 percent of extremely poor children are not orphans, old-age benefits may not be the most efficient programs for protecting these vulnerable children.

Food-based programs tend to have extensive localized coverage, but they often suffer from targeting weaknesses and high costs. Although some school feeding programs have widespread coverage (Benin, Botswana, Malawi, and Zambia), others cover only a small share of children (Cameroon, Tanzania, and Togo). In Burkina Faso, the school feeding program accounts for 38 percent of all safety net beneficiaries. Similarly, some nutritional and emergency feeding programs (for example, those in Benin and Mozambique) may have wide coverage in specific locations affected by emergencies, whereas others have very low national coverage even when acute severe malnutrition is rampant (Burkina Faso, Cameroon, and Mali). Public works programs are generally small in scope because they can be implemented in only a small number of communities and can employ only up to 200 workers at a time. As a share of all underemployed, coverage is hence generally very low—less than 1 percent. Cash transfer programs generally remain on a pilot scale (for example, in Mali and Sierra Leone), which keeps coverage to a minimum. In Madagascar, although the Tsena Mora food subsidy program has wide coverage in the targeted areas, it exists in only six larger towns. Given that they are the mainstay of African safety nets, more work is needed to determine how food-based programs should be included and coordinated with other safety net programs and whether their existing infrastructure can serve as nodes for formation of national systems.

Significant duplication, overlap, and fragmentation mask low coverage rates. According to some country reports, overall coverage rates of safety nets look high, but overlaps of beneficiaries and the limited duration of some payments inflate the coverage numbers. In Liberia, where food-based programs predominate, the number of beneficiaries of safety net programs as a share of total population (poor and nonpoor) is 23.8 percent (and in Burkina Faso, the equivalent figure is 25 percent). However, after taking into account the large number of people who receive benefits from more than one program as well as the small size of the benefit and the short duration of program support, the actual coverage of households below the poverty line is only 10 percent in rural areas and 7 percent in urban areas of Liberia. In addition, as mentioned previously, several countries have a large number of categorical transfer and public works programs with no coordination between their different groups of beneficiaries, geographic zones, and delivery mechanisms. In Mauritius, despite wide coverage of the population as a whole, considerable overlap of programs and beneficiaries occurs as well as significant gaps in the coverage of vulnerable groups. Because benefits are targeted on the basis of categories of eligibility, poor households that do not fit into these predefined categories are not eligible for assistance. One significant gap is the lack of coverage of the working poor.

Several countries are beginning to scale up their well-performing programs and increase coordination between their safety net programs to reduce overlaps and better reach those most in need. The expansion of Rwanda's Vision 2020 Umurenge Program (VUP) is intended to increase coverage of the poor population from 4 to 18 percent within a couple of years. Kenya's Cash Transfer for Orphans and Vulnerable Children (CT-OVC) program is on track to be scaled up to the national level and grew from having 9,900 beneficiaries in 2005 to 412,470 in 2010. More recently, the government plans to expand the coverage of the National Safety Net Program so that by 2018 it will cover an estimated 17 percent of the poor population in Kenya. In Tanzania, the government is investing in the PSNP, which covers 1.5 million people. Expansion should start with those programs that are already well targeted to the poor and vulnerable. If other programs can improve their targeting and reduce overhead costs, then they might also subsequently be scaled up. Some country assessments present simulations of how much it would cost to operate well-targeted and efficient programs that cover all or a large share of the entire poor and vulnerable population. Chapter 5 discusses these simulations in more detail.

Increasing harmonization between programs is an important step in developing a coherent national safety net system and scaling up programs. This approach was taken in Rwanda, where the government is committed to providing better and more efficient social protection for its citizens by reducing the scale of some inefficient programs while merging beneficiaries within better-performing programs. The government is developing policy guidelines for harmonization as well as a social protection management information system that will help policy makers and program managers reduce overlaps and duplication of beneficiaries. Overlaps are most obvious in the areas of direct support transfers from, for example, the VUP, FARG (Fond d'Assistance aux Rescapées du Génocide, or Assistance Fund for Genocide Survivors), and Rwanda Demobilization and Reintegration Commission programs); housing support; and income-generating activities. The PSNPs in Ethiopia and Tanzania are examples of integrated programs that aim to reduce overlap by providing public works programs to chronically food-insecure households with able-bodied adults and by offering direct support (without a work requirement) to households that are labor constrained. In Kenya, the government is in the process of harmonizing the five principal cash transfer programs with its National Safety Net Program to improve the efficiency

Box 4.1 Harmonization of Safety Net Programs in Rwanda

The safety net assessment for Rwanda analyzed the beneficiaries of the Fond d'Assistance aux Rescapées du Génocide (Assistance Fund for Genocide Survivors, or FARG) and found that simply integrating the FARG direct support with the new Vision 2020 Umurenge Program (VUP) would exclude a large number of current FARG beneficiaries, many of whom were likely to be legitimately needy. Ultimately, the targeting approach of VUP is not consistent enough with that of FARG, and the programs currently serve different populations with slightly different objectives (for example, individual versus household coverage). In this case, consolidating these two programs would mean discontinuing support for some households and, unless the government changes its policy commitment to support some groups of genocide survivors, at this time the FARG cannot simply be folded into the VUP.

However, other potential options exist, given the demographic breakdown of FARG beneficiaries, some of whom are orphans whose eligibility will end by 2015 and the remainder being adults with disabilities and the elderly. Rather than forcibly integrating the two programs with very different target groups in the short term, an option in the medium term might be to include FARG direct support with an old-age or disability pension. The consolidation of these two programs would be much more seamless than integrating the FARG and the VUP at present.

In the short term, the integration of FARG direct support and the VUP could still be partially achieved by consolidating their delivery mechanisms. The two programs would continue unchanged, but in the geographic regions where the VUP is operating, FARG direct support lists would be provided to the VUP, and the VUP would be responsible for the payment process, for financial reporting, and for monitoring.

Source: World Bank 2012b.

of safety net support. Also, both Botswana and Zambia are combining separate donor-driven school feeding programs into single government-owned and -operated programs. The approaches being taken to harmonization in Rwanda are described in box 4.1.

Generosity

Given that most countries have tight budget constraints on safety net spending, important trade-offs have to be made between programs' coverage and their generosity (benefit level). If benefit levels are too low, they are likely to have little effect on the well-being of the intended beneficiaries, especially if administrative costs are high. If benefit levels are too high, they may significantly affect the well-being of beneficiaries but may come at a high fiscal cost and may risk creating work disincentives. In some programs, each beneficiary household (or person) receives the same amount, whereas in others, the value of the benefit depends on the household's poverty level, size, and composition. Differentiating benefit levels according to household characteristics can improve outcomes but requires complicated administrative arrangements and considerable capacity to implement.

The generosity of safety net programs in Africa is highly variable and is difficult to estimate. Even within countries (for instance, Mali), safety net programs can vary significantly in terms of the benefit levels that they provide. Given that only some programs are cash based and that in-kind programs vary in terms of the value of the items they deliver (for example, cereals, meals and snacks, emergency feeding kits, and school uniforms and textbooks), monetizing the average generosity of safety net programs is difficult. Little analysis is available on the relationship between the generosity of the food rations provided and the needs of the beneficiaries, especially for those programs providing emergency food rations or subsidized cereal sales in times of crisis. However, some benchmarks can be established for cash transfer programs and social pensions using data available from other parts of the world.

Some estimates can be made regarding the generosity of cash transfer programs in Africa. Table 4.2 presents data on cash transfer programs, excluding noncontributory social pensions, in selected African countries. Benefits are determined per child, per person, or per household. In several countries (Kenya, Malawi, Mauritius, and Rwanda), programs give larger transfers to larger households so as not to disadvantage households with many dependents (children and elderly members) because they tend to suffer the most from poverty, though this approach is administratively more complex than providing a flat-rate transfer. In general, the range of benefits is between US$2 and US$4 per child per month for young children and between US$4 and US$24 per month for older children. Alternatively, by household, the range of benefits is between US$4 and US$50 per month, depending on the household's size and the program type. The median falls at about US$15. The highest amount is paid in the Mauritania cash transfer pilot, which is implemented by the World Food Programme (WFP) and Catholic Relief Services, and the lowest in the Burkina Faso Nahouri cash transfer pilot, which ended in 2011. Garcia and Moore (2012) found that the value of household-level transfers in African cash transfer programs ranges from US$8 to US$15 per month.[6] They also found that one-time cash transfers tend to be larger than regular (monthly or quarterly) transfers.

Looking solely at the dollar amount transferred, one would find it difficult to judge how benefit levels compare to the needs of the targeted beneficiaries or the levels paid by other programs worldwide. Estimating benefit levels as a share of the poverty line or poverty gap or as a share of the total consumption of poor households allows for an easier comparison.

Available data indicate that the generosity of African cash transfer programs is on par with other cash transfer programs worldwide, although few studies provide information on the effect of the benefit level on recipients' consumption.[7] Some data exist for programs in Burkina Faso, Ethiopia, Kenya, Mauritius, Swaziland, and Zambia (table 4.2). The urban food voucher program in Burkina Faso, a WFP program that was active in 2009 and 2010, provided up to CFAF 9,000 per household per month, which was equivalent to 22 percent

Table 4.2 Generosity of Cash Transfer Programs in Selected Countries, Excluding Social Pensions

Program	Benefit level (local currency)	Benefit level (US$ equivalent)	Payment schedule	Benefit as a share of poverty estimates[a]
Burkina Faso				
Nahouri Province cash transfer pilot	CFAF 1,000, CFAF 2,000, or CFAF 4,000	US$2.20, US$4.40, or US$8.80	Per child per quarter, depending on the age of the child[b]	4%, 8%, or 16% of household per capita expenditures (10.4% average)
Food vouchers to urban poor	CFAF 1,500 per person (ceiling of CFAF 9,000 per household)	US$3 per person (ceiling of US$18 per household)	Per month	22% of consumption of a household at the poverty line or 15–18 days of cereal needs
Ethiopia				
Productive Safety Net Program direct support	Br 50 per month of benefits	US$20 per person per year equivalent	Per household per month	10% of the basket represented by the national poverty line for 2007/08; 40% of annual food needs
Ghana				
Livelihood Empowerment against Poverty Program (LEAP)	¢8 (1 dependent) to ¢15 (4 dependents)	US$7–13	Per household per month	—
Kenya				
Combined: Cash Transfer for Orphans and Vulnerable Children, Hunger Safety Net Programme, Disability Grant, Older Persons' Cash Transfer Programme, and Urban Food Subsidy	K Sh 1,500 average	US$15–26 (depending on program)	Per household per month	12–20% of absolute poverty line, 35% of absolute poverty gap, and 70% of average gap for hard-core poor households[c]
Lesotho				
Orphans and vulnerable children bursaries	M 1,537 average	US$220	Per student per year	—
Child grants	M 120	US$17	Per household per month	—
Public assistance	M 100	US$14	Per household per month	—
Liberia				
Bomi cash transfer pilot	$700, $1,050, $1,400, or $1,750 (average total household payment, $1,750)	US$10, US$15, US$20, or US$25 (average total household payment, US$25)	Per household per month, depending on the size of the household[d]	—
Mali				
Bourse maman	CFAF 5,000	US$8–12	Per household per month	—

table continues next page

Table 4.2 Generosity of Cash Transfer Programs in Selected Countries, Excluding Social Pensions *(continued)*

Program	Benefit level (local currency)	Benefit level (US$ equivalent)	Payment schedule	Benefit as a share of poverty estimates[a]
Mauritania				
Cash transfer pilot (World Food Programme and Catholic Relief Services)	UM 15,000	US$50	Per household per month	—
Mauritius				
Social aid	MUR 1,008 (plus extra for children)	US$33	Per household per month	16% of consumption of the poor
Rwanda				
VUP (Vision 2020 Umurenge Program) direct support	RF 7,500–21,000 (depending on household size)	US$12–35	Per household per month	Largely benefits elderly who lack sufficient means to cope
Swaziland				
Public assistance	E 80	US$10	Per person per month	17% of per person consumption at the poverty line; 37% at food poverty line
Young Heroes (double orphan grant)	E 180	US$23	Per child per month	39% of per person consumption at the poverty line; 84% at food poverty line
Togo				
World Association for Orphans cash transfer for education	CFAF 22,000 (primary school); CFAF 75,000 (secondary school)	US$44 (primary school); US$150 (secondary school)	Per child per year in primary or secondary school	—
Zambia				
Social cash transfers	K 60,000 (K 50,000 if no children), equivalent to K 13,274 per person	US$12	Per household per month	14% of per person consumption at the food poverty line; 9% of basic needs poverty line; 20% of consumption of lowest quintile
SPLASH (Sustainable Program for Livelihoods and Solutions for Hunger) vouchers	K 65,000	US$14	Per household per month	18% of per person consumption at the food poverty line; 11% of basic needs poverty line

Source: Country safety net assessments.

Note: — = not available. CFA franc exchange rate rounded to US$1 = CFAF 500.

a. Estimated at the household level unless otherwise indicated.

b. In 2009, the program added a payment of CFAF 1,500 in cash per household for flood-affected households to prevent beneficiaries from selling food vouchers to finance other household costs related to rebuilding the home or other assets lost to the flood.

c. In contrast, the average value of benefits paid by the programs that provide one-off benefits in Kenya is much higher than these regular payments, because the benefit is meant for longer-term specific investments (for example, agricultural inputs such as equipment and seeds or annual school fees).

d. In addition, the household can receive a top-up of $150–300 per child sent to primary or secondary school.

of the consumption of a household at the poverty line, or 15–18 days of the household's cereal needs. In Kenya, estimates are that the average monthly range of benefits for the main cash transfer programs (US$15–26) represents just less than 20 percent of the consumption of households at the 2010 absolute poverty line. The WFP-funded food ration covered just less than 50 percent of the absolute poverty gap.[8] In Mozambique, the generosity of the median transfer of the social pensions, family allowance, and last-resort programs has been estimated at between 18 percent and 27 percent of the average consumption of households in the poorest quintiles. The cash transfer program that is currently being prepared in Cameroon is aiming to set its benefit level at 20 percent of the consumption of an average-size household at the poverty line. These levels are generally on par with those in other cash transfer programs worldwide. For example, in Latin America and the Caribbean, the average transfer varies between 10 percent and 20 percent of the pretransfer income of poor households. In the Kyrgyz Republic (an LIC), total social assistance benefits as a share of the posttransfer consumption for households in the poorest quintile is 10 percent, but in other lower-to-middle-income countries in Eastern Europe and Central Asia, it is more generous at between 24 percent and 52 percent.

Social (noncontributory) pensions are significantly more generous than other cash transfer programs in Africa and differ greatly from those in other countries. Although African pension programs appear generous in terms of the percentage of the international poverty line (US$1.25 purchasing power parity), they are more modest as a share of the income and food poverty lines and as a share of the consumption of poor households (table 4.3). Because social pensions are meant to support those who no longer make a living in the labor force, social pensions are generous compared with incomes at the poverty line, particularly in MICs with established safety net systems. In Mauritius, for example, social pensions are equal to 41 percent of the consumption of those in the bottom quintile and 66 percent of the half-median income poverty line. In Swaziland, they represent 43 percent of the poverty line and 93 percent of the food poverty line. In Lesotho, the monthly payment of M 350 (most recent level) is 2.5 times higher than the estimated food poverty line. In comparison, the social pension programs in MICs in Eastern Europe and Central Asia provide the equivalent of 20 percent of consumption for households in the lowest two quintiles and 27 percent of consumption for households in the lowest quintile (Grosh *et al.* 2008). In Mauritius, it is estimated that the poverty headcount would increase by 13.4 percent if the noncontributory retirement pensions were not available. In both Swaziland and Zambia, qualitative evidence suggests that social pensions have had a positive effect on poor households although no rigorous impact evaluations have been done.

Setting the benefit level (the wage rate) in public works programs is crucial not only in terms of reducing poverty but also in terms of ensuring that only the poor self-select into the program. Table 3.2 in chapter 3 listed the wage levels for

Table 4.3 Generosity of Noncontributory Social Pensions in Selected Countries

Country	Program	Benefit level (local currency)	Benefit level (US$ equivalent)	Benefit as a share of poverty line (%)[a]	Benefit as a share of GDP per capita (%)[a]
Botswana (UMIC)	Old-age pensions (U)	P 220	US$28	133	5
Cape Verde (LMIC)	Old-age pensions (M)	CVEsc 4,500	US$50	156	19
Kenya (LIC)	Older persons pension (M)	K Sh 1,500	US$19	99	25
Lesotho (LMIC)	Old-age pensions (U)	M 350	US$43	180	64
Mauritius (UMIC)	Noncontributory retirement pensions (U)	MUR 2,945	US$95	454	16
Namibia (UMIC)	Old-age pensions (U)	N$450	US$59	207	14
South Africa (UMIC)	Grant for older people (M)	R 1,100	US$144	602	28
Swaziland (LMIC)	Old-age grant (U)	E 200	US$26	124	10
Average	Social pension programs	—	US$58	244	23
Other UMICs	Social pension programs	—	US$115	487	17
Other LMICs	Social pension programs	—	US$43	208	19
Other LICs	Social pension programs	—	US$8	65	14

Sources: Country safety net assessments; HelpAge International's Pension Watch database (http://www.pension-watch.net/about-social-pensions /about-social-pensions/social-pensions-database/).

Note: — = not available. LIC = low-income country; LMIC = lower-middle-income country; M = means tested; U = universal; UMIC = upper-middle-income country.

a. Calculated according to HelpAge International's Pension Watch database, using US$1.25 purchasing power parity per day as the international poverty line.

Africa's cash-for-work programs and estimates of how those levels compare with local and minimum wage levels (as available). Ten of the 23 cash-for-work programs listed (43 percent) set the wage level too high to effectively attract poor workers. However, several programs (for instance, in Botswana and Tanzania) have set the wage rate at a level 10–20 percent lower than the minimum wage to target poor and low-skilled workers. Few studies have been done that analyze the effect of the wage level on the consumption level of the household. However, in the CCT public works program operated by the Malawi Social Action Fund, the wage rate (MK 200 per eight-hour day) can be considered sufficient for poor households to access subsidized fertilizer and purchase some food. In the cash-for-work program in Togo, a wage rate of US$3 per day was set so that it would be equal to 30 percent of the consumption of one person living in a rural area. Because public works programs have to set the wage low enough to attract only the poorest and must limit the number of days of work to concentrate support when it is most needed without distorting labor markets, the overall generosity of public works programs over a longer period is low. Rather, they are designed to provide specific support for a short period (or repeated periods) of time.

Little is known about how benefit levels are set in food-based programs. Despite their importance in terms of the number of beneficiaries that they reach and their high share of total safety net spending, little information is available on the criteria used to set the benefit levels of food and other in-kind programs.[9] Moreover, little analysis has been done of the relationship between the needs of households and the size, type, and frequency of the rations provided. Nor do governments seem to collect any evidence on how these programs affect the poverty levels and well-being of recipient households. In Mali, where most safety net programs provide internationally procured food, the justification for why food is chosen rather than cash (or near cash, such as vouchers) or for the size of the food rations in relation to the specific needs of the food-insecure households is unknown. In Mauritania, in 2008, food distribution (including school feeding) and subsidies accounted for 94 percent of total safety net expenditures. They were provided in response to a severe drought that affected the country that year without monitoring who benefited from the food and the effect the program had on the poor. In Burkina Faso, postoperation reports from cereal banks tend to indicate that the quantities provided are insufficient to cover the needs of recipient households. In Ethiopia, the PSNP provides either cash or food benefits (or sometimes a mix), depending on the seasonal rise in food prices leading up to the hungry season. The daily cash transfer is at a value equivalent to the cost of the food ration, which is 3 kilograms of cereal. The transfer value is the same for households participating in the public works or receiving unconditional support. Both the cash and the food amounts are set at the level required to smooth household consumption or fill the food gap.

Likewise, little is known about the comparative effects of food and cash assistance at the household level. The literature is hampered by the fact that often a strict equivalent comparison between food, cash, and vouchers is not made. A 2009 study compared four programs in Bangladesh with different benefit structures, providing different combinations of cash and food, and varying transfer sizes and regularity (Ahmed *et al.* 2009). The study was inconclusive on the impact of cash and food on indicators such as consumption and poverty level. Most participants expressed a preference for the type of transfer provided by the program in which they were participating. However, as household income increased, beneficiaries' preference for food declined, indicating that the poorest households prefer food transfers. The effect of the choice of transfer on household food consumption depended largely on the size of the transfer and the type of food offered. The study found that cash transfers played an important role in protecting and expanding the asset base of poor households and that cash transfers are more cost-effective than programs that provide food. Ethiopia's PSNP has moved to providing mainly cash benefits over the past couple of years, and it was noted that the shift from food to cash transfers saves money. Given the mix of cash and food transfers to beneficiaries in 2008, estimates suggest that the shift from an all-food program to the current cash and food mix has saved the program almost US$11 million annually.[10]

Some data are available on school feeding programs that compare the caloric and monetary value of the meals provided in schools. In Tanzania, for instance, each child receives a morning snack and lunch for an average of 194 school days a year. The transfer has a value of 718 kilocalories, equivalent to about 40 percent of the minimum daily food requirement. Although the principal aim of the program is to encourage school attendance and achievement rather than to provide transfers, the benefit represents a substantial proportion of the per capita household income of very poor families and can be particularly significant if a family includes several children who are receiving the benefit. In Zambia, the school feeding program provides nutrition equivalent to 24 percent of daily caloric requirements.

More evidence is needed to inform policy makers' decisions about the type and amount of benefits to provide to guide the design of safety net programs. Ex ante simulations, feasibility studies, experiments, and impact evaluations are needed to yield more evidence about what type of benefits (food, cash, vouchers, or other in-kind) to provide, how much of the benefit to provide, to whom it should be provided, and with what frequency and duration. Food-based programs, in particular, should be subject to more studies to determine their marginal effect on poverty indicators and the costs of different benefit structures and generosity levels.

Targeting Efficiency

Once intended beneficiaries have been defined, efficient targeting can maximize beneficiary coverage for a given resource envelope. Some programs aim to have universal coverage, and targeting is not needed. But most safety net programs aim to support specific groups and stand to benefit from being well targeted. For instance, if the program's main objective is to support poor households, then the program should have a targeting mechanism that focuses on impoverished households. If food security is the primary objective, then households vulnerable to food insecurity should be targeted. When a program is well targeted, it maximizes the support reaching each intended beneficiary for a given program budget. Given the constrained budget envelope of most African governments, targeting may also be necessary to justify the poverty-reducing effect of safety net spending. However, targeting is never completely accurate in practice, with both errors of exclusion (not covering an intended beneficiary) and errors of inclusion (covering someone not intended to be a beneficiary) being possible. Furthermore, both the administrative and the political costs associated with targeting can be high, particularly when the targeting criteria are difficult to observe, such as in programs targeting the poor or ultrapoor. Nevertheless, even imperfectly targeted programs can be better at maximizing the support reaching the intended target group than programs without targeting. For a more conceptual discussion about the political economy of targeting, see chapter 5.

Safety net programs can choose from an array of targeting methods. *Categorical targeting* grants eligibility to broad categories of people, such as individuals above a certain age or individuals with disabilities. *Geographical targeting* grants eligibility to all people residing in certain areas, such as areas particularly affected by disasters or with particularly low human development indicators. *Means testing* and *proxy means testing* (PMT) targeting methods are based on a more detailed assessment of each applicant (individual or household) and are typically used when targeting poor households. A means testing program targeting the poor would base eligibility on direct indicators of poverty (such as income or consumption), whereas a PMT program uses indicators related to poverty status.[11] Some programs use *self-selection*, or *self-targeting*, designed in such a way that those not needing the support are automatically discouraged without being prohibited. For example, public works programs can set the wage rate low enough to discourage those who are not needy from participating. Finally, *community-based targeting* relies on the community's assessment of the households' need for program support.

Safety nets in Africa use a wide range of targeting mechanisms and often combine more than one. The most commonly used targeting mechanisms in the countries reviewed are geographic (about 49 percent of programs) and self-targeted (32 percent). These mechanisms are followed by the community-based (about 30 percent), categorical (about 26 percent), (proxy) means testing (around 20 percent), and universal (12 percent of programs) mechanisms (table 4.4). However, 57 percent of programs combined at least two methods. In particular, geographic or categorical targeting is often used together or in combination with other methods. For instance, Tanzania's Most Vulnerable Children program uses geographic targeting to reach the most food-insecure districts, after which the eligibility of individual children is assessed by village committees, with follow-up visits by social welfare officers. Appendix D provides a longer list of targeting methods and targeted groups, by program.

In Africa, community-based targeting is used to a greater extent than in many other parts of the world. McCord and Slater (2009) found that half of all public works programs in Africa used community-based targeting, especially those programs that have strong consumption-smoothing and safety net objectives. Also, in their review of 123 cash transfer programs, Garcia and Moore (2012) noted the widespread use of community-based targeting approaches in Africa (56 percent of cash transfer programs) compared with many other parts of the world. Within Africa, community-based targeting in cash transfer programs is

Table 4.4 Frequency of Targeting Methods
Percent of programs

Targeting method	Frequency
Multiple	57
Geographic	49
Self-targeted	32
Community-based or community-validated	30
Categorical	26
PMT or means testing	20
Universal (excluding subsidies)	12

Source: Calculations based on information from safety net assessments.
Note: These results are based on a review of 100 safety net programs in 22 countries. Because programs can use several targeting mechanisms, they add up to more than 100 percent. General subsidies are excluded.

most widely practiced in LICs (87 percent) and in lower-middle-income countries (56 percent). Upper- and lower-middle-income countries most commonly use categorical targeting, whereas fragile states usually use categorical targeting and self-targeting (in public works programs). Community-based targeting is also used successfully by some of the most promising national safety net programs in Africa, such as the VUP in Rwanda and the PSNP in Ethiopia. Indeed, analysis shows that the targeting in the PSNP is progressive and that the direct support component of the program may be among the best-targeted programs globally (Coll-Black *et al.* 2012).[12]

A growing number of programs targeting the poor and vulnerable use means testing or PMT. Until recently, such targeting was mainly tested in the form of small pilot initiatives. One-fifth of the programs in the countries reviewed used some form of means testing or PMT based on household income, consumption, or other characteristics. Means testing or PMT occurs in three types of programs: (a) social assistance or cash transfer programs in countries with government-driven programs in southern Africa, such as the Child Grants program in Lesotho, the Social Aid and Income Support programs in Mauritius, and the Social Cash Transfer and Farmer Input Support programs in Zambia; (b) small and recent or past donor-supported programs, such as the urban food voucher program in Burkina Faso, Liberia's Bomi cash transfer pilot, Mali's Bourse maman, and the Tanzania Social Action Fund's CCT programs; and (c) government programs currently being scaled up, such as Kenya's CT-OVC program and Rwanda's VUP. Except for the third category of programs, which are increasing their coverage, most poverty-targeted programs are small and reach only a small share of the poor.

The effectiveness of targeting methods used in Africa has not been thoroughly assessed, largely because of limited availability of data required to estimate errors of inclusion and exclusion. A survey of program beneficiaries by itself can reveal only how many beneficiaries do not belong to the intended target group (that is, inclusion errors). A representative household survey is needed to assess targeting errors in full. But such surveys are rare, are infrequent, and often do not collect information on a household's beneficiary status. Even programs that target specific categories of people who would seem easily identifiable can have targeting errors. A case in point is old-age pensions: in practice, even selecting beneficiaries just on the basis of age is not error free, because identification cards are not always used and sometimes misstate age. Sometimes the targeting "error" is that the categorization in use is not consistent with the targeting objective. For instance, Swaziland's Old-Age Grants program is intended to help grandparents caring for orphans, but 83 percent of the elderly do not live with orphans, and 55 percent of orphans do not live with elderly people. Moreover, in several countries, targeted categories often lack clear definitions.

A key question is how well African safety nets are able to identify and reach the poor and vulnerable, especially those in extreme poverty and vulnerability. Often programs seek to target either poor people or some form of vulnerability that is closely related to poverty, such as food insecurity. But direct measures of income or wealth, which can be used in means testing poverty targeting, are rarely available. As a result, programs usually rely on alternative methods, such as categorical, geographic, PMT, or community-based targeting, to reach the poor or the very poor. Assessing the accuracy of such methods is therefore important. In Ethiopia, the conceptual clarity between chronic and transitory food insecurity was necessary to reform the emergency system. Widespread poverty in rural areas of Ethiopia meant food access problems were not temporary or chronic but varied according to the season and year. Indeed, survey data suggested that the food-insecure population ranged from 2.6 million to 26 million, depending on the data source and the definition used.

If a social safety net program specifically seeks to target the poor, then categorical criteria will have to be used in combination with other methods for identifying poor households. Given the ubiquity of categorical targeting programs in Africa, an important policy question is whether targeting to specific categories of the population is also an effective means of targeting poverty. Targeting of households with children or elderly members can be pro-poor, because these categories often do include more poor households than a random group of households. For instance, in Kenya, households with orphans and vulnerable children (OVC) or with children under 18 years of age have significantly higher rates of poverty than the general population. Thus, targeting them would lead to lower inclusion errors than no targeting. However, it could still lead to high exclusion errors, because many poor households may have no OVC or elderly members. Furthermore, the correlation between such categorization and poverty can be weak. Indeed, a simulation of the poverty-targeting effectiveness of different targeting methods in Kenya (box 4.2) suggests that some forms of categorical targeting may not be any better than no (or random) targeting in Kenya. In addition, community-based targeting appears to be more effective at targeting poor households than both PMT and categorical targeting in Kenya. Categorically targeted major safety nets in Mozambique also seem to be weakly pro-poor (box 4.3). Finally, categorical targeting by itself cannot identify the very poor from all poor.

Box 4.2 The Effectiveness of Different Targeting Methods in Kenya

Very little information is available on the cost of different targeting methods in Kenya, and a full quantitative analysis of the trade-offs is not possible. Nevertheless, attempting to quantify the potential effect of different techniques is useful. The simulation assessed the estimated outcomes of different categorical methods, a proxy means testing (PMT) method, a community-based method, perfect targeting (in which households are prioritized depending only on their distance from the poverty line), and random targeting (in which the selection of households is entirely random). Table B4.2.1 shows the predicted change in the absolute poverty headcount, poverty gap, and food poverty gap for each of the different targeting methods.

box continues next page

Box 4.2 The Effectiveness of Different Targeting Methods in Kenya *(continued)*

Table B4.2.1 Results of Targeting Methods Simulation

Targeting method	Reduction in absolute poverty headcount (%)	Reduction in absolute poverty gap (%)	Reduction in food poverty gap (%)
Categorical			
People with a disability or chronic illness in household	8.60	12.22	13.11
Orphans and vulnerable children in household	8.00	13.93	14.30
People over 60 in household	8.86	15.25	15.06
Children under 18 in household	9.07	15.70	16.21
Proxy means testing	9.28	15.41	15.71
Community-based targeting	10.04	18.33	18.19
Perfect targeting	9.64	30.44	31.09
Random targeting	8.26	12.89	12.91

The PMT and community-based targeting mechanisms appear more effective at targeting poor households than does categorical targeting. Within this broad finding, a number of interesting trends emerge. First, the categorical methods have roughly the same effect on poverty headcount as random targeting, although they perform better on the poverty gaps. Of the categorical targeting methods, the ones that target older people or children under 18 have the largest effect on both the headcount and the gaps, and this effect is comparable with the results of the PMT. This result occurs because significant numbers of older people and children are living in extreme poverty. Second, the effect of the perfect targeting method on absolute poverty is only marginally greater than that of the PMT or categorical targeting methods on poverty headcount; however, perfect targeting had significantly greater effect on the poverty gaps. Community targeting performs better than the PMT and categorical methods on all poverty measures.

To form a basis for decision making, the poverty impact of these methods needs to be combined with realistic and complete costing. None of the programs reviewed has a specific budget breakdown, and no data are available on the actual costs involved in using different targeting methods. The available evidence is too weak to support the claims that have been made for or against any particular approach in some of the recent literature. In this respect, Kenya's approach of testing and gradually adapting combinations of targeting approaches makes Kenya an ideal setting for a complete evaluation of the costs and benefits of the various options.

Source: Ministry of State for Planning, National Development, and Vision 2030 2012.

Like categorical targeting, geographic targeting alone may not be sufficient if the aim is to reach poor and vulnerable households. In countries that regularly suffer from food insecurity or climatic shocks (for example, those in the Sahel), many safety net programs target zones and districts that are food insecure. Geographic targeting is easy and can be cheap[13] but can lead to errors of both exclusion and inclusion. Very rough calculations from Tanzania show that

Box 4.3 The Targeting Effectiveness of Mozambique's Major Safety Nets

The major social assistance programs in Mozambique target their beneficiaries based on categorical definitions. The Food Subsidy Program (Programa Subsidio de Alimentos, or PSA) targets the elderly, people with disabilities, and poor pregnant women who cannot work. The Direct Social Assistance Program (Programa Apoio Social Directo, or PASD) provides short-term support to orphans and vulnerable children (OVC) and to poor households that have experienced some kind of shock.

Benefit incidence analysis is helpful in evaluating the *targeting efficiency* of social assistance programs, or the extent to which the poor benefit. A concentration curve (Lorenz) shows the share of total resources (vertical axis) going to percentages of the population ranked by per capita consumption, income, or wealth (horizontal axis). A pro-poor program would be represented by a concentration curve located above the 45-degree-line curve. If the curve lies below the consumption's concentration curve, the program would not be pro-poor. It would also be regressive and would contribute to increasing inequity in the country.

Figure B4.3.1 depicts the concentration curves for the PSA and the PASD. The concentration curves of these programs are above the consumption concentration curve, and therefore both are progressive. However, the concentration curves move around the 45-degree line, and by looking at the graph one cannot say whether the programs are well targeted to the poor (that is, pro-poor).

Figure B4.3.1 Concentration Curves

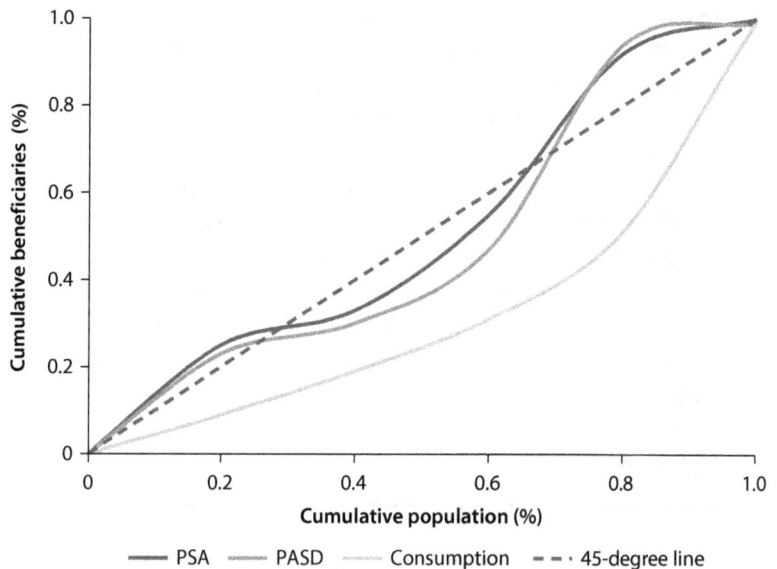

Source: World Bank 2011; estimates based on Mozambique Inquérito ao Orçamento Familiar [Household Budget Survey] 2008/09.
Note: PASD = Direct Social Assistance Program (Programa Apoio Social Directo); PSA = Food Subsidy Program (Programa Subsidio de Alimentos).

box continues next page

Box 4.3 The Targeting Effectiveness of Mozambique's Major Safety Nets *(continued)*

The *targeting accuracy* of a program can be determined from the concentration index. Negative values of the index indicate that a program is pro-poor. The larger the index, in absolute terms, the more accurate the program is in reaching the poor. Figure B4.3.2 shows the concentration indexes for the PSA, the PASD, and other programs in Mozambique. One can see the PSA is pro-poor whereas the PASD is not pro-poor, but both are on the borderline between being pro-poor and not pro-poor. In sum and keeping in mind several estimation caveats, the targeting accuracy of Mozambique's PSA and PASD programs is weak. The beneficiary selection mechanisms need to be improved. Similarly, fuel subsidies are not pro-poor and are regressive.

Figure B4.3.2 Concentration Indexes

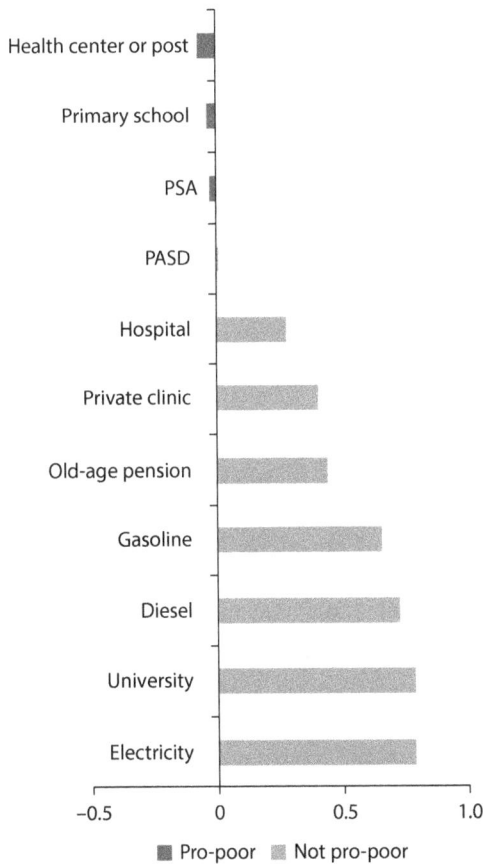

Source: World Bank 2011; estimates based on Mozambique Inquérito ao Orçamento Familiar [Household Budget Survey] 2008/09.
Note: PASD = Direct Social Assistance Program (Programa Apoio Social Directo); PSA = Food Subsidy Program (Programa Subsidio de Alimentos).

operating only in the most food-insecure districts (which most programs do) would miss about 68 percent of the extremely poor in Tanzania.

PMT targeting is potentially more accurate in identifying the poor than is categorical or spatial targeting alone. The PMT index can be more accurate at identifying the poor because it incorporates more information on household characteristics that are associated with poverty (such as type of housing, household size, education level of the household head, and access to sanitation). Furthermore, the process provides a transparent, structured, and reviewable trail of how program eligibility decisions are made, which in most cases is strongly needed. The simulations from Kenya, for example, suggest that PMT (and community-based) targeting would perform better than random or categorical targeting (see box 4.2), but categorical targeting may be equal to PMT in terms of targeting the absolute poorest. In a targeting study exploring the use of PMT in African safety net programs and including seven case study countries, errors vary within each case study with eligibility cutoffs, base population, and region. Exclusion errors broadly ranged from 14 percent in Niger and 15 percent in urban Cameroon to 40 and 41 percent in Ghana and Kenya, respectively. Similarly, inclusion errors ranged from 12 percent in Niger to 52 percent in Malawi (Mills and del Ninno, forthcoming).

However, measuring the core variables used to estimate the PMT scores can be problematic when capacity is weak and poverty widespread. Although often a sunk cost, a quality benchmark national household survey from which to generate PMT weights is expensive. Once basic verifiable variables are identified that perform well in using PMT, however, the marginal cost of basic PMT screening is relatively low. But the gains from using PMT (the additional accuracy in identifying poverty) might not always be enough to justify this additional administrative expense. In several African countries with widespread poverty, such as Lesotho, Madagascar, Mozambique, Swaziland, and Zambia, poor households have a "flat" distribution of consumption and key household characteristics, which implies that such proxy characteristics have limited power to distinguish the poor from the not poor, or the very poor from among the poor. PMT can also seem opaque to households and, for this reason, has less popular support than simpler targeting methods. Among communities participating in the Kenya CT-OVC program, many people interviewed attributed being selected by the PMT to fate, God, luck, or the "computer" in Nairobi. Some community members felt that many more households—some "more deserving"—were not covered by the program but should have been. The objectives, context, poverty profile, data availability, political economy, and capacity in each country will determine what methods are most suitable to reach the specific objectives and groups to be targeted.

Community targeting has the potential to reach the poorest, but the evidence suggests that it would be better to combine it with other methods to minimize elite capture and inclusion errors. Some programs that use community-based targeting in Africa have demonstrated that this method can identify the poor effectively. For instance, the targeting of the social cash transfer scheme in

Malawi is exclusively community based and has proven to be among the most progressively targeted transfer programs in the world, covering 62 percent of the ultrapoor and the labor constrained. Other arguments in favor of community-based targeting are that it is inexpensive and that it fosters community cohesion and greater community ownership of the program. It may also be a good option in situations in which the capacity to undertake other forms of targeting is low or in which households in the lowest quintiles are fairly homogeneous, thus making use of PMT challenging. However, community-targeted programs can fall victim to nepotism or political manipulation, which allegedly occurred in Sierra Leone's cash-for-work program. Although favoritism was also alleged in Malawi, actions were taken to reduce the involvement of village heads in beneficiary selection to improve targeting effectiveness. In addition, analysis of the targeting effectiveness in Ghana shows that community-based targeting appears to be more variable across villages than are PMT methods (Mills and del Ninno, forthcoming). Simulations in box 4.2 show that community-based targeting can yield similarly effective results as those produced by using the PMT in Kenya and can outperform categorical targeting in terms of reaching the poor. In several countries, including Cameroon, Mozambique, and Tanzania, community targeting is currently being combined with PMT to improve the efficiency of identifying the appropriate beneficiaries.

Little is known about the targeting effectiveness of food-based programs (such as cereal bank distribution or subsidized food sales). These programs generally use a combination of geographic targeting (to food-insecure areas), self-targeting (depending on the quality and price of the commodity offered), and community selection or validation of eligible households. The assessment reports from Mali, Mauritania, and Tanzania indicate that no data are available on the actual number or characteristics of the households who receive the subsidized or freely distributed food in these countries. For Malawi's and Tanzania's food and farm subsidy programs, anecdotal reports suggest that although the poor and vulnerable tend to be targeted in principle, village leaders tend to distribute the food more widely to maintain social cohesion. In Burkina Faso, the subsidized cereals may not reach the very poorest because they may not be able to afford to access them, and whether the targeting criteria for vulnerability are being applied is unclear. The same is true for the village cereal banks (Stock Alimentaire Villageois de Sécurité, or SAVS) and special subsidized food boutiques in Mauritania.

Experience with self-targeted programs is mixed. As discussed in chapter 3, some public works programs (such as those in Malawi and Togo) have successfully self-targeted workers in the lowest deciles. Other programs tend to set the wage rate higher than local minimum and market wages, which limits the effectiveness of the self-targeting approach in terms of benefiting the poorest.[14] This has been the case both in Mali's PEJIMO (Programme d'Emploi des Jeunes par l'Approche Haute Intensité de Main d'Œuvre, or Employment Program for Youth by High Labor Force Intensity) and in Cameroon's urban PAD-Y (Projet d'Assainissement de Yaoundé, or Yaoundé Sanitation Project). In Togo, analysis has shown that only a small proportion of the beneficiaries of the country's safety net programs, which are mainly targeted geographically or through self-selection, can be considered poor or vulnerable.

Food and fuel subsidies have extensively been shown to be regressive, thus largely benefiting the nonpoor, who consume more of the subsidized goods than the poor. Mali subsidizes rice, and although rice represents 10.7 percent of average household expenditures, it represents only 6.9 percent of the expenditures of households in the poorest quintile. In Ghana, only 2.3 percent of the subsidies for petrol and diesel products (except kerosene) benefit the poor. In Cameroon, recent data have shown that 80 percent of fuel subsidies benefit people in the wealthiest quintile. Subsidies on rice and fish are also regressive, though to a slightly lesser extent. Other African countries, such as Benin, Liberia, Mozambique, and Togo, also have general price subsidies. Even though rigorous poverty and social impact assessments have not been done in all countries, these subsidies are widely believed to be highly regressive as they are in other low- and middle-income countries (Coady *et al.* 2006).

Overall, the safety net assessments find that ample scope exists for improved targeting in African safety nets and that data are a key constraint in this regard. Data are especially lacking with respect to poverty targeting because unlike other targeting criteria, such as gender or physical disability, poverty is not easily observed and has to be inferred using other, more easily measured characteristics. Also, the structured decision-making process associated with any targeting method contributes to program transparency, accountability, and support. The accuracy of any approach—whether it is based on simple categories, spatial differentiation, or PMT indexes—depends on how easily proxy characteristics can be measured and how well they can predict poverty. Simulations of targeting based on representative household surveys can give a much better sense of the relative accuracy of various targeting methods, for instance, when the distribution of poverty in the lowest quintiles is relatively flat (such as in Lesotho, Madagascar, Mozambique, Swaziland, and Zambia). In these countries, using a combination of methods, including poverty maps to identify vulnerable areas and PMT and community targeting to identify specific communities and households, can be important. Field pilots or impact evaluations that experimentally test between different targeting methods can also help improve targeting. Although more demanding than simulations based on survey data, pilots are more informative because they also yield information on implementation challenges, especially in low-capacity settings.

Better assessment of the relative accuracy of different targeting methods will be a key input for program design, although a number of other considerations are also relevant to the choice of targeting method. For instance, categorical programs may not be optimal for targeting poverty, but they are simple to implement and often enjoy popular support because of their transparency. Programs that are more universal may enjoy higher levels of political support than those that are narrowly targeted. Universal programs and simple categorical targeting are also cheaper to administer than PMT targeting. But to the extent that a program aims to support the poor or an otherwise vulnerable population, universal or simple categorical targeting has a cost, in the sense that it would waste resources on the nonpoor and leave less for those more in need. This cost is often not measured, because inclusion and exclusion rates are largely unknown. Only by quantifying the potential gain in accuracy from more intensive targeting methods can this cost be comprehended and factored into choice of targeting method.

Clearer definitions of targeting objectives and common targeting platforms can be helpful. Several southern African MICs with relatively established safety net systems (such as Botswana, Mauritius, Mozambique, Namibia, South Africa, and Swaziland) have a plethora of categorically targeted programs for specific groups. These groups commonly include OVC, the elderly, people with disabilities, HIV/AIDS patients, pregnant women, and ex-combatants. However, no clear definitions indicate who belongs to these groups. Also, simple indicators of eligibility, such as age, are difficult to verify, which leads to errors of both exclusion and inclusion. In the case of countries such as Ghana, Kenya, Mauritius, and the Seychelles, safety net assessments suggest that establishing one set of criteria to govern whom the safety nets should target would be wise, as well as establishing a common targeting system and a single registry of beneficiaries. This approach would reduce administrative costs and the risk of political influence and increase program coordination, transparency, and fairness in the selection of beneficiaries. Chapter 5 discusses the political economy considerations regarding targeting of safety net programs in Africa.

Flexibility, Predictability, and Crisis Preparedness

Safety net programs should be flexible enough to respond to crises and to provide predictable support. Poor and vulnerable people in Africa repeatedly suffer from a number of shocks, as outlined in chapter 2 (including climatic shocks, food and fuel price increases, global financial crises, and illness and death in the family). Over the past couple of years, food-related crises have been devastating in all of the countries reviewed, either through increases in food prices or through droughts or floods. The prevalence and frequency of shocks in Africa mean that governments need to ensure that programs and mechanisms exist that can quickly provide adequate support to those affected by these shocks. Therefore, it is vital for safety net programs to be designed to be flexible enough so that they can be altered or scaled up to respond to the increased need at such times of crisis. In addition, even for those safety net programs that aim to reduce longer-term poverty, providing beneficiaries with reliable and predictable transfers is crucial to enable them to make the best use of the support.

The recent food, fuel, and financial crises demonstrated that African countries do not have programs capable of responding quickly to shocks. Governments have responded to crises by introducing either ad hoc emergency food-based programs or costly general subsidies or price reductions instead of well-targeted safety net interventions. In Benin, Burkina Faso, Mali, and Niger, governments responded to increased food insecurity by initiating emergency food distribution in affected areas and by using cereal banks to sell food staples at reduced prices without much control over targeting or outcome. In other countries (such as Benin, Cameroon, Mozambique, and Togo), general untargeted food subsidies were introduced and fuel subsidies were increased at a high fiscal cost. In other longer-term safety net programs meant to provide regular support to poor and vulnerable citizens, such as the school input program in Botswana and Mali's Bourse maman CCT, frequent delays in delivering the transfer payments to beneficiaries have caused the beneficiaries hardship and reduced the programs' effectiveness. Several of the safety net systems reviewed have been described as providing transfers in an irregular, erratic, and unpredictable manner.

However, some governments have recognized that more foresight and timely support are needed to respond to crises and are moving toward building more predictable safety net systems. Interestingly, according to a classification done by the World Bank's Social Protection Anchor, the African countries that have strong measures in place for improving safety nets during a crisis are all LICs: Ethiopia, Kenya, Niger, Rwanda, Tanzania, and Zimbabwe (see table B.2 in appendix B). Most of these countries have embarked on the agenda of strengthening their safety nets to enable them to better respond to crises and are receiving support from international donors. The MICs have either moderate or limited measures in place to strengthen their safety nets to respond to crises. Therefore, it is clear that having a broad and well-established safety net system (as is the case in many African MICs) does not necessarily mean that the system is well equipped to protect the poorest against shocks. Having one or two well-targeted and flexible programs that are capable of reaching those groups most affected by crises may be more appropriate and effective.

Many African countries are now looking at Ethiopia's innovative and predictable PSNP to learn how to increase the flexibility of their own safety nets and are benefiting from Ethiopia's experience providing both food and cash. In most African countries, food-based responses to various crises remain predominant even though no strong evidence indicates that providing food is the most effective and efficient type of benefit. In Mauritania, the program Emel ("hope" in Arabic) is the national crisis response program. A key characteristic of the safety net component of this program that provides free or subsidized food is that it has been, to a large extent, self-financed. With the increased frequency and scale of the climatic shocks that Mauritania faces, what was meant to be a short-term, one-off emergency drought response program has become a large-scale, quasi-permanent intervention. Niger has developed a national contingency plan to improve its emergency response, including ensuring access to food, helping protect household assets, and developing early warning indicators. Although the Cellule Crise Alimentaire, which manages the crisis response program in Niger, facilitates mainly public works and food distribution, both of which have relatively poor targeting, reforms are under way to improve the crisis response system. Other countries, including Rwanda and Tanzania, are looking to this experience to strengthen their capacity to respond to climate change (box 4.4).

Box 4.4 The Role of Safety Nets in Promoting Climate Change Adaptation

Safety nets are increasingly recognized by African countries as an important instrument to respond to climate change. The drought in the Horn of Africa in 2011 and the current drought in the Sahel are devastating examples of the negative impacts that climate change may have on poor and vulnerable populations. Safety nets are increasingly being used to respond to these shocks, as was done in Ethiopia and Kenya in response to the 2011 drought and is currently being done in Mali and Niger.

In addition to this crisis response function, safety nets are increasingly seen to be an important tool to build the resilience of poor and vulnerable households to the impacts of climate change. In Ethiopia and Rwanda, public works are improving water management and reducing soil erosion. Safety nets are also contributing to climate change adaptation by enabling households to diversify risk, enhance income, and build skills and assets.

Source: World Bank 2012a.

Time is needed to create safety net programs and systems to efficiently help households affected by shock. Therefore, countries should have operational safety net programs with adequate tools (targeting, registry, and so on) that are able to properly address a shock. Such systems are best developed during stable times so that the systems can be activated and programs can quickly scale up when a crisis occurs to (a) identify the affected households, (b) transfer the adequate benefit at the right time, and (c) be transparent and efficient.

Public works programs, if carefully designed and implemented, have the potential to serve as crisis response instruments, given their short-term and self-targeting nature. The ability of public works programs to respond to crises has been shown in several countries worldwide, including Argentina, Ethiopia, Latvia, and Mexico. Although public works programs are common in Africa, their objectives have tended to focus on creating community assets and promoting longer-term development in poor and vulnerable communities. The exception is Ethiopia, where the large PSNP is flexibly designed to fight droughts and predictable seasonal poverty and food insecurity while also tackling the underlying causes of food insecurity from a longer-term development perspective. Public works programs in other countries, however, have served more ad hoc crisis response functions. Niger used both food- and cash-for-work programs as a response to the 2005 food crisis. Moreover, conflict-affected states such as Liberia, Madagascar, and Sierra Leone have a number of small and uncoordinated cash-for-work and food-for-work programs focused on reconstruction and social cohesion. Coordinated national public works programs that transfer cash (or food) to crisis-affected households during seasonal periods of hardship could be explored as a flexible tool capable of being quickly scaled up and down in response to emergencies.

The Impacts of African Safety Nets

Most (if not all) of the safety net reviews identify the lack of proper M&E systems as a main weakness of African safety net programs. Many countries (including Benin, Burkina Faso, Liberia, Mali, Tanzania, and Togo) do not have accurate administrative data on the number of beneficiaries reached and benefit levels provided by each of their programs. Programs that distribute food through cereal banks or that sell cereals at subsidized prices during emergencies are particularly lacking in data on the number and profile of people who benefit, and information on the effect of the benefit on the welfare status of beneficiaries is completely missing. However, some southern African countries (Botswana, Mauritius, and Mozambique) seem to have more integrated and institutionalized M&E systems. In more recent years, countries have been investing in their M&E systems.

A number of impact evaluations provide solid evidence of the effectiveness of safety net programs, although more impact evaluations are needed. In the past, rigorous impact evaluations were carried out on only a few nationally implemented programs (such as those in Ethiopia and Kenya) and for a number of small pilot transfer programs (such as the CCT and school feeding programs in Burkina Faso, Malawi's Zomba CCT, Tanzania's community-based CCT, and Zambia's cash transfer program in the Monza District). These impact evaluations tend to measure the effect of transfers on households' food consumption and take-up of health and education services. The impact evaluations of small pilot programs are important to document the effectiveness of transfer programs in low-income settings and to inform the possible scale-up of these pilots to national programs. Yet few impact evaluations of programs implemented at scale are available. Even countries with the most advanced administrative monitoring systems do not regularly undertake impact evaluations to inform policy makers and administrators about the effect of their programs on beneficiaries' outcomes. Most large-scale programs (for example, universal school feeding programs) have not yet been subject to rigorous impact assessments. However, in a few larger programs (the CT-OVC and the Hunger Safety Net Programme in Kenya and the PSNP in Ethiopia, for example) impact evaluations are built into program design and yield important information to guide the expansion and modification of these programs. A few impact evaluations are testing how best to design social protection programs. For instance, impact evaluation of a pilot CCT in Burkina Faso tests whether it is more effective to provide the transfers to mothers or to fathers, and the Malawi impact evaluation analyzes whether CCTs are more or less effective than unconditional cash transfers. More impact evaluations explicitly testing alternative design features are needed.

The body of evidence from impact evaluations of African safety net programs is, however, growing quickly. Many African governments, together with the World Bank[15] and other donors, are working actively to improve the impact evaluation evidence base from safety net programs. Currently more than 20 World Bank–supported impact evaluations are ongoing in the social protection sector (including in Ethiopia, Ghana, Lesotho, Malawi, Niger, Nigeria, Sierra Leone, Tanzania, Togo, and Uganda), and several more are in the planning stages (such as in Cameroon, Guinea, Mali, Mozambique, and Swaziland). Most impact evaluations focus on assessing the effects of cash transfer programs on welfare, nutrition practices, or take-up of health and education services. Several studies are focusing on specific issues relevant to safety nets in Africa and other low-income settings, such as the effectiveness of adding accompanying measures to cash transfer programs (Guinea, Niger, and Togo) or the productive impacts of safety nets or of graduation strategies on income-generating activities or employment (Cameroon, Ethiopia, Kenya, and Malawi).

Initial results from the first wave of impact evaluations of cash transfer programs have generally been positive. An evaluation of cash transfer programs in Malawi found that both conditional and unconditional transfers increased girls' schooling. Cash transfers also led to reduced dropout rates and, in turn, delayed the age of marriage for many girls. However, the effect of the conditions was found to be mixed. The evaluation of the Kenya CT-OVC cash transfer program found that the program had mainly positive outcomes, such as consumption, food expenditures, dietary diversity, household asset accumulation, and enrollment rates for secondary students. However, the evaluation found no significant effect on child health indicators or on basic school enrollment or attendance rates. Also, the program was found to benefit mainly small households. Because the cash transfer is set at a flat rate, larger households received a lower per capita transfer amount, which reduced the value of the transfer in their case. The evidence from pilot CCTs in Burkina Faso indicates that cash transfer programs, with and without conditions, increase the enrollment of children ages 9–13 years (the core years for school attendance), especially "more able" children and boys who are traditionally prioritized for school participation by households. However, the CCT was more effective in improving the enrollment of the "marginal child," such as younger or less able children and girls. Compared with control group households, CCTs also significantly increased the number of preventive health care visits during the previous year, whereas unconditional cash transfers did not have such an effect. A CCT program in northern Nigeria has shown significant effects on girls' participation in secondary schools in terms of enrollment, attendance, and even performance.

Positive impacts from school feeding programs have also been documented, despite some mixed results. The study of the WFP's school feeding program (in-school meals and take-home rations for girls) in Burkina Faso showed an increase in girls' enrollment of 5–6 percent without any negative effects on boys' enrollment. However, attendance dropped, and there was no increase in girls' achievement and even a slight decrease in math scores for boys. The evaluation also raised the question of whether school feeding was the most cost-effective method for achieving the desired outcomes. Worldwide, some evidence indicates that school feeding increases school attendance, cognition, and educational attainment, particularly if accompanied by deworming and micronutrient fortification (Bundy et al. 2009).

In Ethiopia, public works participation was found to measurably improve household food security, as measured by changes in self-reported household food gaps, although this effect was strongest among households that received regular, high-value transfers. Growth in caloric acquisition was also 17 percent higher for PSNP households that received recent and regular transfers. In addition, the distress sale of livestock actually decreased among households receiving predictable, high-value transfers, whereas it increased among those that received unpredictable transfers, although PSNP public works recipients reported more distress sales than control groups. Furthermore, the PSNP has had a measurable and positive effect on household assets and investments such as livestock holdings.

In addition, qualitative reviews have sometimes been carried out. These reviews have found that the programs in question have had mainly positive effects on food consumption and schooling. The reviewed programs include the Bomi cash transfer and public works programs in Liberia, Mali's Bourse maman CCT, and Zambia's Kalamo cash transfer pilot. In Ethiopia, PSNP beneficiaries reported that they increased their use of social services such as health facilities and increased the school enrollment and attendance of their children. Evidence also suggests that Swaziland's Old-Age Grants have had a positive effect on food security, nutritional status, and use of education and health services. Also, the old-age pension programs in Lesotho and South Africa have undergone evaluations specifically measuring the effectiveness of targeting and how benefits are shared among household members.

Helping households to become more productive is an increasingly important aspect of safety net provision in Africa, although productive effects of safety nets have yet to be consistently documented. In addition to providing cash or in-kind support to increase households' consumption and to prevent households from resorting to distress sales of their assets in times of crisis, several transfer programs in Africa aim to increase the income generation and productivity of beneficiaries. Safety nets can provide pathways for households to increase their incomes and improve their long-term welfare after graduation. For example, beneficiaries of the PSNP in Ethiopia are linked to the Household Asset Building Program. This link is intended to help them improve the productivity of their farms and to increase their long-term food security. Similarly, in Tanzania, beneficiaries of the PSNP can participate in small groups to promote community saving. The objective is to increase their ability to save for their future needs and investments. Community savings promotion is also being discussed in the development of a new program in Mozambique. In the cash transfer pilot that is being prepared in Cameroon, beneficiaries will be encouraged to participate in awareness and training activities to learn about income generation, ways to access microfinancing, and small business skills. These complementary activities not only are important for raising household living standards after the 24 months of cash support comes to an end, but also are critical elements to garner political and public support for the program to be an accepted intervention for sustainable poverty reduction in Cameroon.

New research and evaluation exploring the productive aspects of safety nets in Africa are promising. Overall, little rigorous evaluation evidence is available to date on potential productivity-enhancing aspects of African safety net programs. The most destitute groups—those that are often the focus of tightly targeted programs—may also be the ones that face the most difficulty in engaging in productive activities. The World Bank, together with several other partners, is currently engaged in a new research agenda that has shown positive effects of cash transfer programs on measures of productivity (such as boosting the local economy and labor market) in Kenya, Lesotho, and Malawi. Box 4.5 provides a deeper discussion. Other research on complementary activities that are aimed at enhancing productive activities of safety net beneficiaries is ongoing in 10 countries, including Ethiopia and Ghana.

Box 4.5 Can Cash Transfers Be Productive in Africa?

Most safety net programs focus on reducing current levels of poverty. However, they may also have the potential to increase productivity and reduce poverty in the long term. Public works are considered productive even in the short term because, besides transferring income to disadvantaged households, they help create small community investments. Cash transfer programs (often conditional) can help poor families invest in the human capital of their children, for instance, through more regular school attendance. However, some groups of the very poor and destitute may not be able to participate productively in society and may use income support to purchase food and other necessities (the protective role of safety nets). Improving consumption could, however, be considered productive in itself; for instance, better nutritional intake helps children develop and improve their prospects. Old-age support to grandparents in Kenya and South Africa is used to support the schooling of their grandchildren.

Helping households become more productive is an increasingly important aspect of safety nets in Africa. This potential remains to be fully exploited, but some findings from impact evaluations and other research show promising results. The hypothesis underlying much of this work is that even a small amount of regular income support—without any conditions—could help households diversify livelihoods and increase their consumption of "goods" (such as small savings or investments in assets and human capital) and move away from "bads" or negative coping strategies (such as reducing exploitive or risky employment and selling assets in times of distress). As such, safety nets can allow households to invest in higher-productivity, higher-return activities. Also, cash transfers may boost the local economy through multiplier effects. The findings indicate the following:

- In Kenya and Malawi, cash transfers led to increased investment in agricultural assets, including crop implements and livestock. Moreover, both programs fostered increased food consumption and improved dietary diversity, with a greater share of household consumption acquired from own-farm production. The program in Malawi led to a shift for adults and children from agricultural wage labor to own-farm wage activities, whereas the program in

box continues next page

Box 4.5 Can Cash Transfers Be Productive in Africa? *(continued)*

Kenya reduced child labor. The program in Kenya also positively influenced participation in nonfarm enterprises for female-headed households.

- In Ethiopia, impact evaluation finds that households with access to both the PSNP and the complementary packages of agricultural support were more likely to be food secure, to borrow for productive purposes, to use improved agricultural technologies, and to operate their own nonfarm business activities.

- Qualitative fieldwork from cash transfer programs in Ghana, Kenya, and Zimbabwe found that cash transfers led to increased investment in economic activities and increased social capital and risk-sharing arrangements. Also, the transfers allowed households to reduce debt levels and increase creditworthiness.

- The income multipliers of cash transfers on the local economy were estimated at 1.81–2.23, respectively, in Kenya and Lesotho. The key insight is that nonbeneficiaries and the local economy also benefit significantly from cash transfer programs through trade and production links.

Nevertheless, few safety net programs in Africa include additional productive components (such as training activities or links for beneficiaries to credit or small business support) that encourage sustainable productive employment and investment. Although initial results are promising, more research is needed. Impact evaluations of new cash transfer programs in Cameroon and Niger will explicitly test whether these programs have productive effects. They will assess the effect of accompanying measures, such as whether awareness-raising campaigns for beneficiaries can help them improve risk management strategies and engage in productive activities.

Sources: Kenya: Asfaw *et al.* 2013; Ethiopia: Gilligan, Hoddinott, and Taffesse 2009; Ghana, Kenya, and Zimbabwe: OPM 2013a, 2013b, and 2013c; Kenya and Lesotho: Taylor, Kagin, and Filipski 2013 and Taylor, Thome, and Filipski 2013; Malawi: Boone *et al.* 2013 and Covarrubias, Davis, and Winters 2012.

Summary of Main Messages

Main messages of the chapter include the following:

- African safety net programs use a wide range of targeting mechanisms and often combine a number of approaches. The most common are geographic targeting, self-targeting, community targeting, and categorical targeting. Poverty-targeted programs using income or consumption measures are still rare, but some countries (Kenya and Rwanda) are moving forward with scaling up their well-targeted programs and harmonizing a number of their programs to minimize duplication and reduce ineffective and inefficient interventions and benefits.

- Improving the targeting of African safety net programs will involve combining a number of methods (such as categorical, geographic, PMT, or community-based targeting) that together can distinguish the most appropriate and poorest groups. The choice of targeting method should depend on the program's objective and the institutional capacity of implementing agencies and will have to be customized to the particular poverty profile and political economy of each country. The structured decision-making process associated with any targeting method can contribute to program transparency and accountability, the ability to scale up a program, and the ability to rapidly respond to shocks.

- A key question is how well African safety nets are able to identify and reach the poor and vulnerable, especially those in extreme poverty and vulnerability. Direct measures of income or wealth, which can be used in means testing poverty targeting, are rarely available. It is therefore important to assess the accuracy of all targeting methods used.

- Coverage by safety nets of the poor and vulnerable in Africa is generally very low but is growing. Nevertheless, in several southern African MICs, social pension programs provide significant benefits to a large number of the elderly. However, because such programs are designed to support all those who cannot participate in the labor force, leakage to the nonpoor is substantial and costly.

- For safety net programs to effectively meet the large-scale need in African countries on a national basis, well-functioning programs should be selectively and gradually scaled up. It is feasible for a small number of well-run coordinated programs to address the needs of the poorest. Ethiopia's PSNP, combining public works and direct support transfers, is a good example.

- The generosity of safety net programs is often hard to measure, but the benefit levels in Africa's cash transfer programs seem to be on a par with levels in programs in other regions. Very little information is available about the generosity, coverage, and targeting effectiveness of food distribution and emergency relief programs that are common in countries such as Benin, Burkina Faso, Cameroon, Kenya, Mali, Niger, and Togo.

- Most African safety net programs lack flexibility and predictability, but several countries are moving toward building safety net systems and programs that provide more predictable benefits and that are flexible enough to respond to crises. With the support of donors, several LICs, including Ethiopia, Kenya, Madagascar, Niger, and Rwanda, are in the process of strengthening the crisis response functions of their safety nets. Public works programs have the potential to play a larger role in providing safety net support during seasonal shocks in Africa, provided that they can be better targeted to the poor and scaled up to include more people.

- Establishing safety net systems that can flexibly respond to crises takes time. Most countries in Africa were not able to use safety nets to respond effectively to the recent global crises but had to resort to inefficient and expensive universal handouts. To increase crisis preparedness, governments need to create and develop safety net systems during stable times so that they are ready and available to respond when crises hit.

- Despite weaknesses in M&E of safety net programs in Africa, the landscape is quickly changing. More and more impact evaluations are being undertaken, thus contributing to a growing body of evidence on safety net programs in Africa. Where known, the impact of safety nets on poverty and welfare indicators has generally been positive but mixed. Information systems need to be improved, and more basic data need to be collected on the number and type of beneficiaries who are covered as well as on program outcomes so that policy makers and planners can use this information to improve program design and coordination and to attract financial resources and donor support.

Notes

1. In numerical terms, this comes to 26 of 34 programs in Sierra Leone and 31 of 37 programs in Mozambique (World Bank 2011, 2012c).
2. These figures are from the World Bank's Europe and Central Asia Social Protection database and Latin America and the Caribbean Social Protection database.
3. At the start of the PSNP, *households in chronic food insecurity* were defined as households having a three-month annual food gap or more and receiving food aid for three consecutive years.
4. These programs include the Public Welfare Assistance Scheme, social cash transfers, the Food Security Pack, and the Peri-Urban Community Self-Help program.
5. For example, according to HelpAge International's Pension Watch database (http://www.pension-watch.net/about-social-pensions/about-social-pensions/social-pensions-database/) coverage is 6 percent in Argentina, 5 percent in Brazil, 10 percent in Uruguay, 20 percent in Costa Rica, 51 percent in Chile, 12 percent in Moldova, and 16 percent in Thailand.
6. This range represents the benefit levels paid in five programs in Ethiopia, Lesotho, Mali, Senegal, and Zambia.
7. This finding is consistent with findings reported in Garcia and Moore (2012).
8. The WFP ration rates for all programs are set at 50 percent or 75 percent of average household nutritional requirements for the main macronutrients (calories and protein).
9. Food-based programs—specifically emergency response programs—generally use the Sphere standards. The Sphere standards are internationally recognized standards for emergency response that commit the implementing agency to provide 2,100 kilocalories, including protein and fat, which is often translated into an amount of cereal, pulses, and oils.
10. These estimates assume that the value of the food and cash transfers are equivalent to ensure that any estimated savings are not due to differences in the value of the monthly cash or food transfers but rather reflect efficiency gains in program implementation.
11. Such proxy indicators may include information about the household dwelling and educational achievement of the household head, for example. PMT targeting is generally used when reliable data on household consumption and income are not available.

12. Coll-Black *et al.* (2012) used the Coady-Grosh-Hoddinott indexes and compared the score for the PSNP against those for the programs reviewed in Coady, Grosh, and Hoddinott (2004).

13. Picking geographic areas from an already established poverty map using political or emergency triggers (such as the occurrence of a natural disaster) can be cheap. However, reliable geographic targeting requires accurate analysis and maps of poverty and vulnerability (or food insecurity) and may even require census data.

14. These findings are consistent with findings by McCord and Slater (2009).

15. The International Food Policy Research Institute is also analyzing the relative effectiveness of food versus cash transfers in some African countries. Several other impact evaluations are also ongoing, including those of the Lesotho OVC Child Grant program and Zambia's social cash transfer scheme.

References

Ahmed, Akhter U., Agnes R. Quisumbing, Mahbuba Nasreen, John F. Hoddinott, and Elizabeth Bryan. 2009. *Comparing Food and Cash Transfers to the Ultra Poor in Bangladesh*. Washington, DC: International Food Policy Research Institute.

Asfaw, Solomon, Benjamin Davis, Josh Dewbre, Giovanni Federighi, Sudhanshu Handa, and Paul Winters. 2013. "The Impact of the Kenya CT-OVC Programme on Productive Activities and Labour Allocation." PtoP project brief, From Projection to Production Project, Food and Agriculture Organization of the United Nations, Rome.

Boone, Ryan, Katia Covarrubias, Benjamin Davis, and Paul Winters. 2013. "Cash Transfer Programs and Agricultural Production: The Case of Malawi." *Agricultural Economics* 44 (3): 365–78.

Bundy, Donald, Carmen Burbano, Margaret Grosh, Aulo Gelli, Matthew Jukes, and Lesley Drake. 2009. *Rethinking School Feeding: Social Safety Nets, Child Development, and the Education Sector*. Washington, DC: World Bank.

Coady, David P., Margaret Grosh, and John Hoddinott. 2004. *Targeting of Transfers in Developing Countries*. Washington, DC: World Bank.

Coady, David P., Moataz El-Said, Robert Gillingham, Kangni Kpodar, Paulo A. Medas, and David Locke Newhouse. 2006. "The Magnitude and Distribution of Fuel Subsidies: Evidence from Bolivia, Ghana, Jordan, Mali, and Sri Lanka." IMF Working Paper 06/247, International Monetary Fund, Washington, DC. http://www.imf.org/external /pubs/ft/wp/2006/wp06247.pdf.

Coll-Black, Sarah, Daniel O. Gilligan, John F. Hoddinott, Neha Kumar, Alemayehu Seyoum Taffesse, and William Wiseman. 2012. "Targeting Food Security Interventions in Ethiopia: The Productive Safety Net Programme." In *Food and Agriculture in Ethiopia: Progress and Policy Challenges*, edited by Paul A. Dorosh and Shahidur Rashid, 280–317. Philadelphia: University of Pennsylvania Press.

Covarrubias, Katia, Benjamin Davis, and Paul Winters. 2012. "From Protection to Production: Productive Impacts of the Malawi Social Cash Transfer Scheme." *Journal of Development Effectiveness* 4 (1): 50–77.

Fiszbein, Ariel, and Norbert Schady. 2009. *Conditional Cash Transfers: Reducing Present and Future Poverty*. Washington, DC: World Bank.

Garcia, Marito, and Charity M. T. Moore. 2012. *The Cash Dividend: The Rise of Cash Transfer Programs in Sub-Saharan Africa*. Washington, DC: World Bank.

Gilligan, Daniel O., John F. Hoddinott, and Alemayehu Seyoum Taffesse. 2009. "The Impact of Ethiopia's Productive Safety Net Programme and Its Linkages." *Journal of Development Studies* 45 (10): 1684–1706.

Grosh, Margaret, Carlo del Ninno, Emil Tesliuc, and Azedine Ouerghi. 2008. *For Protection and Promotion: The Design and Implementation of Effective Safety Nets*. Washington, DC: World Bank.

McCord, Anna, and Rachel Slater. 2009. *Overview of Public Works Programmes in Sub-Saharan Africa*. London: Overseas Development Institute.

Mills, Brad, and Carlo del Ninno. Forthcoming. "Effective and Inclusive Social Assistance Targeting Mechanisms in Sub-Saharan Africa." World Bank, Washington, DC.

Ministry of State for Planning, National Development, and Vision 2030. 2012. *Kenya Social Protection Sector Review*. Nairobi: Republic of Kenya.

OPM (Oxford Policy Management). 2013a. "Qualitative Research and Analyses of the Economic Impact of Cash Transfer Programmes in Sub Saharan Africa: Ghana Country Case Study Report." PtoP project brief, From Projection to Production Project, Food and Agriculture Organization of the United Nations, Rome.

———. 2013b. "Qualitative Research and Analyses of the Economic Impact of Cash Transfer Programmes in Sub Saharan Africa: Kenya Country Case Study Report." PtoP project brief, From Projection to Production Project, Food and Agriculture Organization of the United Nations, Rome.

———. 2013c. "Qualitative Research and Analyses of the Economic Impact of Cash Transfer Programmes in Sub Saharan Africa: Draft Zimbabwe Country Case Study Report." PtoP project brief, From Projection to Production Project, Food and Agriculture Organization of the United Nations, Rome.

Taylor, J. Edward, Justin Kagin, and Mateusz Filipski. 2013. "Evaluating General Equilibrium Impacts of Kenya's Cash Transfer Program for Orphans and Vulnerable Children (CT-OVC)." PtoP project brief, From Projection to Production Project, Food and Agriculture Organization of the United Nations, Rome.

Taylor, J. Edward, Karen Thome, and Mateusz Filipski. 2013. "Evaluating Local General Equilibrium Impacts of Lesotho's Child Grants Program." PtoP project brief, From Projection to Production Project, Food and Agriculture Organization of the United Nations, Rome.

World Bank. 2011. *Mozambique: Social Protection Assessment—Review of Social Assistance Programs and Social Protection Expenditures*. Washington, DC: World Bank.

———. 2012a. *Managing Risk, Promoting Growth: Developing Systems for Social Protection in Africa—The World Bank's Africa Social Protection Strategy, 2012–2022*. Washington, DC: World Bank.

———. 2012b. "Rwanda Social Safety Net Assessment: Draft Report." World Bank, Washington, DC.

———. 2012c. "Sierra Leone: Social Protection Assessment." World Bank, Washington, DC.

———. 2012d. "Zambia: Using Productive Transfers to Accelerate Poverty Reduction." World Bank, Washington, DC.

CHAPTER 5

Financing, Cost, and Sustainability

Spending on safety nets is difficult to quantify, particularly because it varies greatly over time. Because African countries tend to have relatively weak information systems, keeping track of how much is spent on each program is also difficult. Much of the information on spending for individual countries that is quoted in this chapter has been extracted from country safety net reports and is presented with important caveats. All data should be interpreted as approximations.

Most developing countries spend in the range of 1–2 percent of their gross domestic product (GDP) on safety nets (Grosh *et al.* 2008). However, many African countries spend less than 1 percent of GDP (excluding general subsidies). When expenditures are low, more spending may be justified. But this situation does not necessarily mean that existing programs should be expanded to cover more people, because many programs are either universal or targeted by category (therefore benefiting many nonpoor recipients). In resource-rich countries that spend large amounts on general fuel and food subsidies, targeted safety nets can be important mitigating mechanisms to facilitate subsidy reform.

Countries finance safety nets in different ways. They may reallocate expenditures from some other budget item, increase taxes, or obtain international financing. In Africa, the share of safety nets funded by international donors is very large. Therefore, this chapter shows trends in financing by donors as well as by governments. Moreover, safety nets should preferably be financed countercyclically so that in times of crisis, when the needs of the poor are the greatest, they can be expanded. However, in many African countries, very few safety net programs are fully funded even in stable times.

This chapter's main findings indicate spending on safety nets in Africa is low—except in middle-income countries (MICs) in southern Africa—but increasing. Many countries use costly general subsidies to redistribute income, which fails to benefit the poor. Nevertheless, well-targeted safety nets are affordable in Africa if spending on inefficient universal and categorical programs can be reallocated to programs that target the extremely poor and specific vulnerable groups. New wealth generated from extractive industries will also bring more fiscal space in a large number of African countries. Leveraging donor funding for safety nets will continue to be essential, especially in low-income countries (LICs), and should be coordinated into a collective financing envelope or "basket" that can be used to smooth the funding of safety nets over time. Ensuring that funding supports the harmonization of programs into one coherent system will make safety net programs more effective and sustainable over the long term. But successfully reforming safety nets also depends on political viability. Shifting away from emergency and categorical programs and moving toward better-targeted instruments requires an in-depth understanding of administrative and political challenges.

Spending on Safety Nets

In most African countries, especially LICs, spending on social safety nets is low in comparison with that in other countries of the world. As shown in table 5.1, spending averages about 1.7 percent as a share of GDP and 4.4 percent of total government spending in most African countries. Average spending on safety nets in LICs is about 1.1 percent of GDP and 3.7 percent of total government spending. Compared to other developing countries, where average spending generally falls between 1 and 2 percent of GDP, these figures are on the low end (Grosh *et al.* 2008).[1,2] Safety net spending in Africa is also low compared with spending on health and education. In Mali, safety net spending constitutes only 8 percent of spending on health and education, and in Burkina Faso, health and education spending is 14 times higher than spending on safety nets.

Even this level of spending can be a nontrivial amount for LICs. Given the large extent of poverty (that is, the need for safety nets) and the low national income (that is, resources available to distribute), this level of spending may seem inadequate for meeting the needs of the many poor. However, because the tax base is also low, spending 1 percent of GDP is nontrivial for many governments, especially in fiscally constrained and highly indebted countries. To justify increasing budget envelopes for safety nets (or even keeping them at current levels), countries must ensure that spending is more efficient and produces significant results. Nevertheless, with the boom of extractive industries, the natural resource revenue will bring more fiscal space in several African countries, which could be used to finance targeted investments in the poor.

In comparison, in southern African countries with government-driven safety net systems, spending is similar to that in other MICs worldwide. In African MICs, in which safety nets largely consist of categorical and universal programs, spending is significantly higher—about 2.7 percent of GDP and 7.0 percent of total government spending. These spending levels are in line with those of MICs throughout the world and may be considered relatively adequate and affordable. Nevertheless, even with generous government allocations for safety net programs, spending should be efficient and achieve the maximum impact at the lowest available cost.

Because spending varies depending on crisis cycles, spending on safety nets in Africa has been increasing over the past couple of years. Figure 5.1 plots the

Table 5.1 Cost and Financing of Safety Nets

Country	Spending on social safety nets (% of GDP, including government and donor spending)			Share of total government spending, excluding subsidies (%)	Share financed by government, excluding subsidies (%)	Share financed by donors (%)	Years covered
	Excluding general subsidies	Including general subsidies	General subsidies only				
Benin	0.3	0.9	0.5	1.1	35	65	Average 2005–10
Botswana	3.7	3.7	0.0	9.5	100	0	Average 2009/10–2012/13
Burkina Faso	0.6	1.3	0.7	<1.0	20	80	Average 2005–09
Cameroon	0.2	1.6	1.4	1.5	23	77	Average 2008–10
Ethiopia	1.2[a]	1.2[a]	0.0	—	0	100	2009
Kenya	0.8	0.8	0.0	1.0	29	71	2010
Lesotho	4.6	4.6	0.0	8.0	—	—	2010/11
Liberia	1.5	1.5	0.0	4.4	6	94	Average 2008–11
Madagascar	1.1	1.1	0.0	5.0	—	—	2010
Mali	0.5	0.5	0.1	—	40	60	Average 2006–09
Mauritania	1.3	3.2	1.9	4.6	62	38	Average 2008–13
Mauritius	4.4	5.2	0.8	9.0	—	—	2008/09
Mozambique	1.7	3.1	1.4	—	38	62	2010
Niger	—	—	—	1.0–5.0	33	67	Average 2001–06
Rwanda	1.1	1.1	0.0	—	—	—	2010/11
Sierra Leone	3.5	5.6	2.1	13.1	15	85	2011
South Africa	3.5	—	—	—	—	—	2010
Swaziland	2.1	2.1	0.0	—	—	—	2010/11
Tanzania	0.3	0.3	0.0	1.0	—	—	2011
Togo	0.5	1.3	0.8	1.8	25	75	Average 2008–10
Zambia	0.2	2.1	1.9	—	25	75	2010/11

table continues next page

Table 5.1 Cost and Financing of Safety Nets *(continued)*

Country	Spending on social safety nets (% of GDP, including government and donor spending)			Share of total government spending, excluding subsidies (%)	Share financed by government, excluding subsidies (%)	Share financed by donors (%)	Years covered
	Excluding general subsidies	Including general subsidies	General subsidies only				
Average	1.7	2.2	0.6	4.4	32	68	—
Average for LICs	1.1	1.7	0.6	3.7	27.5	72.5	—
Average for MICs	2.7	3.2	0.7	7.0	49.3	50.7	—
Average for established systems	3.9	4.5	0.4	9.3	100	0	—
Average for emerging systems	1.5	1.7	0.2	2.8	28	72	—
Average for early stage or no plans	1.0	2.1	1.0	4.5	26.4	73.6	—
Average for Eastern Europe and Central Asia	1.8[b]	1.8[b]	—	—	—	—	Latest 2008–10
Average for Latin America and the Caribbean	1.1[c]	1.1[c]	—	—	—	—	2010
Average for Middle East and North Africa	0.7	6.4[d]	—	—	—	—	Latest

Sources: Country safety net assessments; Silva, Levin, and Morgandi 2013; Woolard and Leibbrandt 2010; World Bank's Europe and Central Asia Social Protection database; World Bank's Latin America and the Caribbean Social Protection database.

Note: — = not available. Numbers may not add up because of rounding errors. Except general budget support, the spending data presented include donor financing but exclude funding by the private sector.
a. Includes only the Productive Safety Net Program and does not include spending on other safety net programs.
b. Covers government spending only, including subsidies in very rare cases, where data are available. Data are for the latest year between 2008 and 2010.
c. Data are for 2010 for 10 countries in Latin America and the Caribbean.
d. Data are for the latest year available for 11 countries in the Middle East and North Africa. Spending includes general subsidies and ration cards.

Figure 5.1 Safety Net Spending Trends in Selected Countries, 2005–2011

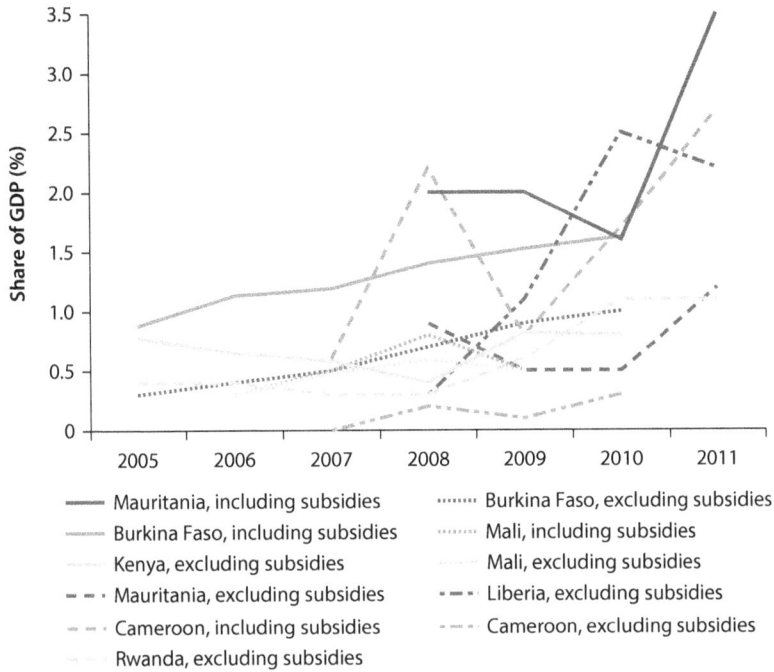

Sources: Ministry of State for Planning, National Development, and Vision 2030 2012; World Bank 2011a, 2011b, 2012a, 2012b, 2013a.
Note: Data on Cameroon in 2011 include spending only on fuel subsidies.

increasing spending levels in seven countries since 2005. The increase is mainly due to three main factors: (a) an increase in general government subsidies in response to the food, fuel, and financial crises; (b) an increase in food-related emergency programs in response to rising food prices and food insecurity in many countries; and (c) an increase in donor spending on safety nets. The rise in spending varies from country to country. In Liberia, the country with the sharpest rise in safety net spending, the increase is mainly attributable to new budget allocations for public works, school feeding, and other food distribution programs by donors in the postconflict environment. In Kenya, safety net spending doubled between 2008 and 2010, mainly because of the relief and recovery response to the 2008 drought and the new cash transfer programs that have started since 2009. In Benin and Burkina Faso, spending has increased more steadily because of a gradual expansion of donor-funded programs, although Benin also increased its subsidies. In Cameroon, in contrast, the large increases in food and fuel subsidies that were prompted by the crisis are the driver of overall spending trends, which remain highly volatile.

The bulk of spending is accounted for by emergency and food-based programs or categorical and universal transfers, and very little spending on safety nets is allocated to programs aimed at reducing chronic poverty and vulnerability (table 5.2). In many West African countries (Benin, Burkina Faso, Cameroon,

Table 5.2 Percentage of Social Safety Net Spending, by Program Type, Selected Countries

Country	School feeding	Public works programs	Fee waivers	Cash transfers and vouchers	Food and in-kind distributions	Nutrition programs	Other
Benin	56	16	12	1	8	3	4
Botswana	12	8	0	22	0	1	57[a]
Cameroon	8	6	44	1	40	<1	0
Lesotho[b]	42	0	0	47[c]	0	10	1
Liberia	34	17	0	5	9	33	2
Mali	18	15	0	0	36	31	0
Mauritania	12	8	7	5	59	8	0
Mauritius	0.5	0	0	87	0	0	13[d]
Sierra Leone	17	21	32	0.2	13	9	7
Togo	6	6	14	0	59	14	1
Zambia	2	—	0	2	27	1	69

Source: Country safety net assessments.

Note: — = not available. These figures include both government and donor financing, as applicable, but exclude general subsidies.

a. This figure includes scholarships.

b. The figures for Lesotho are approximations, calculated by the authors.

c. This figure includes some in-kind and food transfers and medical fee waivers through the Public Assistance Program.

d. This figure includes in-kind programs such as housing, school supplies, tertiary grants, and bus subsidies.

Liberia, Mali, Mauritania, Niger, Sierra Leone, and Togo), the majority of safety net spending is allocated to emergency and food-based programs. In 2005, in Burkina Faso, 90 percent of safety net spending was on food-based programs, and this allocation remained high (70 percent) in 2009. The equivalent figure for Togo is 72 percent, for Liberia 75 percent, for Niger 80 percent, and for Mauritania 94 percent (latest years available). During the 2008 crisis, almost 80 percent of safety net spending in Cameroon (excluding subsidies) was allocated to emergency programs that largely provided food staples for free or at a reduced price. In Kenya, although poverty-targeted cash transfers to combat long-term vulnerability and poverty have seen steady growth, the bulk of funding is still spent on relief and recovery efforts. Between 2005 and 2010, 53 percent of safety net spending went to the General Food Distribution program. However, in several MICs in southern Africa (Botswana, Lesotho, and Mauritius), the largest share of spending is allocated to cash transfer programs because of the focus on old age and on categorical and universal programs in those countries. In Botswana, for example, two-thirds of the health spending envelope is devoted to programs targeted to chronically vulnerable groups such as the elderly, orphans, and schoolchildren in need. Botswana also has large scholarship programs that are counted in the overall safety net budget. In addition, in Mauritius, cash transfer programs account for 87 percent of spending because of generous old-age pensions.

In several countries, general food and fuel subsidies take up the lion's share of safety net spending even though they do not benefit the poorest segments of the population. In 2011, energy subsidies amounted to 1.5 percent of regional GDP, or 5.5 percent of total government revenues, in Sub-Saharan Africa (IMF 2013).

In Burkina Faso, spending on general subsidies represented over 90 percent of government safety net spending between 2005 and 2009. In Cameroon, food and fuel subsidies cost the government over 1.4 percent of GDP and over 6 percent of total government expenditures between 2008 and 2010. It is estimated that in 2011 fuel subsidies alone escalated to 2.7 percent of Cameroon's GDP. Benin, Mauritania, Mozambique, and Togo also use expensive general subsidies to distribute revenue, even though a large volume of evidence shows the regressivity of such untargeted subsidies (see chapter 4). Evidence from Benin, Cameroon, and Togo indicates that increases in subsidies that have been made in response to crises have crowded out other more regular social spending. In Zambia, transfers for farm inputs are partially targeted to farmers, but very large errors of inclusion benefit better-off farmers. Together the Maize Price Support Scheme and the Farmer Input Support Program account for about 93 percent of safety net spending in Zambia.

Financing by Governments and Donors

Donors are the main financiers of safety nets in Africa (not including general subsidies). The most important organizations include the World Food Programme (WFP), the United Nations Children's Fund (which receives much of its funding through bilateral government programs), and a number of bilateral and smaller relief organizations. As seen in table 5.1, donors provide 68 percent of spending on safety nets in Africa. This share increases to almost three-fourths if MICs are excluded because they generally have generous government programs, usually for the elderly. Several countries depend increasingly on donor funds to finance their safety nets, including Burkina Faso, where donor funding has increased almost fivefold in recent years. In Ethiopia, the Productive Safety Net Program is almost 100 percent financed by donors. Mauritania, an LIC, is an exception: an average of 62 percent of safety net spending (not including fuel subsidies) in 2010–12 was domestically funded. The WFP supports school feeding programs, food-for-work programs, voucher programs, and other food distribution programs in almost every country in Africa. The World Bank is also increasingly supporting targeted safety net programs in countries such as Kenya, Niger, and Tanzania. Private sector partners, including Equity Bank in Kenya, also provide a small share of funding.

Both governments and donors have mainly prioritized food-based programs. Donors tend to focus on therapeutic feeding and nutrition-related safety nets, and governments on cereal banks and on provision of staple foods at reduced prices. This focus is evident in many of the countries bordering the Sahel, which repeatedly suffer from food insecurity. International donors are also supporting small, poverty-targeted cash transfer programs such as the Bourse maman conditional cash transfer (CCT) in Mali, the Zomba CCT in Malawi, the Bomi cash transfer in Liberia, and the Nahouri cash transfers in Burkina Faso. In recent years, the WFP has implemented food voucher programs in several countries in response to food price increases, especially those affecting urban households (in Burkina Faso, Mauritania, and the Republic of Congo, for instance). Donors are scaling up their funding for poverty-targeted cash transfers in Ethiopia, Kenya, Niger, and Tanzania. Recently, many donors have begun to fund the provision of cash transfers or vouchers rather than in-kind benefits, given the lower transaction costs involved and the greater flexibility that cash transfers give to households.

The need for donors to finance safety nets, especially in LICs and in many lower-MICs, will continue at least in the short and medium terms. Governments and donors should seek to pool their funding as much as possible to align all resources with the priorities set out in the country strategies and to support the harmonization of programs and the building of a coherent safety net system. Pooling donor funds can also make it easier for countries to respond to emergencies and thus reduce the need for ad hoc emergency aid. This kind of contingent financing for emergencies has been used in Ethiopia to respond to droughts and is also being explored in Kenya. The main lesson from Ethiopia's experience is that pooling donor funds for a single objective such as food security allows governments to take a more planned, effective, and unified approach to crises than a haphazard relief-oriented approach. In the medium to long term, however, especially in MICs, funding should be secured from domestic sources to transition into a fully government-driven system. This transition has yet to take place in African countries.

Sustainability: What Would Be Needed to Meet the Needs in the Medium Term?

The high costs of universal programs such as subsidies and old-age pensions risk becoming unsustainable in the medium and long terms. In several countries, demographic changes such as the aging of the population and the fiscal pressure of the recent global recession have caused universal programs to become fiscally unsustainable, a problem that could crowd out targeted programs. In Lesotho, government revenues have drastically declined over the past couple of years, thereby making the expansion of existing safety net programs or the introduction of new ones fiscally impossible. The old-age pensions, school feeding, and tertiary bursary programs account for the vast majority of spending on direct transfer programs, though the benefits of all three programs accrue mainly to the better off. The same problem occurs in Swaziland, where although there is more fiscal space, the global recession has caused old-age grants to be paid intermittently and has resulted in the program prioritizing beneficiaries with bank accounts (generally the nonpoor). In addition, public assistance benefits to poor households with no elderly members have been suspended.

In Madagascar, the cost of social security benefits for formal sector workers increased from 44 percent to 86 percent of total social protection spending between 2007 and 2010, thus squeezing the share that is available for poverty-targeted programs. In Mauritius, the country with the highest noncontributory old-age pension spending on the continent (about 3 percent of GDP), these costs increased by 30 percent in real terms between 2004/05 and 2008/09 and are expected to double by 2025.

Reallocating resources from universal programs to poverty-targeted programs can significantly increase the extent to which safety nets can reach the poorest. The increasing costs of social protection indicate a pressing need to rationalize spending and to improve the quality and increase the efficiency of existing programs. Safety net assessments for countries all over the region have indicated a need to carefully review the cost-effectiveness of universal and categorical programs to assess their effects in terms of reducing poverty and inequity. Then countries must start reallocating spending to programs that are targeted to the poorest and most vulnerable. The capacity constraints in most African countries and the political challenges involved in tight poverty targeting argue in favor of prioritizing certain subgroups of the poor, such as households with vulnerable children.

As more African countries are profiting from mineral resource wealth, programs such as safety nets that invest in the poor will be increasingly affordable. In addition to the oil- and energy-exporting countries, over the next 10 years about 30 countries in Sub-Saharan Africa are expected to depend on exports of mineral resources (over 20 percent of exports) (World Bank 2013b). Invested well, to address long-run poverty and improve human capital outcomes for the poor, these funds could help propel African countries forward quickly. However, these prospects involve significant political economy considerations and forward-looking strategic planning (see the next section for a discussion on political economy).

Simulations show that fiscally sustainable yet effective safety nets can be provided in Africa.[3] Targeting safety nets only to the extremely poor or food insecure or to specific groups such as poor families with children or the underemployed may make safety nets fiscally sustainable within current and future estimated budget envelopes. For instance, in Zambia, a cost of only about 1 percent of GDP (just about half the proposed 2012 budget for the Farmer Input Support Program) is estimated as necessary to cover the poorest 20 percent of the population. In Cameroon, an estimated cost of 0.5 percent of GDP is needed to provide CFAF 1,000 per month to half the chronically poor. This figure is significantly less than the 1.6 percent of GDP that was spent on average between 2008 and 2010, including on subsidies.

However, providing adequate safety net coverage to all of the poor would cost substantially more, especially in West Africa. For instance, in Benin the cost to provide CFAF 1,000 per person per month to all of the poor and vulnerable is estimated at the equivalent of 1.0–1.2 percent of GDP. In Togo, the estimate is higher—1.8 percent of GDP—to provide the same transfer amount to all of the chronically poor, and an additional 1.0 percent of GDP is needed to cover transitory poor. These levels are significantly higher than the amount that the government and donors currently spend on safety nets if subsidies are excluded but not much higher than what they spend if general subsidies are included.

The Political Economy of Safety Nets in Africa

To be successful, safety net programs need to be technically sound, administratively and financially feasible, and politically viable.[4] Political decision making and preferences determine how to allocate finite budgets between social protection and other expenditures, and within the social protection budget, governments must determine how to allocate funds between different types of targeted, universal, and categorical programs. Throughout Africa, each country's context—including the former colonial regime, the extent of democratization, and the occurrence of past conflicts (as in Rwanda and Sierra Leone)—influences social policy. For instance, in the past, Kenyan politicians have used selective food aid distribution to secure electoral support, thus denying access to some vulnerable groups in the process (De Waal 1997). In South Africa, politics strongly shaped the development of the social pension scheme in the early 1990s after the end of apartheid. Other southern African countries, such as Lesotho and Swaziland, have adopted generous pension schemes along the lines of the South African model although they were not strongly politically motivated. Also, because of the character of governance in Africa, development partners and donors have a strong influence, especially in highly indebted countries and in many countries in West Africa.

In reality, reallocating safety net spending away from emergency food aid, universal categorical programs, and subsidies and toward poverty-targeted programs such as cash transfers is difficult. First, targeting can be costly and administratively complex. Second, many African countries still categorize safety nets as "handouts" and are concerned that they may engender an attitude of dependency in recipients, although in southern Africa, cash transfers are much more acceptable because of the inherited rights-based social policy that prioritizes categorical groups. Third, increasing the targeting efficiency of safety nets involves taking away benefits from many current recipients, which is politically very challenging and could lead to social unrest and reduced electoral support for the government in power. Experience from programs in Colombia and Sri Lanka that have transformed from universal and costly to better targeted and poverty focused show that leakage of benefits to the better off can be an important way for governments to sustain political support, and narrow, albeit effective programs may completely lose political viability and become dismantled (Hickey 2007). Box 5.1 raises a number of issues for African countries to consider in moving forward with energy subsidy reform and the use of mineral resource revenues. In moving forward, countries will need to get the balance right between (a) effectively targeting these funds to the poorest through safety nets or other investments in social services and (b) building both fiscally and politically sustainable social protection systems.

The role of safety nets in the context of subsidy reform and use of natural resource proceeds should be further explored with the unique political economy of each country in mind. In moving forward with efforts to rationalize public spending in Africa to better reach the poorest, safety nets are one

Box 5.1 Moving Forward with Subsidy Reform: What Can Africa Learn from Other Countries?

Indonesia, 2005

Reforming fuel subsidies has been a persistent policy challenge in Indonesia. Indonesia has attempted to tackle subsidy reform a number of times during this period to improve the fiscal position and achieve other policy objectives such as improving energy efficiency and protecting the environment.

Reforms since 1997. The first two attempts at cutting subsidies (in 1998 and 2003) were unsuccessful. Drastic cuts instead of a gradual approach, poor communication, and general dissatisfaction with the government led to violent protests, and the measures were finally rolled back. Concerned over the increasing fiscal pressure from fuel subsidies, the government undertook two large fuel price increases in 2005. As a result, the price of diesel fuel doubled and that of kerosene nearly tripled. Protests again took place in opposition to the reform but with less intensity than before. The government was led by President Susilo Bambang Yudhoyono, who was first elected in 2004 and won a convincing reelection in 2009.

Mitigating Measures. The 2005 reforms were accompanied by unconditional cash transfers for 19.2 million poor households (35 percent of the population). Other measures included a health insurance program for the poor, a school operational assistance program, and an expanded rural infrastructure support project. A number of analyses have credited the reduced intensity of protests in 2005 to the creation of these welfare programs.

Lessons. A rapid reduction in subsidies can generate opposition to reform, whereas a popular government and a clear communication strategy increase the likelihood of success. Targeted cash transfers have proved to be effective and popular mitigating measures.

The Philippines, 1996

The Philippines is a net oil importer. Until the late 1990s, the downstream oil sector was heavily regulated, resulting in price subsidies of fuel products when international oil prices rose. The Oil Price Stabilization Fund (OPSF) stabilized domestic prices of fuel products by collecting or paying out the difference between regulated domestic prices and actual import costs. Increases in domestic prices were politically difficult to implement. As a result, the national government had to regularly replenish the OPSF.

Reforms. Initially, the political environment was not conducive to reform of fuel subsidies, because President Fidel Ramos had won the election by only a small margin and his party was a minority in both chambers of the Philippine congress. Nevertheless, a public communication campaign began at an early stage and included a nationwide roadshow to inform the public of the problems caused by oil price subsidies. Although the president's party was a minority in congress, he set up a coordination body between the executive and the two chambers of congress and used it to prioritize the oil deregulation bill and forge consensus on it. In 1996, the government passed the law to abolish the OPSF and to allow the prices to move freely.

box continues next page

Box 5.1 Moving Forward with Subsidy Reform: What Can Africa Learn from Other Countries?
(continued)

The industry remains liberalized today, and movements in international oil prices have been passed through to domestic prices.

Mitigating Measures. The 1996 law included a transition period during which fuel product prices were adjusted monthly using an automatic pricing mechanism. During that period, the government provided transfers to the OPSF to absorb price increases in excess of a threshold. More recently, the authorities announced several measures to mitigate the impact of the food and fuel crises in mid-2008. The government launched a package of pro-poor spending programs that are financed by windfall value added tax revenue from high oil prices. The policy package included electricity subsidies for indigent families, college scholarships for low-income students, and subsidized loans to convert engines of public transportation vehicles to less costly liquefied petroleum gas. In addition, the government distributed subsidized rice to low-income families and started a conditional cash transfer program.

Lessons. The experience of the Philippines underscores the importance of planning, persistence, and a good communication plan in achieving a successful outcome. The survival of the reform to date can be attributed to its comprehensiveness and mitigating measures for the poor during the 2008 fuel price hike, which helped maintain popular support.

Source: IMF 2013.

---

important mitigating aspect that countries may want to have in place. Careful political economy considerations are needed when balancing tightly targeted programs with other investments that benefit a wider set of people and contribute to improved social outcomes. For example, more and more African countries are benefiting from newfound mineral resource wealth. These countries will need to get the balance right between (a) effectively targeting these funds to the poorest through safety nets or other investments in social services and (b) building a social protection system that is both fiscally and politically sustainable.

Consequently, initiatives to reform safety nets to be more effective should aim to take the middle ground. The trick is to develop safety net programs in a way that promotes economic transformation and supports the groups that most citizens agree are in need. Concentrating the benefits through targeting to the poorest and most vulnerable may be important politically to justify spending in fiscally constrained environments. Nevertheless, a certain level of national coverage is generally politically appealing. Striking the balance between covering enough people and targeting the right people with the right amount of benefits will make safety net systems both effective and sustainable. In countries with government-driven systems and with an existing social contract between the state and the citizens, the challenge lies in sustaining the contract while including the poor and keeping costs down. In countries where systems are fragmented and little trust exists between the citizens and the state, the key will be to create a sustainable social contract to enhance the role of social protection in overall poverty reduction.

To address these social and political concerns, policy makers may find that programs with a work requirement (such as public works) or with conditions that require beneficiaries to invest in their children's health and education (for example, CCTs) are attractive options. For example, reform of public works programs that previously were not particularly well targeted to the poor is ongoing in Tanzania. CCT programs are being tested and expanded; they have been piloted in Burkina Faso and Malawi. Nevertheless, the poorest and most vulnerable groups of society are often those that are likely to have the most difficulties in fulfilling program coresponsibilities and hence risk being excluded from receiving support if the program conditions are tightly enforced. Adopting mechanisms such as self-targeting, geographic targeting, and community-based targeting, which are less radical than direct poverty targeting through proxy means testing, may be useful. (Targeting mechanisms were discussed in more detail in chapter 4.)

Well-performing safety nets that provide support to the most vulnerable groups can be important mitigating mechanisms to facilitate reform of expensive general subsidy programs. In the first instance, governments may wish to establish programs that target the poorest income groups while gradually reducing the amount spent on subsidies or other regressive programs. The timing of price adjustments and the communication strategy used by the government in reforming general subsidies are very important elements of efforts to make subsidy reform politically feasible and acceptable to the public. In addition, having in place effective mitigating measures to compensate poor people who would otherwise suffer from price increases is crucial to prevent any increases in poverty. Safety nets have effectively been used in Indonesia (energy reform in 2005 and 2008) as well as in Jordan and Tunisia (food price reforms) while raising prices on staple goods. In other countries, such as in Nigeria, where increased fuel prices led to nationwide rioting in January 2012, no concrete safety net scheme was in place to protect the poorest from the increase in prices.

Ultimately, African countries need to make real trade-offs in designing safety net systems. Decision makers choose what they want their safety net systems to look like on the basis of what is best suited for their particular contexts and political, cultural, historical, and social preferences. These choices should be made with full information about the pros and cons of the approaches—in particular, those related to targeting and sophistication of program design, the expected impacts, and the costs that are likely incurred. For instance, universal or categorical programs, such as old-age pensions to everyone over the age of 65 or benefits to all families with children of primary school age, may be easier to undertake administratively even in capacity- and data-constrained environments. Providing cash to a large number of households may also be politically appealing. Nonetheless, universal and categorical programs are likely very expensive and ineffective ways of trying to reduce poverty. They may also encounter political resistance as "handouts" (as occurred, for instance, in Cameroon). On the contrary, well-targeted programs that provide cash only to specific eligible groups (defined using proxy means testing) and that include some form of coresponsibilities, such as conditions on health checkups or participation in microfinance training, may yield much better effects at a lower relative fiscal cost (because they are not universal). Although CCT programs that seek to enhance the productivity and promotion of poor households may be justified on the basis of success stories from other countries showing improved indicators of long-run poverty, such programs are highly complex to implement in LICs and may not be consistent with existing social contracts in countries that have strong preferences for redistribution and equity, such as in southern Africa.

Summary of Main Messages

Main messages of the chapter include the following:

- Spending on safety nets in Africa is low (except in MICs in southern Africa) but is highly variable over time and has been increasing since the global crisis. However, in many countries, general subsidies are costly and do not proportionately benefit the poor.

- Donors finance a large share of safety nets in Africa (excluding general subsidies), and such financing will continue to be necessary at least in the medium term, especially in LICs. Pooling and smoothing donor funding for safety nets would enable governments to prepare for crises in advance while continuing to build systems and scale up programs for the longer term.

- The concentration of safety net spending on scattered emergency and food-based programs means that neither donors nor governments have focused on funding sustainable safety nets designed to reduce long-term chronic poverty. A better allocation of social protection spending would make safety net programs more effective and more sustainable over the long term and make possible harmonization of disparate programs into a coherent national safety net.

- Well-targeted safety nets are affordable in Africa if inefficient universal and categorical programs can be rationalized and if this spending can be redirected to the poor and to specific vulnerable groups (depending on the objective of specific programs). Likewise, well-performing safety nets providing support to the most vulnerable groups can be important mitigating mechanisms to facilitate reform of expensive general subsidy programs. As more African countries are profiting from mineral resource wealth, more fiscal space will be available for programs such as safety nets that invest in the poor.

- Successfully reforming safety nets also depends on political viability. Shifting away from emergency and categorical programs toward better-targeted development-oriented instruments requires an in-depth understanding of administrative and political challenges. Careful political economy considerations are important when balancing tightly targeted programs with other investments that can benefit a wider set of people and contribute to improved social outcomes.

- Scaling up spending on safety nets in Africa should be focused on those programs that are well targeted and provide the most important effects while gradually reducing regressive or ineffective programs.

Notes

1. The World Bank's Africa Social Protection Strategy (2012–22) argues that, given the low level of spending on safety nets in African countries compared with international standards, safety nets are affordable in Africa and that experience suggests that national coverage in most countries can be achieved at the cost of only 1 or 2 percent of GDP (World Bank 2012c).

2. Average spending in Africa is on par with many other LICs around the world. However, when compared only to spending in lower-middle-income countries, safety net spending in Africa is generally lower. For instance, the Kyrgyz Republic and Tajikistan spend only 1.0 percent and 0.6 percent of GDP, respectively, on social assistance. However, in six lower-middle-income countries in Eastern Europe and Central Asia, social assistance spending in 2008 and 2009 ranged between 1.2 percent and 2.7 percent of GDP (Europe and Central Asia Social Protection database). Spending on safety nets (excluding subsidies) in the Republic of Yemen is about 1.5 percent of GDP (2008 and 2009), and in the West Bank and Gaza, it is just below 1 percent (Silva, Levin, and Morgandi 2013). In Honduras, safety net spending in 2010 was only 0.4 percent of GDP (Latin America and the Caribbean Social Protection database).

3. These estimates include a number of caveats. For instance, they assume equal distribution of benefits at current poverty line and poverty gap levels, they do not include administrative costs (15 percent is generally needed), and they assume perfect targeting (which is almost impossible to achieve in reality).

4. See Ouerghi (2005) and Hickey (2007) for a deeper discussion.

References

De Waal, Alex. 1997. *Famine Crimes: Politics and the Disaster Relief Industry in Africa.* Oxford, U.K.: James Curry.

Grosh, Margaret, Carlo del Ninno, Emil Tesliuc, and Azedine Ouerghi. 2008. *For Protection and Promotion: The Design and Implementation of Effective Safety Nets.* Washington, DC: World Bank.

Hickey, Sam. 2007. "Conceptualizing the Politics of Social Protection in Africa." BWPI Working Paper 4, Brooks World Poverty Institute, University of Manchester, Manchester, U.K.

IMF (International Monetary Fund). 2013. *Case Studies on Energy Subsidy Reform: Lessons and Implications*. Washington, DC.

Ministry of State for Planning, National Development, and Vision 2030. 2012. *Kenya Social Protection Sector Review*. Nairobi: Republic of Kenya.

Ouerghi, Azedine. 2005. "The Political Economy of Targeted Safety Nets." Social Safety Nets Primer Note 20, World Bank, Washington, DC.

Silva, Joana, Victoria Levin, and Matteo Morgandi. 2013. *Inclusion and Resilience: The Way Forward for Social Safety Nets in the Middle East and North Africa*. Washington, DC: World Bank.

Woolard, Ingrid, and Murray Leibbrandt. 2010. "The Evolution and Impact of Unconditional Cash Transfers in South Africa." Working Paper 51, Southern Africa Labour and Development Research Unit, University of Cape Town, Cape Town, South Africa.

World Bank. 2011a. *Burkina Faso: Social Safety Nets*. Washington, DC: World Bank.

———. 2011b. *Mali: Social Safety Nets*. Washington, DC: World Bank.

———. 2012a. "Cameroun: Filets Sociaux." World Bank, Washington, DC.

———. 2012b. *Lesotho: A Safety Net to End Extreme Poverty*. Washington, DC: World Bank.

———. 2012c. *Managing Risk, Promoting Growth: Developing Systems for Social Protection in Africa—The World Bank's Africa Social Protection Strategy, 2012–2022*. Washington, DC: World Bank.

———. 2013a. *Islamic Republic of Mauritania: Summary Analysis of Safety Net Programs and Costs*. Washington, DC: World Bank.

———. 2013b. "Securing the Transformational Potential in Africa's Mineral Resources." PowerPoint presentation, World Bank, Washington, DC.

CHAPTER 6

Moving Forward: Building Better Safety Nets in Africa

In this review, we analyzed the objectives, features, systems, performance, and financing of safety nets according to studies in 22 African countries. The purpose of the review was to assess the status of safety nets in Africa and their strengths and weaknesses and to identify areas for improvement in an effort to guide governments and donors in strengthening African safety net systems and helping them protect and promote poor and vulnerable people.

Despite two decades of strong economic growth, high poverty levels persist in Africa, especially in rural areas. Much of the economic growth is not benefiting a large share of the African population. In addition to high levels of chronic poverty, widespread vulnerability to a range of risks, such as environmental and economic shocks, can be found. New sources of vulnerability are emerging because of factors such as demographic trends, climate change, and governance challenges, which Africa's integration into the global economy has exposed. The effects of such shocks can be deep and long lasting. Also, as countries prosper, economic inequality may increase, and social structures and traditional safety nets may erode as a result of economic and social developments.

The uneven distribution of the growth dividend suggests that targeted efforts, such as safety nets, are necessary parts of poverty reduction strategies. Well-targeted safety nets are needed in Africa to protect and promote the chronically poor and vulnerable. Together with sustained growth, they have the potential to speed up poverty reduction and help the poor invest in human and physical capital. Given the World Bank's new goals for reducing extreme poverty to 3 percent by 2030, using safety nets for concentrating investments toward the poor will be essential in Africa. Safety nets can also provide support in times of shock and social change to those who are temporarily thrown into poverty and help them develop strategies to build up their resilience and avoid drawing down on their assets during times of hardship. Some groups are particularly vulnerable to the negative effects of shocks and persistent poverty, such as orphans, populations affected by HIV/AIDS, widows, and elderly people with no family support.

Although governments are increasingly aware of this need to provide safety nets, until recently, many African countries approached social protection on a largely ad hoc basis. Safety nets have not been used as programs to help reduce poverty on a larger scale in Africa. But when the recent global economic and food and fuel price crises threatened progress in poverty reduction, safety nets increasingly began to be viewed as core instruments for poverty reduction in the region. Given the extent of poverty and vulnerability, safety nets in Africa cannot reach all the poor but need to focus on the extreme poor and specific vulnerable groups for maximum impact and affordability. As new natural resource wealth is discovered and revenues increase, fiscal space for financing investments in the poor will become more and more affordable in Africa.

The Need for a Systematic Approach to Safety Nets

In most African countries, government-led social safety nets are a relatively new phenomenon, and although they are increasing, overall levels of spending and coverage remain low, except in some middle-income countries (MICs). Although exceptions exist, such as universal old-age pension programs in MICs and some of the programs targeted to specific groups, the coverage of most individual programs is low relative to the total number of eligible beneficiaries countrywide. In particular, the limited evidence available suggests that less than a quarter of poor and vulnerable households in Africa have access to safety nets. Significant duplication, overlap, and fragmentation further mask low coverage rates. Average spending on safety nets in low-income countries (LICs) is about 1.1 percent of gross domestic product (GDP), which is low given the extent of poverty and in comparison to the spending in other developing countries, which generally falls on average between 1 and 2 percent of GDP (Grosh *et al.* 2008).

The development of safety nets in Africa differs because of country contexts and is driven by the specific political economy and sociocultural background of each country. The policy frameworks, approaches, and institutional arrangements that govern safety net systems are not homogeneous across the continent. For instance, MICs in southern Africa have strong government-driven systems based on horizontal equity, whereas in LICs and fragile states, donors tend to influence the social protection more with most programs focusing on emergency relief, especially in West Africa and the Sahel. Any measures to strengthen safety nets need to be designed in ways that take into account these context-specific factors to effectively meet the needs of the targeted groups.

Despite the heterogeneity in context and policy across the continent, the concept of safety nets as a core instrument for poverty reduction is taking hold, and dialogue and debate on social protection are expanding. More and more African countries are preparing social protection strategies that serve as a basis on which to build effective and efficient safety net systems. Experience from some African countries, such as Rwanda, shows that clear action plans with careful costing and implementation measures are crucial for putting these strategies into operation.

Safety nets in Africa generally tend not to be housed together in well-designated institutions and tend to lack coordinating bodies such as interministerial steering committees. Responsibility for government safety net programs is generally spread over a number of different ministries, such as the president's office; the prime minister's office; the ministry of finance; the ministries of social affairs, women and family, and employment; and other cross-sectoral ministries, each with its own mandate. Many of these ministries often lack significant political decision-making power within the government. Meanwhile, fragmented donor support has left LICs with a host of isolated programs and pilots, lacking coordination or a political champion. For instance, both Liberia and Madagascar have more than five different public works programs, each operated by different donor organizations and ministries.

As a result, few countries have well-planned safety net systems that are capable of taking a strategic approach to reducing poverty and vulnerability. Instead, safety net systems are generally composed of a large number of small and fragmented programs that tend to be donor driven. Our analysis suggests that 50 percent of the countries reviewed have no system of social safety net programs. However, 36 percent are making progress in building a system, and 14 percent have a system in place.

Programs aimed at providing support to the chronically poor and vulnerable and helping them move out of poverty are uncommon outside MICs such as Botswana, South Africa, and Swaziland (which have social pension programs). In LICs, such as those in West Africa, safety nets are focused on emergency relief and food-related issues. In a handful of countries, such as Ethiopia and Tanzania, however, sustainable and more institutionalized programs are starting to appear that are backed by influential ministries, such as the ministry of finance and the ministry of economy and planning. And although national poverty-targeted cash transfer programs are not common, some that do exist and are currently being expanded, such as Kenya's Cash Transfer for Orphans and Vulnerable Children (CT-OVC) program and Rwanda's Vision 2020 Umurenge Program (VUP). Across the countries, school feeding programs; public works programs; programs providing transfers to specific groups, such as children and the elderly; and other in-kind transfer programs are the most common, but additionally, 17 of the 22 countries reviewed have general subsidies (food, fuel, or input) that are mostly untargeted. About 82 percent of the countries have categorical transfer programs that target specific vulnerable groups such as orphans, people affected by HIV, the elderly, indigents, and people with disabilities. Because of limitations in demographic data and weak enforcement capacity, however, these programs often lack clear criteria for establishing household vulnerability levels.

Many LICs and fragile countries tend to react to crises and disasters, providing support only as emergency relief. Thus, they do not have in place long-term safety net programs. Therefore, shock response mechanisms tend to be weak, inflexible, and unpredictable. In addition, very little information is available about the effectiveness of food distribution and emergency relief programs that are common in West Africa (for example, in Benin, Burkina Faso, Cameroon, Mali, and Mauritania).

Increasing the accuracy of the targeting of African safety net programs is likely to involve combining a number of targeting methods that together can distinguish the appropriate households and individuals. Which targeting approach is chosen will depend on the program's objective and the institutional capacity of the implementing agencies. Also, the approach will have to be customized to the particular poverty profile and political economy of the country. Household-level income and consumption data are often not precise enough to be reliable as the sole basis for identifying those most in need. Assessing the targeting accuracy of programs is important irrespective of which targeting method is used. To achieve their goals at a reasonable cost, safety nets need to be accurately targeted, cover the identified groups, provide adequate benefits, and be flexible enough to adjust to changing needs and respond to shocks.

Well-targeted safety nets are affordable in Africa, especially if inefficient universal and categorical spending can be reduced or redirected to the extremely poor and to specific vulnerable groups and if fragmented programs can be harmonized. In LICs, where poverty is high and government income low, attracting donor funds will continue to be vital to support the safety net agenda, both in the short run and the longer run. With the exception of universal programs, such as those providing old-age benefits and general subsidies, donors finance a large share of safety nets in Africa—over 80 percent in Burkina Faso, Liberia, Mali, and Sierra Leone. In MICs, however, current public budgets are sufficient to provide adequate support for the poorest. For instance, in Cameroon, estimates are that providing adequate safety nets to half the chronic poor would cost as little as 0.5 percent of GDP.

In many countries, general subsidies are costly mechanisms for redistributing income and often do not benefit the poor. This is the case for the fuel subsidies in Cameroon, Mauritania, and Sierra Leone. Reducing poorly targeted programs and subsidies can make fiscal space for more effective and better-targeted safety nets. Likewise, well-performing safety nets providing support to the most vulnerable groups can be important mitigating mechanisms to facilitate reform of expensive general subsidy programs. Growing natural resource discoveries across Africa (see World Bank 2013) are also likely to create additional fiscal space for safety nets.

Several countries are actively increasing the effectiveness of their existing programs and are building a coherent safety net system. A number of countries are actively expanding the scale of their existing programs, including some that are relatively well targeted (such as the programs run by the Tanzania Social Action Fund, Ghana's Livelihood Empowerment against Poverty program, or Kenya's CT-OVC program). Also, more countries are moving toward building safety net systems and programs that are predictable and that are flexible enough to respond to crises. Ethiopia's Productive Safety Net Program (PSNP) has long been a pioneer in this respect. More broadly, household-level income and consumption data are often not precise enough to be reliable as the sole basis for identifying those most in need. Thus, increasing the accuracy of the targeting of African safety net programs is likely to involve combining a number of targeting methods that together can distinguish the most vulnerable and poorest households and individuals. Which targeting approach is chosen will depend on the program's objective and the institutional capacity of the implementing agencies. The approach will have to be customized to the particular poverty profile and political economy of the country in question.

The Way Forward: How to Build Safety Net Systems in Africa

Moving ahead, countries in Africa must start by articulating a long-term vision for a system of safety nets and a strategy for achieving that vision. African governments should continue to prepare social protection strategies and put them into operation. To achieve the vision, taking into consideration the characteristics and size of the most vulnerable groups in the population and existing program coverage, policy makers should be guided by the following choices:

- The type of safety net programs and how best to scale them up, harmonize objectives, and minimize overlap
- The appropriate financing mechanisms over the medium to long term
- Institutional arrangements—in particular defining the roles and responsibilities of ministries and implementing agencies and the method of coordination

Another key step for governments is to integrate, harmonize, and consolidate their safety net programs. The review shows that a small number of coordinated and well-functioning programs can effectively and feasibly meet the needs of the poorest. In part, countries can achieve this goal by consolidating programs that have some overlap in their objective or target populations or by harmonizing their benefits, services, and eligibility conditions. For instance, Rwanda's support to the poor is largely channeled in the form of cash transfers and public works through the VUP, its flagship social protection program. The VUP and FARG (Fond d'Assistance aux Rescapées du Génocide, or Assistance Fund for Genocide Survivors) are slowly being harmonized (with their beneficiary lists being merged) to reduce duplication and cost, thereby enabling their expansion on a much wider scale. Furthermore, building links between programs can help maximize synergies, such as by making graduation from one program to another easier for people. Preparing the strategy for such harmonization will require an assessment of existing coverage, expenditure levels, impact, efficiency, interaction, and effectiveness of programs to identify gaps and areas where reforms are necessary.

Scaling up safety nets in Africa should be focused on those programs that are well targeted and provide the most needed benefits, while gradually reducing regressive or ineffective programs. As mentioned previously, because of Africa's widespread poverty and vulnerability, safety nets cannot reach all of the poor but need to focus on the poorest and most vulnerable to ensure maximum impact and affordability. The allocation of safety net spending on fragmented emergency programs in many African countries illustrates the lack of focus, from either donors or governments, on creating safety nets aimed at reducing long-term chronic poverty. This situation is now starting to change. Ethiopia, Kenya, Rwanda, and Tanzania are building national programs for enhanced efficiency and coverage.

To create safety net systems, countries must build strong operational tools, adopting common platforms as much as possible. Building blocks, such as beneficiary registries and targeting and payment systems, that programs can use to effectively deliver support to targeted groups are the basis for a safety net system. Furthermore, adopting common platforms across programs can lead to economies of scale and increase institutional efficiencies. For instance, some countries in the region are already experimenting with single beneficiary registries, harmonized targeting systems, and unified payment mechanisms. Similarly, some countries are adopting common systems for collecting contributions, disseminating information, and performing monitoring and evaluation (M&E). Over time, these systems can be linked to national databases, such as those for civil registration, or to a range of poverty-targeted programs.

Safety net systems need to be created and developed during stable times so that they are ready and available to respond when crises hit. It takes time to create safety net programs and systems to effectively and efficiently help households affected by shock. Most countries in Africa (including Benin, Cameroon, Mauritania, and Sierra Leone) did not have safety nets capable of effectively responding to the recent global crises but had to resort to inefficient and expensive universal handouts. Pooling funding from donors as much as possible is crucial to make building the system over the long run feasible while still being able to respond to emergencies as they arise.

Data collection and the M&E systems that support safety net programs also need to be improved. Basic and core data on the number and type of beneficiaries reached and information about program targeting and impact are imperative to improve the design and coordination of programs, to keep decision makers informed, and to attract financial resources and donor support. For instance, an assessment of target accuracy is necessary to determine which programs should be scaled up. So is an assessment of their effect or final outcome. Although the body of evidence from impact evaluations of African safety net programs is growing quickly, more is needed to provide more and better lessons for the design and scale-up of larger government programs.

The role of safety nets in the context of subsidy reform and use of mineral resource proceeds should be explored further with the unique political economy of each country in mind. In moving forward with the efforts in Africa to rationalize public spending for better reaching the poorest, safety nets are one important mitigating aspect that countries may want to have in place. Careful political economy considerations are important when balancing tightly targeted programs with other investments that can benefit a wider set of people and contribute to improved social outcomes. As more and more African countries are benefiting from newfound mineral resource wealth, it will be especially important to get the balance right between (a) effectively targeting these funds to the poorest through safety nets or other investments in social services and (b) building a social protection system that is both fiscally and politically sustainable.

Recommendations by Country Context

Because great variation exists in the state of safety nets across Africa, countries need to pursue the reform agenda most suitable to their particular context. One size does not fit all, and the way social protection systems evolve will depend on country characteristics, such as level of development, institutional capacity, and political economy. MICs tend to have broader range and deeper coverage of social protection programs than do LICs. In comparison, LICs have fewer resources relative to the number of poor and vulnerable individuals and are more constrained in administrative capacity. Besides the level of economic development, the objectives, size, and target groups of social protection programs depend on prevailing views about entitlements to social protection, which are influenced by notions of justice, perceived causes of poverty, and concerns with inequality, among other factors. Safety net strategies should also consider differences in a country's capacity to plan, coordinate, implement, and deliver social protection programs and to develop policy. Countries with weak capacity—which tend to be LICs—should focus on delivering well a limited set of simple programs and should add more complex, innovative elements only once more capacity has been built.

Hence, the path of safety net development and reform should be based on careful analysis of each country's specific needs, challenges, and constraints. The 22 safety net assessments provide thoughtful country-specific recommendations for doing so. However, some recommendations can be made that are broadly grouped according to the country typology used in this review (see table 1.1 in chapter 1). These recommendations are intended to serve as guidance for other countries on how to develop their safety net systems and learn from the experience in these 22 African countries.

The following recommendations apply to countries that are classified as "early stage or no plans."[1] Such countries have no solid plans for a national safety net system or no adequate programs in place. They mainly consist of LICs and fragile states but also include some MICs whose main form of income redistribution is through general subsidies.

- *Develop and put into operation a safety net strategy.* This strategy should assign clear institutional responsibilities for safety net programs and policies, with specific roles and responsibilities for involved ministries and agencies. The strategy should be used as the basis for building strong financial and political support for the safety net agenda. It should also be embedded in the country's broader poverty reduction agenda.

- *Build key organizational tools on which safety net programs should be based.* These tools include basic targeting mechanisms, a registry, a payment system, and a strong monitoring system. They can channel transfers from various programs to the targeted poor and vulnerable groups that enhance efficiency, accountability, and transparency. Multiple programs should migrate toward using a single registry, a common payment system, and a coordinated M&E system, even though the programs may support different groups of people.

- *Coordinate scattered donor support.* Safety net development in this group of countries will continue to depend on donor support, at least in the medium term. With the long-term view of moving toward a coordinated system of safety nets, these countries must begin harmonizing the funding given and approaches taken by donors, guided by the government's safety net strategy and the establishment of underlying systems. In postconflict countries, establishing government systems to track and monitor existing donor programs can offer a practical foundation for government interventions and can build country ownership in low-capacity and fragile contexts.

- *Develop a few key safety net programs that are based on a careful analysis of the country's needs.* This small number of key safety net interventions should (a) provide regular support to people in chronic and extreme poverty and (b) be able to expand and contract to provide assistance to poor and vulnerable households in the case of emergencies or seasonal fluctuations in income and consumption. Which programs are chosen and how they are implemented should be based on the country's poverty profile, the experience of pilot programs, and feasibility studies. Particular efforts should be made to develop robust targeting methods for these programs so that, when the programs are considered functioning well and when the political economy and fiscal resources allow, they can be scaled up to become efficient national programs. However, this expansion does not necessarily have to take place right away. Other existing smaller programs should be strengthened, especially to gather basic monitoring data to inform decisions about their future.

- *Other context-specific recommendations.* Countries with generous general subsidies and with emergency aid programs should consider reallocating some of those funds to more targeted interventions. Moreover, because human development outcomes tend to be poor in this group of countries, policy makers should seek to establish synergies between safety nets and health, education, and nutrition interventions.

The following recommendations apply to countries that are classified as "emerging" because their safety net systems are in the process of being developed. They consist mainly of LICs but also include some MICs.

- *Continue to reform existing categorical, universal, and ad hoc food emergency programs to make them more effective and efficient tools for reducing poverty.* Improving poverty targeting is especially important. For instance, social pension programs could be more cost-effective if they were targeted only to elderly people and people with disabilities who are also poor, and grants for orphans and vulnerable children as well as other children should target only those in poor and vulnerable families. Efforts to reallocate universal subsidies and expensive ad hoc food emergency programs toward better-targeted and development-oriented safety net support should continue.

- *Continue scaling up a few key, relatively well-targeted programs.* Experience from the 22 countries shows that a small number of complementary and well-coordinated programs is often sufficient for meeting the needs of the poor. Which programs are selected will vary by country, but they should provide regular support to chronically poor families or individuals and be flexible enough to scale up and down to provide shorter-term or repeated support to poor and vulnerable groups in response to shocks. As these programs are being scaled up, they should be continuously assessed to ensure that vulnerable groups are being adequately supported. It may also be appropriate to supplement these core programs with smaller complementary programs and services that focus on helping beneficiaries engage in productive and promotive activities, such as investing in the health and education of children.

- *Continue harmonizing and consolidating fragmented safety net programs.* Even if countries have prepared safety net or social protection strategies, they also need to prepare well-costed action plans. While the core programs are being implemented, these countries should continue to harmonize and consolidate the objectives and operational tools of their various programs. Unique beneficiary registration systems should be explored to reduce duplication and overlap. The capacity to develop robust information systems, M&E systems, and payment systems will also need to be strengthened or built.

- *Coordinate donor funding and technical assistance into one collective financing envelope or "basket."* As occurred in Ethiopia, such coordination can minimize duplication and maximize effectiveness as a first step toward the government taking over financing of the safety net system in the medium to long term. To build sustainability, countries must secure a medium-term funding envelope from domestic sources. Donor support and technical assistance are likely to remain important in the short and medium run to strengthen systems and scale up programs.

The following recommendations apply to countries that are classified as "established" and that already have a national safety net and social protection system in place. They consist mainly of MICs.

- *Strengthen the existing safety net and social protection system to ensure that it is reaching the extremely poor.* Even when countries have well-established programs, large overlaps in programs often occur along with significant inclusion errors, and some gaps can remain, with some members of the poorest and most excluded groups not receiving sufficient support. Within the existing budget it is entirely possible to refine the targeting mechanisms used by universal and categorical programs to provide adequate support to the poorest families and individuals within these groups.

- *Continue harmonizing and consolidating fragmented safety net programs.* As in countries with emerging systems, more effort is needed even in this group of countries to integrate the individual programs into one national system. This effort may require policy makers to reduce the number of existing programs by assessing their individual targeting effectiveness and impact compared with other interventions within the safety net system.

- *Continue strengthening the effectiveness of targeting, unique registry systems, payment systems, M&E systems, and grievance systems.* This task includes incorporating information technology for better management, accountability, and governance of programs and linking program eligibility and registries to national identification databases.

An Agenda for Learning

Better understanding of the risks and vulnerabilities affecting the population, of the coverage and effects of existing safety nets, and of which safety net instruments work in different contexts is needed to build effective safety net systems. A profile indicating which types of households (or individuals) are vulnerable to major types of risks, such as vulnerability to weather-related shocks, is necessary to determine target groups for safety net programs. Data on the coverage of existing programs are needed to assess the extent to which these groups are supported and where support needs to be extended or made more effective. In moving forward, the role of safety nets in the policy discussion on subsidy reform should be further explored with the specific context of each country in mind. More work is also needed to understand how existing food-based programs and their existing infrastructure should play a part in new and improved safety net systems in Africa. Moreover, impact evaluations are required to assess whether a program is having the desired effect on the outcomes of beneficiaries and how this result depends on elements of program design and the context in which it operates.

Strong monitoring and information systems are necessary elements of the safety nets learning agenda, but they will need to be complemented by analysis that is based on nationally representative surveys and rigorous impact evaluations. The safety net assessments reviewed in this study identify the lack of proper M&E as a main weakness. Many countries (including Benin, Burkina Faso, Liberia, Mali, Tanzania, and Togo) do not even have accurate administrative data on the number of beneficiaries reached and benefit levels provided by their programs. Although this basic information is critical and is generated only through program monitoring and information systems, it is only a part of the necessary information and will have to be complemented by other types of data and analysis:

- *Analysis of representative household surveys.* Data on program beneficiaries have natural limitations. For instance, such data cannot reveal the share of the intended targeted group that is covered by the program. A representative household survey can reveal both the coverage rate of intended beneficiaries and the extent of erroneous coverage of unintended beneficiaries. Moreover, a household survey can potentially collect program-by-program information on benefits reaching the household, thereby giving a comprehensive picture of safety net coverage while also identifying overlaps. Another use for household surveys is in the identification and analysis of the risks and vulnerabilities faced by different types of households.

- *Impact evaluations.* A rigorous impact evaluation that compares the outcomes of beneficiaries to a suitable control group of nonbeneficiaries can tease out the impact of the program on outcomes of interest, such as the effects of a cash transfer program on consumption, health, and education outcomes. Impact evaluations tell not only whether a program works but also how it can be designed to work better. More and more impact evaluations are being undertaken, thereby contributing to a growing body of evidence on safety net programs in Africa. Although in the past most have been for small donor pilots for research purposes, such as Malawi's Zomba cash transfer program or Mali's Bourse maman, larger programs (such as the CT-OVC and the Hunger Safety Net Programme in Kenya, the VUP in Rwanda, and the PSNP in Ethiopia and Tanzania) are now benefiting from impact evaluations yielding important information to guide program modification and adoption in other neighboring countries. More impact evaluations are needed of larger-scale government-provided programs.

Helping households become more productive is an increasingly important objective of safety nets in Africa, and this is one area in particular where more impact evaluations would be useful in building a knowledge base for program design. Besides helping poor households invest in the health and education of their children (usually through conditional cash transfers or school feeding programs), safety nets could have productive effects through helping households diversify livelihoods, acquire assets, reduce negative coping strategies, and invest in higher-productivity and higher-return activities. Complementary measures may also link beneficiaries to credit programs, soft skills, and job training. Several safety programs in Africa aim to increase the income generation and productivity of beneficiaries through a range of instruments (for example, the PSNP in Ethiopia and in Tanzania and the cash transfer pilot that is being prepared in Cameroon). To date, evidence on the productive effects of these complementary interventions is limited, and much of it is from other regions. However, ongoing research programs are investigating the potential productive aspects of safety net programs in Africa (for example, see box 4.5 in chapter 4).

The World Bank is contributing to this learning agenda by promoting knowledge generation and dissemination. The Bank is helping generate new knowledge through new analytical work, which includes a number of impact evaluations. This work has given priority to addressing the key knowledge gaps, such as how to address productivity and employment, particularly among young people. Other research priorities are to assess the relative effectiveness of conditional cash transfers and unconditional cash transfers in Africa and to promote the synergies between climate change and social protection. The Bank is also contributing to the safety nets learning agenda by strengthening its poverty assessments to include analyses of chronic and transitory poverty and vulnerability to inform social protection programming; by conducting assessments of national social protection programs, such as the safety net assessments reviewed here; and by synthesizing recent analytical work. To move beyond the 22 safety net assessments included in this review, future country-level assessments should cover the broader social protection sector, including contributory social insurance and labor market programs.

The Bank is also helping countries learn from international good practices and is facilitating the sharing of knowledge among African countries. Many opportunities exist for South-South learning within and beyond the continent, which the Bank is facilitating. For example, Malawi, Rwanda, and Tanzania have all learned from Ethiopia's PSNP, and the government of Ghana recently indicated its interest in learning from Kenya's experience with youth employment programs. Moreover, African countries can learn from Latin America's experience with cash transfer and labor market programs and from South Asia's experience with public works. The Bank is already actively supporting this kind of exchange of knowledge through the annual South-South Learning Forum on social protection and by supporting initiatives such as the recent Communities of Practice on cash transfers among researchers and implementers and bilateral study tours and visits.

Note

1. See table 1.1 in chapter 1 of this book for the country classification and grouping.

References

Grosh, Margaret, Carlo del Ninno, Emil Tesliuc, and Azedine Ouerghi. 2008. *For Protection and Promotion: The Design and Implementation of Effective Safety Nets.* Washington, DC: World Bank.

World Bank. 2013. "Securing the Transformational Potential in Africa's Mineral Resources." PowerPoint presentation, World Bank, Washington, DC.

APPENDIX A

Definition of Safety Nets

No overall consensus exists on a universal definition of social safety nets, on what they should address, and on how best to tailor safety net programs to local circumstances. Different terminologies—social protection, social security, social assistance, social safety nets, and social transfers—are often used interchangeably. In the present review, the term *safety nets* refers to noncontributory transfer programs targeted in some manner to the poor or vulnerable (Grosh *et al.* 2008) and *social protection* refers to both contributory and noncontributory programs.

Safety nets aim to increase household consumption of basic commodities and essential services—either directly or through substitution effects—rather than to increase household resources per se. Income-generating activities and other livelihood programs thus fall outside the scope of this study because these interventions cannot ensure a direct increase in consumption.[1] Safety nets are also targeted to the poor and vulnerable—in other words, individuals living in poverty and unable to meet their own basic needs or those in danger of falling into poverty, either because of an external shock or socioeconomic circumstances such as age, illness, or disability. Hence, universal subsidies also fall outside the definition of *targeted safety nets* but are included in this review because they are nevertheless important and costly programs used by countries to transfer resources to the population.

Safety nets can serve one or more of the following groups (Grosh *et al.* 2008):

- Chronic poor—that is, people who lack the assets to earn sufficient income, even in good years
- Transient poor—that is, people who earn sufficient income in good years but fall into poverty, at least temporarily, as a result of idiosyncratic or covariate shocks, ranging from an illness in the household or the loss of a job to drought or a macroeconomic crisis
- Vulnerable groups, which include, but are not limited to, people with disabilities, the elderly, orphans, widows, the displaced, refugees, and asylum seekers
- People who have lost advantages as a result of political reforms

The most common types of safety net programs can be classified as follows (modified from Grosh *et al.* 2008):

- Programs that provide unconditional transfers either in cash or in kind:
  - Cash transfers (such as child benefits, family allowances, and social pensions) and near-cash transfers (such as food stamps and commodity vouchers)
  - In-kind food transfers (such as school feeding and take-home rations) and other in-kind transfers (such as school supplies)
- Programs that provide an income:
  - Public works in which the poor and vulnerable work for food or cash
- Programs that protect and enhance human capital and access to basic services:
  - Conditional transfers, which are transfers in cash or in kind to poor or vulnerable households subject to their compliance with specific conditions requiring them to use education or health services
  - Fee waivers for health and education to help beneficiaries access essential public services (for example, fee waivers for health care services or education scholarships)

Social safety nets are a subset of broader social protection policies and programs along with social insurance and social legislation (labor laws and health and safety standards) that ensure minimum civic standards to safeguard the interests of individuals. Social protection is a basic human right. It is designed to reduce poverty and food insecurity and to promote economic growth and human development. Social safety nets are also part of a country's broader poverty reduction strategy. Social safety nets interact and work in parallel with social insurance, health, education, financial services, the provision of utilities and roads, and other policies aimed at reducing poverty and managing risk (figure A.1). Safety net systems usually consist of several programs that ideally complement each other as well as other public or social policies. A good safety net system is more than a collection of well-designed and well-implemented programs; it is more than the sum of its parts because of complementarities.

This review concentrates on publicly financed social safety nets—in other words, those funded by a national or local government or by official international aid. In most developing countries, social transfers take three basic forms:

- Formal support that is provided by governments and is prescribed by law
- Semiformal support that is provided by United Nations agencies or nongovernmental organizations
- Informal support supplied by households and communities to each other

This review does not cover other social protection programs that are complementary to safety nets (such as cereal banks, microcredit programs, and input subsidies), nor does it cover informal safety nets. However, because these

Figure A.1 Social Safety Nets in Development Policy

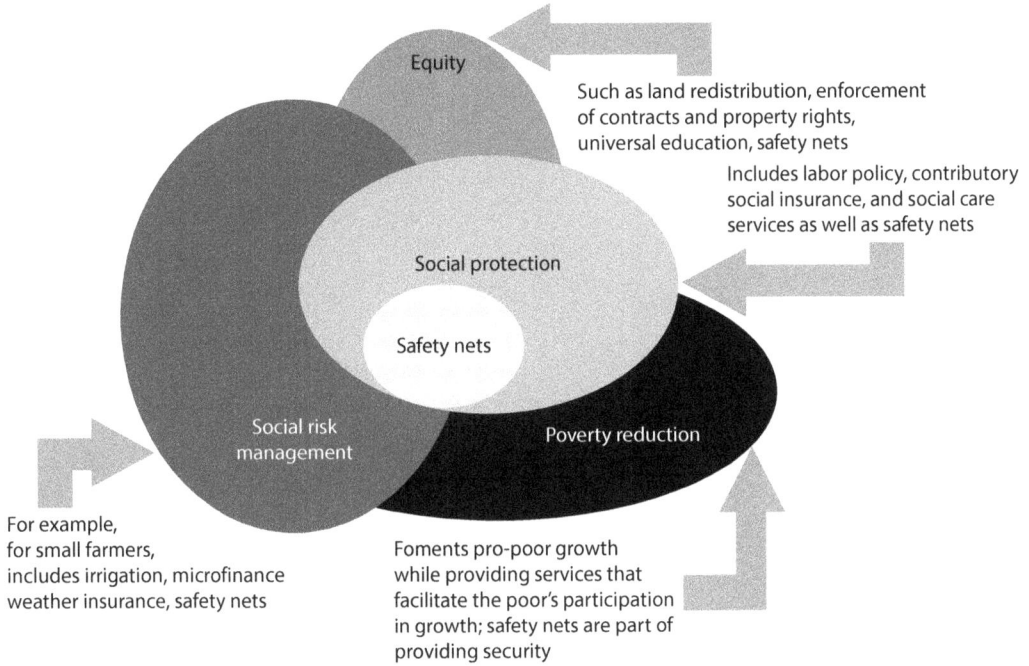

Equity

Such as land redistribution, enforcement
of contracts and property rights,
universal education, safety nets

Includes labor policy, contributory
social insurance, and social care
services as well as safety nets

Social protection

Safety nets

Social risk
management

Poverty reduction

For example,
for small farmers,
includes irrigation, microfinance
weather insurance, safety nets

Foments pro-poor growth
while providing services that
facilitate the poor's participation
in growth; safety nets are part of
providing security

Source: Grosh *et al.* 2008.

programs are relevant to understanding the full picture of social protection and
promotion, their role in poverty reduction is discussed at the margin.

Note

1. Policies and programs intended to increase access to basic services for the entire population (for example, free primary education) also fall outside the scope of this review,
   as do transfer programs targeted to communities and associations, for example, to
   build social assets in vulnerable communities, because such programs are not targeted
   specifically to poor and vulnerable individuals or households.

Reference

Grosh, Margaret, Carlo del Ninno, Emil Tesliuc, and Azedine Ouerghi. 2008. *For Protection
    and Promotion: The Design and Implementation of Effective Safety Nets*. Washington,
    DC: World Bank.

APPENDIX B

Country Typologies

Considering income level, one would expect better-off countries to provide more extensive safety net protection to their populations. Income level is the classification most commonly used for grouping countries throughout the world. According to the World Bank's latest World Development Indicators database, 15 of the 22 countries analyzed in this review are low-income countries (LICs), and 7 are middle-income countries (MICs) (see table B.1). Because richer countries tend to have more capacity and resources as well as lower levels of poverty, one would expect that the MICs would provide more extensive safety net protection to their populations than do the LICs.

However, safety net development in Africa also depends to a large extent on the enabling environment, including such factors as the stability of the government, the type of social contract between the state and its citizens, and the country's colonial heritage. Hence, despite having relatively high levels of gross domestic product per capita, countries such as Cameroon and Zambia do not have effective safety net systems (which are mandated by the government) but rather tend to have a plethora of ad hoc emergency aid and food security programs with hardly any coordination and with no overall safety net or social protection strategy to guide them. These characteristics are also common in LICs and fragile or conflict-affected states. In contrast, several LICs, including Ethiopia, Kenya, Rwanda, and Tanzania, are following the lead of many MICs by building coordinated safety net systems targeted to the poorest people, who suffer from a variety of risks. Even in Ghana, Mali, Mozambique, and Niger, better-coordinated and poverty-targeted safety net systems are starting to emerge.

The countries in Africa tend to be divided geographically in a way that largely reflects their English or French colonial backgrounds.[1] In an analysis of cash transfer programs in Africa, Garcia and Moore (2012) found that two country models dominate. The East and Southern African model (which prevails in many MICs but also some LICs) takes a rights-based and categorical approach to safety nets inherited from the countries' colonial regimes. These programs are usually government funded and have strong institutional backing and a long-term focus. These countries also have relatively stable governments, and the

Table B.1 Countries Classified by Income Level

Low-income countries	Middle-income countries
Benin	Botswana
Burkina Faso	Cameroon[b]
Ethiopia[a]	Ghana
Kenya[a]	Lesotho
Liberia	Mauritius
Madagascar	Swaziland
Malawi	Zambia[b]
Mali	
Mauritania	
Mozambique	
Niger	
Rwanda[a]	
Sierra Leone	
Tanzania[a]	
Togo	

Source: World Bank's World Development Indicators database.
a. These low-income countries are building safety net systems.
b. These middle-income countries do not currently have well-coordinated safety net systems.

provision of safety nets is a government mandate. The West and Central African model (prevalent mainly in LICs and fragile states) is dominated by short-term donor-supported programs that are focused on food security and nutrition, are implemented by a variety of agencies, and have little state guidance and oversight. Not all East and Southern African countries have well-developed systems. For example, because of the recurring governance crises in Madagascar over the past decade, its safety net system fits better in the West and Central African model. Also, despite their relatively high income levels, some West and Central African countries, such as Cameroon and the Republic of Congo (which is not included in this review), remain without adequate safety net programs.

The World Bank's Social Protection Anchor classifies countries on the basis of (a) the capacity of their safety nets and (b) the measures that they have taken to improve safety nets' response to crises (table B.2). Most countries covered in this review fall in the category of "weak capacity in social safety nets," except for Botswana, Ethiopia, Kenya, Lesotho, Mauritius, and Rwanda, all of which have more developed systems in place. Moreover, most countries fall under the categories of "moderate measures" or "limited or no measures" to improve social safety nets during a crisis. The exceptions are Ethiopia, Kenya, Niger, Rwanda, and Tanzania, all of which recently have made important improvements to their safety net systems to ensure that they are better able to respond to shocks and systemic crises. The World Bank's crisis-readiness classification corresponds closely with the income and geography-based typologies discussed previously. The East and Southern African countries generally have "strong measures " or "moderate measures" to improve social safety nets during a crisis, whereas the lower-income West

Table B.2 Country Typology Based on Their Crisis Preparedness and Safety Net Capacity

Tier	Strong measures to improve social safety nets during a crisis	Moderate measures to improve social safety nets during a crisis	Limited or no measures to improve social safety nets during a crisis
Tier I, no social safety nets in place	None	Comoros	Central African Republic; Chad[a]; Congo, Rep.; Côte d'Ivoire; Equatorial Guinea[a]; Eritrea[a]; Gambia, The; Guinea; **Mauritania**; Somalia[a]; Sudan
Tier II, weak capacity in social safety nets	**Niger**, **Tanzania**, Zimbabwe	**Ghana**, **Liberia**, **Malawi**, **Mozambique**, **Sierra Leone**, **Togo**, Uganda	Angola; **Benin**; **Burkina Faso**; Burundi; **Cameroon**; Congo, Dem. Rep.; Gabon[a]; Guinea-Bissau; **Madagascar**; **Mali**; Nigeria; São Tomé and Príncipe; Senegal; **Swaziland**; **Zambia**
Tier III, increasing capacity in social safety nets	**Ethiopia**, **Kenya**, **Rwanda**	Cape Verde,[a] **Lesotho**, **Mauritius**	None
Tier IV, high capacity in social safety nets	None	**Botswana**, Namibia, South Africa	None

Source: World Bank 2011b. (The original table also covers countries in regions outside Africa.)
Note: Countries in bold are included in this review.
a. A major information gap exists.

and Central African countries have "moderate measures" or "limited or no measures" to improve social safety nets during a crisis. The only exception is Zambia, which the Bank classifies as having limited crisis preparedness.

The World Bank's Africa Region puts the countries with which it is working into four categories according to how well advanced their social safety net systems are (table B.3). Again, the income- and geography-based typologies correspond relatively well to this system-based model. Although only a few southern African countries have established national systems, safety net systems are starting to emerge in several LICs, both in the West and Central African model and in the East and Southern African model. However, a large number of LICs are classified as having no solid plans for establishing a national safety net system.

In this review, we group countries using a combination of the income- and system-based models. This typology combines income, a factor that is exogenous to the development of a safety net system but that is an important aspect of the enabling environment, and the extent of development of the country's current safety net system.[2] This typology is presented in table 1.1 in the main text as well as in table B.4. This country typology is used throughout the analysis to illustrate some important underlying differences between sets of countries and to help explain why some countries are more able to establish effective and efficient safety net programs and coordinated systems. The typology compares safety net objectives, policies, programs, and measures of effectiveness across the 22 countries.

Table B.3 Country Typology Based on the Extent of Development of the Safety Net System

Status of safety net system	Criteria for categorization	Countries[a]
Level 1, national safety net system in place	Has adequate policies and delivery capacity	**Botswana, Mauritius**, Namibia, Seychelles, South Africa
Level 2, safety net system development in progress	Has one or more programs in place and has harmonized donor involvement working toward a consolidated safety net system	**Ethiopia, Ghana, Kenya, Lesotho, Mali, Mozambique, Niger, Rwanda, Swaziland, Tanzania**, Uganda
Level 3, no solid plans for a national safety net system	Has some individual projects or elements of programs or is putting such projects in place	Angola; **Benin; Burkina Faso;** Comoros; Congo, Dem. Rep.; **Liberia; Madagascar; Malawi;** Nigeria; Senegal; **Sierra Leone;** Sudan; **Togo; Zambia;** Zimbabwe
Level 4, no adequate safety net programs in place	Does not have adequate safety net programs or mechanisms to support vulnerable groups	**Cameroon;** Central African Republic; Chad; Congo, Rep.; Côte d'Ivoire; Eritrea; Gambia, The; Guinea; **Mauritania;** Somalia; Republic of South Sudan

Source: World Bank 2011a.
Note: Countries in bold are included in this review.
a. The World Bank does not currently provide any support for social safety net programs or system strengthening for Burundi, Cape Verde, Equatorial Guinea, Eritrea, Gabon, Guinea-Bissau, Mauritania, Namibia, São Tomé and Príncipe, Somalia, South Africa, Republic of South Sudan, or Sudan. Some of these countries are missing in the categorization table because of lack of data.

Table B.4 Country Typology Used in This Review

Level	Low-income countries	Lower- and upper-middle-income countries
Level 1: "Established"—national safety net system in place	None	Botswana, Mauritius
Level 2: "Emerging"—safety net system development in progress	Ethiopia, Kenya, Mali, Mozambique, Niger, Rwanda, Tanzania	Ghana, Lesotho, Swaziland
Levels 3 and 4: "Early stage or no plans"—no solid plans for a national safety net system or no adequate programs in place	Benin, Burkina Faso, Liberia, Madagascar, Malawi, Mauritania, Sierra Leone, Togo	Cameroon, Zambia

Sources: World Bank 2011b; World Bank's World Development Indicators database.
Note: Compared to the original model used by the Bank's Africa Region, the number of levels is reduced to three: "Established" = level 1, "Emerging" = level 2, and "Early stage or no plans" = levels 3 and 4.

Notes

1. Exceptions in the countries included in this review are Madagascar, which would fall into the French colonial group in West and Central Africa, though it is not geographically close to them, and Mozambique, which has a Portuguese colonial history.

2. The World Bank's Africa Social Protection Strategy (2012–22) also differentiates between safety net policies and systems in Africa in LICs and those in MICs and concludes that social protection programs in MICs tend to have deeper coverage than those in LICs (World Bank 2012). Social protection programs in LICs have only limited coverage, and administrative constraints undermine governance arrangements and limit the provision of basic services to the poor.

References

Garcia, Marito, and Charity M. T. Moore. 2012. *The Cash Dividend: The Rise of Cash Transfer Programs in Sub-Saharan Africa.* Washington, DC: World Bank.

World Bank. 2011a. "Safety Nets in Africa." Brief to Robert Zoellick, Annex 1, World Bank, Washington, DC.

———. 2011b. "Update on World Bank Work on Social Safety Nets and Country Assessments of the Readiness of Safety Net Systems." World Bank, Washington, DC.

———. 2012. *Managing Risk, Promoting Growth: Developing Systems for Social Protection in Africa—The World Bank's Africa Social Protection Strategy, 2012–2022.* Washington, DC: World Bank.

Poverty Headcount Data

Figure C.1 Poverty Headcount at US$1.25 per Day Purchasing Power Parity

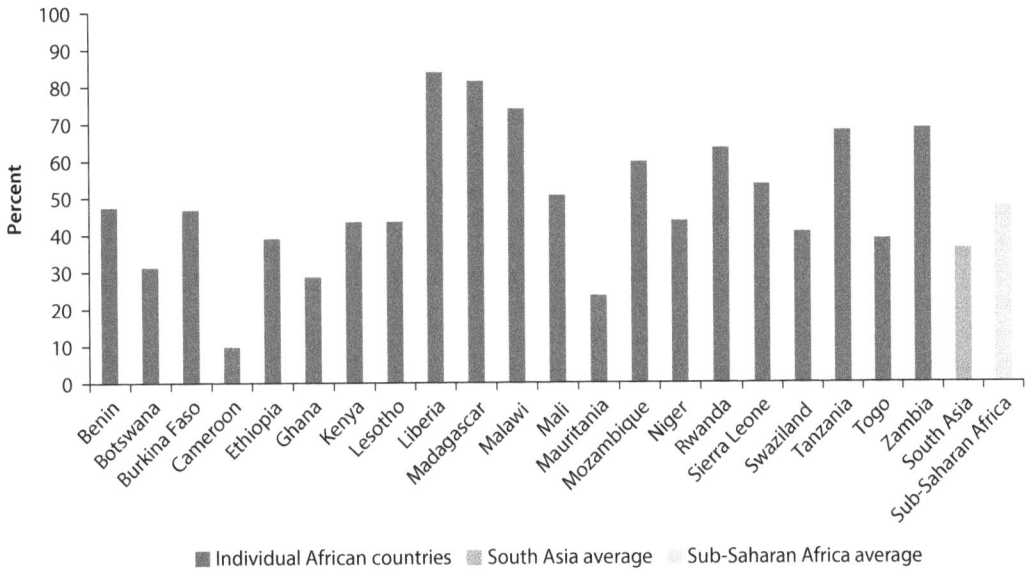

Individual African countries South Asia average Sub-Saharan Africa average

Source: World Bank's PovcalNet database.
Note: Regional averages are projections for 2008 using latest data available, 2005 US$1.25 per day purchasing power parity. Data on Mauritius are not available from PovcalNet.

Figure C.2 Poverty Headcount at US$2 per Day Purchasing Power Parity

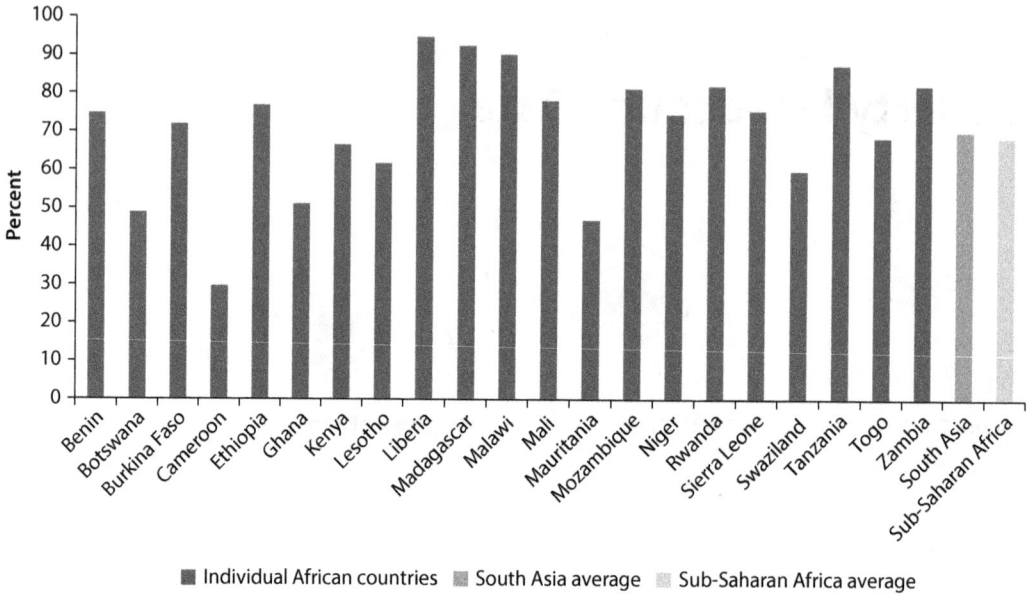

Source: World Bank's PovcalNet database.
Note: Regional averages are projections for 2008 using latest data available, 2005 US$2 per day purchasing power parity. Data on Mauritius are not available from PovcalNet.

Targeting Methods and Targeted Groups, by Program

Program	Targeting methods	Targeted groups	Comment on targeting effectiveness
Benin			
Girls cash transfer (Swiss Agency for Development and Cooperation)	Geographic and categorical selection based on application and by a multiactor commission	Schoolgirls in difficult situations in poor areas	Good targeting despite few resources
Support for indigents	Self-application and social surveys	Indigent adults and children	No information available
Cereal stocks	Geographic targeting and self-targeting based on commodity and price	Populations in the most vulnerable regions of the country suffering from food insecurity and floods	No information available
School feeding	Geographic targeting and school-based targeting	Primary school children in the most disadvantaged zones	Open to all children in the same school for equity reasons; in the poorest zones, canteens will not feed the poorest who are not in school
School feeding—take-home rations	Geographic, school-based, and categorical targeting	Schoolgirls and other disadvantaged children in the most disadvantaged zones	No information available
Urban public works (Projet de Gestion Urbaine Décentralisée, or Decentralized City Management Project)	Geographic targeting and self-targeting using wage rate	Unemployed high school and college graduates and artisans after their training	Weak targeting to the poor because wages are almost twice the minimum wage
Rural public works (Danish International Development Agency)	Geographic targeting and self-targeting using wage rate	Rural workers during agricultural lean seasons	Maximum wage almost twice the regional wage level; 55% workers poor; another 38% vulnerable
Botswana			
Vulnerable Group Feeding Program	Categorical targeting (not means tested)	Children younger than 5 years of age, pregnant and lactating women, tuberculosis patients, primary school children	No information available
Old-age pensions	Categorical targeting (not means tested)	People age 65 and older	For many, pension is recipient's only source of cash income and supports primary needs such as food
Veterans benefits	Categorical targeting (not means tested)	Veterans of the two World Wars and their survivors	No information available

table continues next page

Program	Targeting methods	Targeted groups	Comment on targeting effectiveness
Orphan care program	Categorical targeting (not means tested)	Orphans under the age of 18	No information available
Community home-based care	Categorical targeting and means tested	Mainly terminal HIV patients	No information available
Ipelegeng public works	Self-targeting using wage rate, rationed because of excess demand	Rural and urban poor workers	Wages deemed low enough to encourage self-selection by the poor
Burkina Faso			
Urban food voucher program	Geographic targeting and proxy means testing using a household vulnerability score, with community verification	No information available	Evaluation showed worse targeting than expected but that all beneficiary households were needy; large exclusion errors, ill-adapted screening questionnaire
Programme Pistes Rurales: Désenclavement à l'Est (Rural Access Roads Program)	Self-targeting using wage rate	No information available	Wage rate set slightly below minimum wage
Food for Assets	Self-targeting using wage rate	No information available	No information available
Targeted food subsidized sales	Geographic targeting and self-targeting based on commodity and price, with eligibility criteria defined by the provincial council of emergency relief and rehabilitation; interested eligible households need to register	No information available	May not reach the very poorest since they may not have the financial resources to access the proposed subsidized cereals; unclear whether criteria for vulnerability apply
Targeted free food distribution	Assistance to vulnerable populations made on the basis of requests received from charities	Vulnerable households and people affected by small-scale disasters (farmer-breeder conflicts, fire)	No information available
School feeding	Geographic and school-based targeting	Primary school children in the most disadvantaged zones	No information available
School feeding—take-home rations	Geographic and school-based, categorical targeting	Schoolgirls and other disadvantaged children in the most disadvantaged zones	No information available
Health fee waivers	Categorical targeting	Indigents	Not enforced because of lack of mechanisms to identify the indigent
Health fee waivers	Community-based approach	No information available	No information available

table continues next page

157

Program	Targeting methods	Targeted groups	Comment on targeting effectiveness
Cameroon			
School feeding	Geographic and school-based targeting	Primary school children in four northern provinces	No information available
School feeding—take-home rations (World Food Programme)	Geographic, school-based, and categorical targeting	Schoolgirls and other disadvantaged children in four northern provinces	No information available
Feeding programs	Categorical targeting	Orphans and vulnerable children (OVC), HIV patients	No information available
Projet d'Assainissement de Yaoundé (Yaoundé Sanitation Project)	Geographic targeting and self-targeting using wage rate	Urban poor	Almost 200% of regular pay—too high to attract the poorest
Food for work	Self-targeting using wage rate	Rural poor	No information available
Ethiopia			
Productive Safety Net Program (public works and direct support)	Geographic targeting, community-based targeting, and self-targeting using wage rate (for public works)	Rural food insecure	87% of public works participants food insecure
Ghana			
Livelihood Empowerment against Poverty	Proxy means testing and community-based targeting	No information available	Well targeted: 57.5% of outlays benefit the poor
Indigent exemption to National Health Insurance Scheme	No information available	No information available	Well targeted: more than 50% of outlays benefit the poor
Free school uniforms for primary schools in poor areas	No information available	No information available	Well targeted: imputation predicts that 50% of outlays benefit the poor
Kenya			
Protracted Relief and Recovery Operation and school feeding (World Food Programme)	Geographic targeting	Schoolchildren and poor women and children in the most food-insecure districts	No information available
Hunger Safety Net Programme	Geographic targeting	No information available	No information available
School feeding	Geographic targeting	No information available	No information available

table continues next page

Program	Targeting methods	Targeted groups	Comment on targeting effectiveness
Lesotho			
Old-Age Pensions	Categorical targeting and universal targeting to all people over the age of 70 except former civil servants	People over the age of 70	Almost half of the benefits go to nonpoor households; covers only 4.4% of the very poor
OVC bursaries	Categorical targeting, with district-level quota each year; district bursary administrators identify beneficiaries	Orphaned secondary students	Poverty status of beneficiaries not known, but poverty among orphans does not appear to be much higher than among other children
Child Grants Program	Geographical, categorical, and community targeting and proxy means testing	Poor households with OVC	Too early to determine efficiency; covers only 3.9% of very poor (ongoing impact evaluation)
Public Assistance	Case-by-case basis, at discretion of district offices using set criteria	Destitute people	No information available
Fertilizer–National Subsidy	Untargeted	Untargeted	No information available
Agricultural Input Fairs	Selection by Ministry of Agriculture and Food Security staff in consultation with chiefs and community counselors using set criteria	Vulnerable but viable famers	Targeting efficiency unknown
School feeding	All government schools	All primary students	22% of students in the poorest quintile; 43% in the two poorest quintiles
Liberia			
Bomi pilot cash transfer program	Community-based and interview-based means testing	Labor-constrained ultrapoor households	Initially only used community targeting, which led to large inclusion errors; adding proxy means testing at the household level improved targeting and effectiveness but is costly
Ministry of Health and Social Welfare support stipend to orphanages	Categorical targeting, but support provided at the orphanage level if orphanages meet certain criteria	Orphans	No information available
Save the Children cash transfer	Categorical targeting	Child mothers associated with armed groups in certain regions	No information available

table continues next page

Program	Targeting methods	Targeted groups	Comment on targeting effectiveness
Liberia Emergency Employment Program and Liberia Employment Action Program public works	Self-targeting using wage rate	Mainly former combatants	Little known about the actual capability of beneficiaries to leverage short-term employment, through savings or investments, to reduce their vulnerability
YES (Youth Employment Skills)	Selection based on at-risk, unemployment, vulnerability status, and self-targeting using wage rate	At-risk adults between 18 and 35	80.0% of participants were in the three lowest quintiles, but only 14.5% were from the lowest quintile
Livelihood Asset Rehabilitation	Community selection; households chosen on the basis of access to food market or ability to produce food	Food-insecure populations	No information available
Maternal and Child Health Nutrition	No information available	Malnourished pregnant or lactating women and all pregnant teenagers (15–19 years) and their children (6–24 months of age) in counties with critical chronic malnutrition rates	No information available
School feeding (World Food Programme)	Geographic and school-based targeting	Primary school children in the most food-insecure counties	No information available
School feeding (World Food Programme)—take home	Geographic, school-based, and categorical targeting	Primary school girls in the most food-insecure counties	No information available
Madagascar			
Tsena Mora	Geographic targeting in large urban areas, with beneficiaries selected by the staff of the sales points using preexisting lists of vulnerable residents	Households with 3–5 non-working-age dependents, households with unstable income, and women who work in the informal sector	Not known but significant leakage to the nonpoor suspected
School feeding (World Food Programme)	Geographic targeting to southern districts with poor education and food security indicators, using vulnerability maps	All pupils attending assisted schools	No information available

table continues next page

Program	Targeting methods	Targeted groups	Comment on targeting effectiveness
All public works programs	Multistage: geographic targeting and self-targeting of participants by advertising the wage rate; when demand for work exceeds supply, beneficiary households selected through a process of consultation with community leaders	Multiple groups	Wage rate set above market rate
Malawi			
Social Cash Transfer Schemes	Community-based targeting	Ultrapoor and labor-constrained households	Errors of exclusion of ultrapoor households but still one of the most progressively targeted cash transfer programs globally, with 62% of ultrapoor and labor-constrained households covered
Farm Input Support Program	Community-based targeting, including chiefs	Poor farmers	Input subsidies widely used as political tools by politicians, and beneficiaries known to have been urged by chiefs to share benefits with other community members, thus reducing targeting effectiveness and creating errors of inclusion
Public Works Programme (Malawi Social Action Fund)	Geographic targeting, self-targeting using wage rate, and community selection	Food-insecure and vulnerable rural households with labor in poor areas	93% of households targeted correctly to poor and vulnerable
Village Savings and Loans schemes	Self-targeting	Organized groups in poor communities	No information available
Mali			
Bourse maman conditional cash transfer	Community-based targeting and proxy means testing	Girls and boys of poor families already enrolled in primary school (grades 1–6) in nine pilot schools located in poor areas of Kayes and Mopti, where school services exist but demand remains low	Exclusion errors quite significant because of funding constraints and poor targeting methods
Food distribution through cereal banks	Geographic targeting and self-targeting based on commodity, price, and self-application	Food-insecure communities	No information available on actual number of beneficiaries

table continues next page

Program	Targeting methods	Targeted groups	Comment on targeting effectiveness
Programme d'Emploi des Jeunes par l'Approche Haute Intensité de Main d'Œuvre (Employment Program for Youth by High Labor Force Intensity)	Selection by local authorities and self-targeting	People 15–40 years of age in poor and vulnerable areas	Wage set much higher than minimum and market wage; no attempt to enroll the poorest individuals in the program
Health fee waivers	Categorical targeting	Elderly and indigent	No information available
Mauritania			
Cash transfer pilot (World Food Programme and Catholic Relief Services)	Geographic targeting, community targeting, and proxy means testing	Urban households affected by drought and food-price increases	No information available
Mauritius			
Social Aid	Means-tested targeting; the law stipulates categories of eligibility that include household heads unable to support their dependents, abandoned spouses, households experiencing a sudden loss of employment, dependents of prisoners, and drug addicts	Poor and indigent	Reaches only 2.3% of poor households and especially excludes the working poor, who often have many children, because employment makes them ineligible; 29% of beneficiaries are poor (after transfers) and 80% of households are in the two poorest quintiles
Income Support	Social Aid beneficiaries automatically eligible for Income Support; otherwise selection based on amount of electricity consumption	Poor and indigent	No information available
Noncontributory Pensions	Categorical and universal targeting	All people 60 years of age and older, invalids, widows and orphans, dependent children, and guardians	No information available
National Solidarity Fund	Means-tested targeting	Vulnerable families	No information available
School Feeding Program	Universal targeting	All primary students	No information available
Overseas Medical Care	Universal targeting	Persons requiring medical care	No information available
Bus subsidy	Universal targeting	Students, elderly, people with disabilities	No information available

table continues next page

Program	Targeting methods	Targeted groups	Comment on targeting effectiveness
In-kind school support (textbooks, supplies, and grants)	Means-tested targeting	Poor students	No information available
Mozambique			
Food Subsidy Program	Categorical targeting	Elderly, people with disabilities, and poor pregnant women who cannot work	Targeting accuracy poor
Direct Social Assistance Program	Categorical targeting	OVC and poor people who experience some shock (such as a death, illness, unemployment, or a house fire)	Targeting accuracy poor
Food for work	Geographic targeting and self-targeting using wage rate	No information available	No information available
Rwanda			
Vision 2020 Umurenge Program (VUP)–Direct Support	Geographic, *Ubudehe* targeting approach based on household labor capacity and access to land, livestock, housing, and other assets	Poor households without available labor	Largely benefits households with elderly members who lack sufficient means to care for themselves
VUP–Public Works	Geographic, *Ubudehe* targeting approach based on household labor capacity and access to land, livestock, housing, and other assets	Poor households with available labor	Significant leakage to ineligible beneficiaries
FARG (Fond d'Assistance aux Rescapées du Génocide, or Assistance Fund for Genocide Survivors)	Categorical targeting with community selection validated by sector executive secretary and district	Needy genocide survivors (orphans, old-age survivors unable to work, survivors with disabilities)	No information available
Sierra Leone			
National Social Assistance Program's (Youth Employment Support Project) Cash for Work	Geographic targeting (World Food Programme's Comprehensive Food Security and Vulnerability Analysis) and self-selection, with community involvement in some sites	Unemployed and at-risk youths	Evaluation found 54% of beneficiaries in the top two quintiles and only 27% in the bottom two (evaluation did not consider geographic targeting)
Swaziland			
Old-Age Grant	Categorical and universal targeting	All people over 60 years of age	No information available
Public Assistance	Means testing	Poor people with disabilities, indigents	No information available

table continues next page

Program	Targeting methods	Targeted groups	Comment on targeting effectiveness
Child Welfare Grants	Categorical targeting	Children in foster care	No information available
OVC Education Grant	Categorical and community targeting	OVC	No information available
School Feeding Program	Universal targeting	Primary and high school students	No information available
Food- and Cash-for-Work Programs	Geographic targeting and self-targeting	Food-insecure households	No information available
Food Distribution	Geographic targeting and self-targeting	Food-insecure households	No information available
Health Fee Waivers	Categorical and means-tested targeting	Elderly and the indigent	No information available
Tanzania			
School feeding	Geographic and school-based targeting	Primary school children in drought-prone and food-insecure districts	No evaluation showing whether program benefits primarily the poor, the very poor, or the nonpoor, although Comprehensive Food Security and Vulnerability Analysis data suggest benefits are concentrated in the second-lowest wealth quintile rather than the poorest
Food for Assets	Geographic targeting, community-guided household targeting, and self-selection using wage rate	Households with available labor in food-insecure districts	No assessment of the poverty status of people receiving transfers
Most Vulnerable Children	Geographic targeting, with eligibility of individual children assessed by village committees and follow-up visits by social welfare officers	Households of OVC in food-insecure districts	No information available
Tanzania Social Action Fund (TASAF) vulnerable groups	Geographic and community-guided household targeting	Small groups of vulnerable individuals, such as widows, AIDS sufferers, and unemployed youths	No information available
TASAF public works program	Geographic targeting, community-guided household targeting, and self-selection using wage rate	Able-bodied poor in food-insecure districts	No evidence yet whether the program benefits the poor

table continues next page

Program	Targeting methods	Targeted groups	Comment on targeting effectiveness
TASAF conditional cash transfer	Geographic targeting, community-based targeting, proxy means testing, and categorical targeting	Low-income elderly people with children	No information available
National Food Subsidy program	Geographic targeting, with households identified by village committees and confirmed by local government	Households in food-insecure districts and farmers with less than 1 hectare of land	No good data on accuracy of targeting; anecdotal reports suggest that although the poor and vulnerable tend to be targeted, village committees tend to spread the food more widely to maintain social cohesion, resulting in smaller benefits and wider coverage
Togo			
Targeted food distribution	Geographic targeting	Malnourished children, pregnant women, and the most vulnerable in northern regions with food insecurity and floods	No information available
School feeding	Geographic and school-based targeting	Schoolchildren in poor communities in regions affected by floods and food prices	No information available
Cash-for-work program	Geographic targeting and self-targeting using wage rate	Disadvantaged youths in poor rural communities	At least 75% of workers live below the poverty line
Zambia			
Social Cash Transfer Scheme	Geographic, categorical, and community targeting and proxy means testing	Labor-constrained households and households with members with HIV or tuberculosis, families with children under the age of 5, the elderly, households headed by women, and elderly people caring for orphans	No information available
Pilot Old-Age Pension	Categorical and universal targeting	All people over 65 years old	No information available
STEPS (Sustainability through Economic Strengthening, Prevention, and Support) OVC and OVC Bursary Program	Categorical and community targeting	OVC and people with HIV/AIDS	Simulations show that targeting elderly or female-headed households with orphans or households with people with disabilities would make 56% of the nonextreme poor eligible for the program while 38% would be ineligible

table continues next page

Program	Targeting methods	Targeted groups	Comment on targeting effectiveness
School Feeding Program	Geographic targeting	Primary students	No information available
SPLASH (Sustainable Program for Livelihoods and Solutions for Hunger) food security for vulnerable groups (vouchers and food; World Food Programme)	Geographic targeting	Households with undernourished members or members receiving antiretroviral therapy or treatment for tuberculosis	No information available
PUSH (Peri-Urban Community Self-Help)	Geographic targeting, self-targeting, and proxy means testing	Urban poor who are unemployed	No information available
Food Security Pack	Categorical targeting	Poor farmers with vulnerability characteristics	No information available
Farmer Input Support Program (FISP)	Proxy means testing	Smallholder farmers	Only 14% of smallholder farmers received FISP fertilizer, compared with more than 50% of those in the largest farm size categories; smallholder farmers also received much less of it (an average 169 kilograms versus 657 kilograms for the largest farmers)

Source: Country safety net assessments.

Environmental Benefits Statement

The World Bank is committed to reducing its environmental footprint. In support of this commitment, the Publishing and Knowledge Division leverages electronic publishing options and print-on-demand technology, which is located in regional hubs worldwide. Together, these initiatives enable print runs to be lowered and shipping distances decreased, resulting in reduced paper consumption, chemical use, greenhouse gas emissions, and waste.

The Publishing and Knowledge Division follows the recommended standards for paper use set by the Green Press Initiative. Whenever possible, books are printed on 50 percent to 100 percent postconsumer recycled paper, and at least 50 percent of the fiber in our book paper is either unbleached or bleached using Totally Chlorine Free (TCF), Processed Chlorine Free (PCF), or Enhanced Elemental Chlorine Free (EECF) processes.

More information about the Bank's environmental philosophy can be found at http://crinfo.worldbank.org/wbcrinfo/node/4.

green press INITIATIVE

www.ingramcontent.com/pod-product-compliance
Lightning Source LLC
Chambersburg PA
CBHW080613270326
41928CB00016B/3033